BORN A CRIME

BORN A CRIME

STORIES FROM A SOUTH AFRICAN CHILDHOOD

TREVOR NOAH

SPIEGEL & GRAU
NEW YORK

Copyright © 2016 by Trevor Noah

Published in the United States by Spiegel & Grau, an imprint of Random House,
a division of Penguin Random House LLC, New York.

SPIEGEL & GRAU and Design is a registered trademark of Penguin Random House LLC.

Library of Congress Cataloging-in-Publication Data

Names: Noah, Trevor, author.

Title: Born a crime: stories from a South African childhood / by Trevor Noah.

Description: First edition. | New York : Spiegel & Grau, 2016.

Identifiers: LCCN 2016031399 | ISBN 9780399588174 |
ISBN 9780399590443 (international) | ISBN 9780399588181 (ebook)

Subjects: LCSH: Noah, Trevor | Comedians—United States—Biography. |
Comedians—South Africa—Biography. | Television personalities—United States—
Biography.

Classification: LCC PN2287.N557 A3 2016 | DDC 791.4502/8092 [B]—dc23 LC record
available at https://lccn.loc.gov/2016031399

Printed in the United States of America on acid-free paper

spiegelandgrau.com

1 2 3 4 5 6 7 8 9

First Edition

Book design by Susan Turner

For my mother. My first fan.
Thank you for making me a man.

IMMORALITY ACT, 1927

**To prohibit illicit carnal intercourse
between Europeans and natives and
other acts in relation thereto.**

B E IT ENACTED by the King's Most Excellent
Majesty, the Senate and the House of Assembly of
the Union of South Africa, as follows:—

1. Any European male who has illicit carnal
intercourse with a native female, and any native
male who has illicit carnal intercourse with a
European female . . . shall be guilty of an offence
and liable on conviction to imprisonment for a
period not exceeding five years.

2. Any native female who permits any European
male to have illicit carnal intercourse with her and
any European female who permits any native male
to have illicit carnal intercourse with her shall
be guilty of an offence and liable on conviction
to imprisonment for a period not exceeding four
years. . . .

CONTENTS

I

II

PART I

The genius of apartheid was convincing people who were the over-whelming majority to turn on each other. Apart hate, is what it was. You separate people into groups and make them hate one another so you can run them all.

At the time, black South Africans outnumbered white South Africans nearly five to one, yet we were divided into different tribes with different languages: Zulu, Xhosa, Tswana, Sotho, Venda, Ndebele, Tsonga, Pedi, and more. Long before apartheid existed these tribal factions clashed and warred with one another. Then white rule used that animosity to divide and conquer. All nonwhites were systematically classified into various groups and subgroups. Then these groups were given differing levels of rights and privileges in order to keep them at odds.

Perhaps the starkest of these divisions was between South Africa's two dominant groups, the Zulu and the Xhosa. The Zulu man is known as the warrior. He is proud. He puts his head down and fights. When the colonial armies invaded, the Zulu charged into battle with nothing but spears and shields against men with guns. The Zulu were slaughtered by the thousands, but they never stopped fighting. The Xhosa, on the other hand, pride themselves on being the thinkers. My mother is Xhosa. Nelson Mandela was Xhosa. The Xhosa waged a long war against the white man as well, but after experiencing the futility of battle against a better-armed foe, many Xhosa chiefs took a more nimble approach. "These white people are here whether we like it or not," they said. "Let's see what tools they possess that can be useful to us. Instead of being resistant to English, let's learn English. We'll understand what the white man is saying, and we can force him to negotiate with us."

The Zulu went to war with the white man. The Xhosa played chess with the white man. For a long time neither was particularly successful, and each blamed the other for a problem neither had created. Bitterness festered. For decades those feelings were held in check by a common enemy. Then apartheid fell, Mandela walked free, and black South Africa went to war with itself.

———————

I
RUN

Sometimes in big Hollywood movies they'll have these crazy chase scenes where somebody jumps or gets thrown from a moving car. The person hits the ground and rolls for a bit. Then they come to a stop and pop up and dust themselves off, like it was no big deal. Whenever I see that I think, *That's rubbish. Getting thrown out of a moving car hurts way worse than that.*

I was nine years old when my mother threw me out of a moving car. It happened on a Sunday. I know it was on a Sunday because we were coming home from church, and every Sunday in my childhood meant church. We *never* missed church. My mother was—and still is—a deeply religious woman. Very Christian. Like indigenous peoples around the world, black South Africans adopted the religion of our colonizers. By "adopt" I mean it was forced on us. The white man was quite stern with the native. "You need to pray to Jesus," he said. "Jesus will save you." To which the native replied, "Well, we do need to be saved—saved from *you*, but that's beside the point. So let's give this Jesus thing a shot."

My whole family is religious, but where my mother was Team Jesus all the way, my grandmother balanced her Christian faith with the traditional Xhosa beliefs she'd grown up with, communicating with the spirits of our ancestors. For a long time I didn't understand why so many black people had abandoned their indigenous faith for Christianity. But the more we went to church and the longer I sat in those pews the more I learned about how Christianity works: If you're Native American and you pray to the wolves, you're a savage. If you're African and you pray to your ancestors, you're a primitive. But when white people pray to a guy who turns water into wine, well, that's just common sense.

My childhood involved church, or some form of church, at least four nights a week. Tuesday night was the prayer meeting. Wednesday night was Bible study. Thursday night was Youth church. Friday and Saturday we had off. (Time to sin!) Then on Sunday we went to church. Three churches, to be precise. The reason we went to three churches was because my mom said each church gave her something different. The first church offered jubilant praise of the Lord. The second church offered deep analysis of the scripture, which my mom loved. The third church offered passion and catharsis; it was a place where you truly felt the presence of the Holy Spirit inside you. Completely by coincidence, as we moved back and forth between these churches, I noticed that each one had its own distinct racial makeup: Jubilant church was mixed church. Analytical church was white church. And passionate, cathartic church, that was black church.

Mixed church was Rhema Bible Church. Rhema was one of those huge, supermodern, suburban megachurches. The pastor, Ray McCauley, was an ex-bodybuilder with a big smile and the personality of a cheerleader. Pastor Ray had competed in the 1974 Mr. Universe competition. He placed third. The winner that year was Arnold Schwarzenegger.

Every week, Ray would be up onstage working really hard to make Jesus cool. There was arena-style seating and a rock band jamming out with the latest Christian contemporary pop. Everyone sang along, and if you didn't know the words that was okay because they were all right up there on the Jumbotron for you. It was Christian karaoke, basically. I always had a blast at mixed church.

White church was Rosebank Union in Sandton, a very white and wealthy part of Johannesburg. I *loved* white church because I didn't actually have to go to the main service. My mom would go to that, and I would go to the youth side, to Sunday school. In Sunday school we got to read cool stories. Noah and the flood was obviously a favorite; I had a personal stake there. But I also loved the stories about Moses parting the Red Sea, David slaying Goliath, Jesus whipping the money changers in the temple.

I grew up in a home with very little exposure to popular culture. Boyz II Men were not allowed in my mother's house. Songs about some guy grinding on a girl all night long? No, no, no. That was forbidden. I'd hear the other kids at school singing "End of the Road," and I'd have no clue what was going on. I knew *of* these Boyz II Men, but I didn't really know who they were. The only music I knew was from church: soaring, uplifting songs praising Jesus. It was the same with movies. My mom didn't want my mind polluted by movies with sex and violence. So the Bible was my action movie. Samson was my superhero. He was my He-Man. A guy beating a thousand people to death with the jawbone of a donkey? That's pretty badass. Eventually you get to Paul writing letters to the Ephesians and it loses the plot, but the Old Testament and the Gospels? I could quote you anything from those pages, chapter and verse. There were Bible games and quizzes every week at white church, and I kicked everyone's ass.

Then there was black church. There was always some kind of black church service going on somewhere, and we tried them all. In the township, that typically meant an outdoor, tent-revival-style church. We usually went to my grandmother's church, an old-school Methodist congregation, five hundred African grannies in blue-and-white blouses, clutching their Bibles and patiently burning in the hot African sun. Black church was rough, I won't lie. No air-conditioning. No lyrics up on Jumbotrons. And it lasted forever, three or four hours at least, which confused me because white church was only like an hour—in and out, thanks for coming. But at black church I would sit there for what felt like an eternity, trying to figure out why time moved so slowly. *Is it possible for time to actually stop? If so, why does it stop at black church and not at white church?* I eventually decided black people needed more time with Jesus because we suffered more. "I'm here to fill up on my blessings for the week," my mother used to say. The more time we spent at church, she reckoned, the more blessings we accrued, like a Starbucks Rewards Card.

Black church had one saving grace. If I could make it to the third or fourth hour I'd get to watch the pastor cast demons out of people. People possessed by demons would start running up and down the aisles like madmen, screaming in tongues. The ushers would tackle them, like bouncers at a club, and hold them down for the pastor. The pastor would grab their heads and violently shake them back and forth, shouting, "I cast out this spirit in the name of *Jesus!*" Some pastors were more violent than others, but what they all had in common was that they wouldn't stop until the demon was gone and the congregant had gone limp and collapsed on the stage. The person had to fall. Because if he didn't fall that meant the demon was powerful and the pastor needed to come at him even harder. You could be a linebacker in the NFL. Didn't matter. That pastor was taking you *down*. Good Lord, that was fun.

Christian karaoke, badass action stories, and violent faith healers—man, I loved church. The thing I didn't love was the lengths we had to go to in order to get to church. It was an epic slog. We lived in Eden Park, a tiny suburb way outside Johannesburg. It took us an hour to get to white church, another forty-five minutes to get to mixed church, and another forty-five minutes to drive out to Soweto for black church. Then, if that wasn't bad enough, some Sundays we'd double back to white church for a special evening service. By the time we finally got home at night, I'd collapse into bed.

This particular Sunday, the Sunday I was hurled from a moving car, started out like any other Sunday. My mother woke me up, made me porridge for breakfast. I took my bath while she dressed my baby brother Andrew, who was nine months old. Then we went out to the driveway, but once we were finally all strapped in and ready to go, the car wouldn't start. My mom had this ancient, broken-down, bright-tangerine Volkswagen Beetle that she picked up for next to nothing. The reason she got it for next to nothing was because it was always breaking down. To this day I hate secondhand cars. Almost everything that's ever gone wrong in my life I can trace back to a secondhand car. Secondhand cars made me get detention for being late for school. Secondhand cars left us hitchhiking on the side of the freeway. A secondhand car was also the reason my mom got married. If it hadn't been for the Volkswagen that didn't work, we never would have looked for the mechanic who became the husband who became the stepfather who became the man who tortured us for years and put a bullet in the back of my mother's head—I'll take the new car with the warranty every time.

As much as I loved church, the idea of a nine-hour slog, from mixed church to white church to black church then doubling back to white church again, was just too much to contemplate. It was bad enough in a car, but taking public transport would be twice as long and twice as hard. When the Volkswagen refused to start, inside my head I was praying, *Please say we'll just stay home. Please say we'll just stay home.* Then I glanced over to see the determined look on my mother's face, her jaw set, and I knew I had a long day ahead of me.

"Come," she said. "We're going to catch minibuses."

My mother is as stubborn as she is religious. Once her mind's made up, that's it. Indeed, obstacles that would normally lead a person to change their plans, like a car breaking down, only made her more determined to forge ahead.

"It's the Devil," she said about the stalled car. "The Devil doesn't want us to go to church. That's why we've got to catch minibuses."

Whenever I found myself up against my mother's faith-based obstinacy, I would try, as respectfully as possible, to counter with an opposing point of view.

"Or," I said, "the Lord knows that today we *shouldn't* go to church, which is why he made sure the car wouldn't start, so that we stay at home as a family and take a day of rest, because even the Lord rested."

"Ah, that's the Devil talking, Trevor."

"No, because Jesus is in control, and if Jesus is in control and we pray to Jesus, he would let the car start, but he hasn't, therefore—"

"No, Trevor! Sometimes Jesus puts obstacles in your way to see if you overcome them. Like Job. This could be a test."

"Ah! Yes, Mom. But the test could be to see if we're willing to accept what has happened and stay at home and praise Jesus for his wisdom."

"No. That's the Devil talking. Now go change your clothes."

"But, Mom!"

"Trevor! *Sun'qhela!*"

Sun'qhela is a phrase with many shades of meaning. It says "don't undermine me," "don't underestimate me," and "just try me." It's a command and a threat, all at once. It's a common thing for Xhosa parents to say to their kids. Any time I heard it I knew it meant the conversation was over, and if I uttered another word I was in for a hiding—what we call a spanking.

At the time, I attended a private Catholic school called Maryvale College. I was the champion of the Maryvale sports day every single year, and my mother won the moms' trophy every single year. Why? Because she was always chasing me to kick my ass, and I was always running not to get my ass kicked. Nobody ran like me and my mom. She wasn't one of those "Come over here and get your hiding" type moms. She'd deliver it to you free of charge. She was a thrower, too. Whatever was next to her was coming at you. If it was something breakable, I had to catch it and put it down. If it broke, that would be my fault, too, and the ass-kicking would be that much worse. If she threw a vase at me, I'd have to catch it, put it down, and then run. In a split second, I'd have to think, *Is it valuable? Yes. Is it breakable? Yes. Catch it, put it down, now run.*

We had a very Tom and Jerry relationship, me and my mom. She was the strict disciplinarian; I was naughty as shit. She would send me out to buy groceries, and I wouldn't come right home because I'd be using the change from the milk and bread to play arcade games at the supermarket. I loved videogames. I was a master at *Street Fighter*. I could go forever on a single play. I'd drop a coin in, time would fly, and the next thing I knew there'd be a woman behind me with a belt. It was a race. I'd take off out the door and through the dusty streets of Eden Park, clambering over walls, ducking through backyards. It was a normal thing in our neighborhood. Everybody knew: That Trevor child would come through like a bat out of hell, and his mom would be right there behind him. She could go at a full sprint in high heels, but if she really wanted to come after me she had this thing where she'd kick her shoes off while still going at top speed. She'd do this weird move with her ankles and the heels would go flying and she wouldn't even miss a step. That's when I knew, *Okay, she's in turbo mode now.*

When I was little she always caught me, but as I got older I got faster, and when speed failed her she'd use her wits. If I was about to get away she'd yell, *"Stop! Thief!"* She'd do this to her own child. In South Africa, nobody gets involved in other people's business—unless it's mob justice, and then everybody wants in. So she'd yell "Thief!" knowing it would bring the whole neighborhood out against me, and then I'd have strangers trying to grab me and tackle me, and I'd have to duck and dive and dodge them as well, all the while screaming, "I'm not a thief! I'm her son!"

The last thing I wanted to do that Sunday morning was climb into some crowded minibus, but the second I heard my mom say *sun'qhela* I knew my fate was sealed. She gathered up Andrew and we climbed out of the Volkswagen and went out to try to catch a ride.

I was five years old, nearly six, when Nelson Mandela was released from prison. I remember seeing it on TV and everyone being happy. I didn't know why we were happy, just that we were. I was aware of the fact that there was a thing called apartheid and it was ending and that was a big deal, but I didn't understand the intricacies of it.

What I do remember, what I will never forget, is the violence that followed. The triumph of democracy over apartheid is sometimes called the Bloodless Revolution. It is called that because very little white blood was spilled. Black blood ran in the streets.

As the apartheid regime fell, we knew that the black man was now going to rule. The question was, which black man? Spates of violence broke out between the Inkatha Freedom Party and the ANC, the African National Congress, as they jockeyed for power. The political dynamic between these two groups was very complicated, but the simplest way to understand it is as a proxy war between Zulu and Xhosa. The Inkatha was predominantly Zulu, very militant and very nationalistic. The ANC was a broad coalition encompassing many different tribes, but its leaders at the time were primarily Xhosa. Instead of uniting for peace they turned on one another, committing acts of unbelievable savagery. Massive riots broke out. Thousands of people were killed. Necklacing was common. That's where people would hold someone down and put a rubber tire over his torso, pinning his arms. Then they'd douse him with petrol and set him on fire and burn him alive. The ANC did it to Inkatha. Inkatha did it to the ANC. I saw one of those charred bodies on the side of the road one day on my way to school. In the evenings my mom and I would turn on our little black-and-white TV and watch the news. A dozen people killed. Fifty people killed. A hundred people killed.

Eden Park sat not far from the sprawling townships of the East Rand, Thokoza and Katlehong, which were the sites of some of the most horrific Inkatha–ANC clashes. Once a month at least we'd drive home and the neighborhood would be on fire. Hundreds of rioters in the street. My mom would edge the car slowly through the crowds and around blockades made of flaming tires. Nothing burns like a tire—it rages with a fury you can't imagine. As we drove past the burning blockades, it felt like we were inside an oven. I used to say to my mom, "I think Satan burns tires in Hell."

Whenever the riots broke out, all our neighbors would wisely hole up behind closed doors. But not my mom. She'd head straight out, and as we'd inch our way past the blockades, she'd give the rioters this look. *Let me pass. I'm not involved in this shit.* She was unwavering in the face of danger. That always amazed me. It didn't matter that there was a war on our doorstep. She had things to do, places to be. It was the same stubbornness that kept her going to church despite a broken-down car. There could be five hundred rioters with a blockade of burning tires on the main road out of Eden Park, and my mother would say, "Get dressed. I've got to go to work. You've got to go to school."

"But aren't you afraid?" I'd say. "There's only one of you and there's so many of them."

"Honey, I'm not alone," she'd say. "I've got all of Heaven's angels behind me."

"Well, it would be nice if we could *see* them," I'd say. "Because I don't think the rioters know they're there."

She'd tell me not to worry. She always came back to the phrase she lived by: "If God is with me, who can be against me?" She was never scared. Even when she should have been.

That carless Sunday we made our circuit of churches, ending up, as usual, at white church. When we walked out of Rosebank Union it was dark and we were alone. It had been an endless day of minibuses from mixed church to black church to white church, and I was exhausted. It was nine o'clock at least. In those days, with all the violence and riots going on, you did not want to be out that late at night. We were standing at the corner of Jellicoe Avenue and Oxford Road, right in the heart of Johannesburg's wealthy, white suburbia, and there were no minibuses. The streets were empty.

I so badly wanted to turn to my mom and say, "You see? This is why God wanted us to stay home." But one look at the expression on her face, and I knew better than to speak. There were times I could talk smack to my mom—this was not one of them.

We waited and waited for a minibus to come by. Under apartheid the government provided no public transportation for blacks, but white people still needed us to show up to mop their floors and clean their bathrooms. Necessity being the mother of invention, black people created their own transit system, an informal network of bus routes, controlled by private associations operating entirely outside the law. Because the minibus business was completely unregulated, it was basically organized crime. Different groups ran different routes, and they would fight over who controlled what. There was bribery and general shadiness that went on, a great deal of violence, and a lot of protection money paid to avoid violence. The one thing you didn't do was steal a route from a rival group. Drivers who stole routes would get killed. Being unregulated, minibuses were also very unreliable. When they came, they came. When they didn't, they didn't.

Standing outside Rosebank Union, I was literally falling asleep on my feet. Not a minibus in sight. Eventually my mother said, "Let's hitchhike." We walked and walked, and after what felt like an eternity, a car drove up and stopped. The driver offered us a ride, and we climbed in. We hadn't gone ten feet when suddenly a minibus swerved right in front of the car and cut us off.

A Zulu driver got out with an *iwisa*, a large, traditional Zulu weapon—a war club, basically. They're used to smash people's skulls in. Another guy, his crony, got out of the passenger side. They walked up to the driver's side of the car we were in, grabbed the man who'd offered us a ride, pulled him out, and started shoving their clubs in his face. "Why are you stealing our customers? Why are you picking people up?"

It looked like they were going to kill this guy. I knew that happened sometimes. My mom spoke up. "Hey, listen, he was just helping me. Leave him. We'll ride with you. That's what we wanted in the first place." So we got out of the first car and climbed into the minibus.

We were the only passengers in the minibus. In addition to being violent gangsters, South African minibus drivers are notorious for complaining and haranguing passengers as they drive. This driver was a particularly angry one. As we rode along, he started lecturing my mother about being in a car with a man who was not her husband. My mother didn't suffer lectures from strange men. She told him to mind his own business, and when he heard her speaking in Xhosa, that really set him off. The stereotypes of Zulu and Xhosa women were as ingrained as those of the men. Zulu women were well-behaved and dutiful. Xhosa women were promiscuous and unfaithful. And here was my mother, his tribal enemy, a Xhosa woman alone with two small children—one of them a mixed child, no less. Not just a whore but a whore who sleeps with white men. "Oh, you're a *Xhosa*," he said. "That explains it. Climbing into strange men's cars. Disgusting woman."

My mom kept telling him off and he kept calling her names, yelling at her from the front seat, wagging his finger in the rearview mirror and growing more and more menacing until finally he said, "That's the problem with you Xhosa women. You're all sluts—and tonight you're going to learn your lesson."

He sped off. He was driving fast, and he wasn't stopping, only slowing down to check for traffic at the intersections before speeding through. Death was never far away from anybody back then. At that point my mother could be raped. We could be killed. These were all viable options. I didn't fully comprehend the danger we were in at the moment; I was so tired that I just wanted to sleep. Plus my mom stayed very calm. She didn't panic, so I didn't know to panic. She just kept trying to reason with him.

"I'm sorry if we've upset you, *bhuti*. You can just let us out here—"

"No."

"Really, it's fine. We can just walk—"

"No."

He raced along Oxford Road, the lanes empty, no other cars out. I was sitting closest to the minibus's sliding door. My mother sat next to me, holding baby Andrew. She looked out the window at the passing road and then leaned over to me and whispered, "Trevor, when he slows down at the next intersection, I'm going to open the door and we're going to jump."

I didn't hear a word of what she was saying, because by that point I'd completely nodded off. When we came to the next traffic light, the driver eased off the gas a bit to look around and check the road. My mother reached over, pulled the sliding door open, grabbed me, and threw me out as far as she could. Then she took Andrew, curled herself in a ball around him, and leaped out behind me.

It felt like a dream until the pain hit. *Bam!* I smacked hard on the pavement. My mother landed right beside me and we tumbled and tumbled and rolled and rolled. I was wide awake now. I went from half asleep to *What the hell?!* Eventually I came to a stop and pulled myself up, completely disoriented. I looked around and saw my mother, already on her feet. She turned and looked at me and screamed.

"Run!"

So I ran, and she ran, and nobody ran like me and my mom.

It's weird to explain, but I just knew what to do. It was animal instinct, learned in a world where violence was always lurking and waiting to erupt. In the townships, when the police came swooping in with their riot gear and armored cars and helicopters, I knew: *Run for cover. Run and hide.* I knew that as a five-year-old. Had I lived a different life, getting thrown out of a speeding minibus might have fazed me. I'd have stood there like an idiot, going, "What's happening, Mom? Why are my legs so sore?" But there was none of that. Mom said "run," and I ran. Like the gazelle runs from the lion, I ran.

The men stopped the minibus and got out and tried to chase us, but they didn't stand a chance. We smoked them. I think they were in shock. I still remember glancing back and seeing them give up with a look of utter bewilderment on their faces. *What just happened? Who'd have thought a woman with two small children could run so fast?* They didn't know they were dealing with the reigning champs of the Maryvale College sports day. We kept going and going until we made it to a twenty-four-hour petrol station and called the police. By then the men were long gone.

I still didn't know why any of this had happened; I'd been running on pure adrenaline. Once we stopped running I realized how much pain I was in. I looked down, and the skin on my arms was scraped and torn. I was cut up and bleeding all over. Mom was, too. My baby brother was fine, though, incredibly. My mom had wrapped herself around him, and he'd come through without a scratch. I turned to her in shock.

"What was *that*?! Why are we running?!"

"What do you mean, 'Why are we running?' Those men were trying to kill us."

"You never told me that! You just threw me out of the car!"

"I did tell you. Why didn't you jump?"

"Jump?! I was asleep!"

"So I should have left you there for them to kill you?"

"At least they would have woken me up before they killed me."

Back and forth we went. I was too confused and too angry about getting thrown out of the car to realize what had happened. My mother had saved my life.

As we caught our breath and waited for the police to come and drive us home, she said, "Well, at least we're safe, thank God."

But I was nine years old and I knew better. I wasn't going to keep quiet this time.

"No, Mom! This was *not* thanks to God! You should have listened to God when he told us to stay at home when the car wouldn't start, because clearly the Devil tricked us into coming out tonight."

"No, Trevor! That's not how the Devil works. This is part of God's plan, and if He wanted us here then He had a reason . . ."

And on and on and there we were, back at it, arguing about God's will. Finally I said, "Look, Mom. I know you love Jesus, but maybe next week you could ask him to meet us at our house. Because this really wasn't a fun night."

She broke out in a huge smile and started laughing. I started laughing, too, and we stood there, this little boy and his mom, our arms and legs covered in blood and dirt, laughing together through the pain in the light of a petrol station on the side of the road in the middle of the night.

Apartheid was perfect racism. It took centuries to develop, starting all the way back in 1652 when the Dutch East India Company landed at the Cape of Good Hope and established a trading colony, Kaapstad, later known as Cape Town, a rest stop for ships traveling between Europe and India. To impose white rule, the Dutch colonists went to war with the natives, ultimately developing a set of laws to subjugate and enslave them. When the British took over the Cape Colony, the descendants of the original Dutch settlers trekked inland and developed their own language, culture, and customs, eventually becoming their own people, the Afrikaners—the white tribe of Africa.

The British abolished slavery in name but kept it in practice. They did so because, in the mid-1800s, in what had been written off as a near-worthless way station on the route to the Far East, a few lucky capitalists stumbled upon the richest gold and diamond reserves in the world, and an endless supply of expendable bodies was needed to go in the ground and get it all out.

As the British Empire fell, the Afrikaner rose up to claim South Africa as his rightful inheritance. To maintain power in the face of the country's rising and restless black majority, the government realized they needed a newer and more robust set of tools. They set up a formal commission to go out and study institutionalized racism all over the world. They went to Australia. They went to the Netherlands. They went to America. They saw what worked, what didn't. Then they came back and published a report, and the government used that knowledge to build the most advanced system of racial oppression known to man.

Apartheid was a police state, a system of surveillance and laws designed to keep black people under total control. A full compendium of those laws would run more than three thousand pages and weigh approximately ten pounds, but the general thrust of it should be easy enough for any American to understand. In America you had the forced removal of the native onto reservations coupled with slavery followed by segregation. Imagine all three of those things happening to the same group of people at the same time. That was apartheid.

———

2

BORN A CRIME

I grew up in South Africa during apartheid, which was awkward because I was raised in a mixed family, with me being the mixed one in the family. My mother, Patricia Nombuyiselo Noah, is black. My father, Robert, is white. Swiss/German, to be precise, which Swiss/Germans invariably are. During apartheid, one of the worst crimes you could commit was having sexual relations with a person of another race. Needless to say, my parents committed that crime.

In any society built on institutionalized racism, race-mixing doesn't merely challenge the system as unjust, it reveals the system as unsustainable and incoherent. Race-mixing proves that races can mix—and in a lot of cases, *want* to mix. Because a mixed person embodies that rebuke to the logic of the system, race-mixing becomes a crime worse than treason.

Humans being humans and sex being sex, that prohibition never stopped anyone. There were mixed kids in South Africa nine months after the first Dutch boats hit the beach in Table Bay. Just like in America, the colonists here had their way with the native women, as colonists so often do. Unlike in America, where anyone with one drop of black blood automatically became black, in South Africa mixed people came to be classified as their own separate group, neither black nor white but what we call "colored." Colored people, black people, white people, and Indian people were forced to register their race with the government. Based on those classifications, millions of people were uprooted and relocated. Indian areas were segregated from colored areas, which were segregated from black areas—all of them segregated from white areas and separated from one another by buffer zones of empty land. Laws were passed prohibiting sex between Europeans and natives, laws that were later amended to prohibit sex between whites and all nonwhites.

The government went to insane lengths to try to enforce these new laws. The penalty for breaking them was five years in prison. There were whole police squads whose only job was to go around peeking through windows—clearly an assignment for only the finest law enforcement officers. And if an interracial couple got caught, God help them. The police would kick down the door, drag the people out, beat them, arrest them. At least that's what they did to the black person. With the white person it was more like, "Look, I'll just say you were drunk, but don't do it again, eh? Cheers." That's how it was with a white man and a black woman. If a black man was caught having sex with a white woman, he'd be lucky if he wasn't charged with rape.

If you ask my mother whether she ever considered the ramifications of having a mixed child under apartheid, she will say no. She wanted to do something, figured out a way to do it, and then she did it. She had a level of fearlessness that you have to possess to take on something like she did. If you stop to consider the ramifications, you'll never do anything. Still, it was a crazy, reckless thing to do. A million things had to go right for us to slip through the cracks the way we did for as long as we did.

Under apartheid, if you were a black man you worked on a farm or in a factory or in a mine. If you were a black woman, you worked in a factory or as a maid. Those were pretty much your only options. My mother didn't want to work in a factory. She was a horrible cook and never would have stood for some white lady telling her what to do all day. So, true to her nature, she found an option that was not among the ones presented to her: She took a secretarial course, a typing class. At the time, a black woman learning how to type was like a blind person learning how to drive. It's an admirable effort, but you're unlikely to ever be called upon to execute the task. By law, white-collar jobs and skilled-labor jobs were reserved for whites. Black people didn't work in offices. My mom, however, was a rebel, and, fortunately for her, her rebellion came along at the right moment.

In the early 1980s, the South African government began making minor reforms in an attempt to quell international protest over the atrocities and human rights abuses of apartheid. Among those reforms was the token hiring of black workers in low-level white-collar jobs. Like typists. Through an employment agency she got a job as a secretary at ICI, a multinational pharmaceutical company in Braamfontein, a suburb of Johannesburg.

When my mom started working, she still lived with my grandmother in Soweto, the township where the government had relocated my family decades before. But my mother was unhappy at home, and when she was twenty-two she ran away to live in downtown Johannesburg. There was only one problem: It was illegal for black people to live there.

The ultimate goal of apartheid was to make South Africa a white country, with every black person stripped of his or her citizenship and relocated to live in the homelands, the Bantustans, semi-sovereign black territories that were in reality puppet states of the government in Pretoria. But this so-called white country could not function without black labor to produce its wealth, which meant black people had to be allowed to live near white areas in the townships, government-planned ghettos built to house black workers, like Soweto. The township was where you lived, but your status as a laborer was the only thing that permitted you to stay there. If your papers were revoked for any reason, you could be deported back to the homelands.

To leave the township for work in the city, or for any other reason, you had to carry a pass with your ID number; otherwise you could be arrested. There was also a curfew: After a certain hour, blacks had to be back home in the township or risk arrest. My mother didn't care. She was determined to never go home again. So she stayed in town, hiding and sleeping in public restrooms until she learned the rules of navigating the city from the other black women who had contrived to live there: prostitutes.

Many of the prostitutes in town were Xhosa. They spoke my mother's language and showed her how to survive. They taught her how to dress up in a pair of maid's overalls to move around the city without being questioned. They also introduced her to white men who were willing to rent out flats in town. A lot of these men were foreigners, Germans and Portuguese who didn't care about the law and were happy to sign a lease giving a prostitute a place to live and work in exchange for a steady piece on the side. My mom wasn't interested in any such arrangement, but thanks to her job she did have money to pay rent. She met a German fellow through one of her prostitute friends, and he agreed to let her a flat in his name. She moved in and bought a bunch of maid's overalls to wear. She was caught and arrested many times, for not having her ID on the way home from work, for being in a white area after hours. The penalty for violating the pass laws was thirty days in jail or a fine of fifty rand, nearly half her monthly salary. She would scrape together the money, pay the fine, and go right back about her business.

My mom's secret flat was in a neighborhood called Hillbrow. She lived in number 203. Down the corridor was a tall, brown-haired, brown-eyed Swiss/German expat named Robert. He lived in 206. As a former trading colony, South Africa has always had a large expatriate community. People find their way here. Tons of Germans. Lots of Dutch. Hillbrow at the time was the Greenwich Village of South Africa. It was a thriving scene, cosmopolitan and liberal. There were galleries and underground theaters where artists and performers dared to speak up and criticize the government in front of integrated crowds. There were restaurants and nightclubs, a lot of them foreign-owned, that served a mixed clientele, black people who hated the status quo and white people who simply thought it ridiculous. These people would have secret get-togethers, too, usually in someone's flat or in empty basements that had been converted into clubs. Integration by its nature was a political act, but the get-togethers themselves weren't political at all. People would meet up and hang out, have parties.

My mom threw herself into that scene. She was always out at some club, some party, dancing, meeting people. She was a regular at the Hillbrow Tower, one of the tallest buildings in Africa at that time. It had a nightclub with a rotating dance floor on the top floor. It was an exhilarating time but still dangerous. Sometimes the restaurants and clubs would get shut down, sometimes not. Sometimes the performers and patrons would get arrested, sometimes not. It was a roll of the dice. My mother never knew whom to trust, who might turn her in to the police. Neighbors would report on one another. The girlfriends of the white men in my mom's block of flats had every reason to report a black woman—a prostitute, no doubt—living among them. And you must remember that black people worked for the government as well. As far as her white neighbors knew, my mom could have been a spy posing as a prostitute posing as a maid, sent into Hillbrow to inform on whites who were breaking the law. That's how a police state works—everyone thinks everyone else is the police.

Living alone in the city, not being trusted and not being able to trust, my mother started spending more and more time in the company of someone with whom she felt safe: the tall Swiss man down the corridor in 206. He was forty-six. She was twenty-four. He was quiet and reserved; she was wild and free. She would stop by his flat to chat; they'd go to underground get-togethers, go dancing at the nightclub with the rotating dance floor. Something clicked.

I know that there was a genuine bond and a love between my parents. I saw it. But how romantic their relationship was, to what extent they were just friends, I can't say. These are things a child doesn't ask. All I do know is that one day she made her proposal.

"I want to have a kid," she told him.

"I don't want kids," he said.

"I didn't ask you to have a kid. I asked you to help me to have my kid. I just want the sperm from you."

"I'm Catholic," he said. "We don't do such things."

"You do know," she replied, "that I could sleep with you and go away and you would never know if you had a child or not. But I don't want that. Honor me with your yes so that I can live peacefully. I want a child of my own, and I want it from you. You will be able to see it as much as you like, but you will have no obligations. You don't have to talk to it. You don't have to pay for it. Just make this child for me."

For my mother's part, the fact that this man didn't particularly want a family with her, was prevented by law from having a family with her, was part of the attraction. She wanted a child, not a man stepping in to run her life. For my father's part, I know that for a long time he kept saying no. Eventually he said yes. Why he said yes is a question I will never have the answer to.

Nine months after that yes, on February 20, 1984, my mother checked into Hillbrow Hospital for a scheduled C-section delivery. Estranged from her family, pregnant by a man she could not be seen with in public, she was alone. The doctors took her up to the delivery room, cut open her belly, and reached in and pulled out a half-white, half-black child who violated any number of laws, statutes, and regulations—I was born a crime.

When the doctors pulled me out there was an awkward moment where they said, "Huh. That's a very light-skinned baby." A quick scan of the delivery room revealed no man standing around to take credit.

"Who is the father?" they asked.

"His father is from Swaziland," my mother said, referring to the tiny, landlocked kingdom in the west of South Africa.

They probably knew she was lying, but they accepted it because they needed an explanation. Under apartheid, the government labeled everything on your birth certificate: race, tribe, nationality. Everything had to be categorized. My mother lied and said I was born in Ka-Ngwane, the semi-sovereign homeland for Swazi people living in South Africa. So my birth certificate doesn't say that I'm Xhosa, which technically I am. And it doesn't say that I'm Swiss, which the government wouldn't allow. It just says that I'm from another country.

My father isn't on my birth certificate. Officially, he's never been my father. And my mother, true to her word, was prepared for him not to be involved. She'd rented a new flat for herself in Joubert Park, the neighborhood adjacent to Hillbrow, and that's where she took me when she left the hospital. The next week she went to visit him, with no baby. To her surprise, he asked where I was. "You said that you didn't want to be involved," she said. And he hadn't, but once I existed he realized he couldn't have a son living around the corner and not be a part of my life. So the three of us formed a kind of family, as much as our peculiar situation would allow. I lived with my mom. We'd sneak around and visit my dad when we could.

Where most children are proof of their parents' love, I was the proof of their criminality. The only time I could be with my father was indoors. If we left the house, he'd have to walk across the street from us. My mom and I used to go to Joubert Park all the time. It's the Central Park of Johannesburg—beautiful gardens, a zoo, a giant chessboard with human-sized pieces that people would play. My mother tells me that once, when I was a toddler, my dad tried to go with us. We were in the park, he was walking a good bit away from us, and I ran after him, screaming, "Daddy! Daddy! Daddy!" People started looking. He panicked and ran away. I thought it was a game and kept chasing him.

I couldn't walk with my mother, either; a light-skinned child with a black woman would raise too many questions. When I was a newborn, she could wrap me up and take me anywhere, but very quickly that was no longer an option. I was a giant baby, an enormous child. When I was one you'd have thought I was two. When I was two, you'd have thought I was four. There was no way to hide me.

My mom, same as she'd done with her flat and with her maid's uniforms, found the cracks in the system. It was illegal to be mixed (to have a black parent and a white parent), but it was not illegal to be colored (to have two parents who were both colored). So my mom moved me around the world as a colored child. She found a crèche in a colored area where she could leave me while she was at work. There was a colored woman named Queen who lived in our block of flats. When we wanted to go out to the park, my mom would invite her to go with us. Queen would walk next to me and act like she was my mother, and my mother would walk a few steps behind, like she was the maid working for the colored woman. I've got dozens of pictures of me walking with this woman who looks like me but who isn't my mother. And the black woman standing behind us who looks like she's photobombing the picture, that's my mom. When we didn't have a colored woman to walk with us, my mom would risk walking me on her own. She would hold my hand or carry me, but if the police showed up she would have to drop me and pretend I wasn't hers, like I was a bag of weed.

When I was born, my mother hadn't seen her family in three years, but she wanted me to know them and wanted them to know me, so the prodigal daughter returned. We lived in town, but I would spend weeks at a time with my grandmother in Soweto, often during the holidays. I have so many memories from the place that in my mind it's like we lived there, too.

Soweto was designed to be bombed—that's how forward-thinking the architects of apartheid were. The township was a city unto itself, with a population of nearly one million. There were only two roads in and out. That was so the military could lock us in, quell any rebellion. And if the monkeys ever went crazy and tried to break out of their cage, the air force could fly over and bomb the shit out of everyone. Growing up, I never knew that my grandmother lived in the center of a bull's-eye.

In the city, as difficult as it was to get around, we managed. Enough people were out and about, black, white, and colored, going to and from work, that we could get lost in the crowd. But only black people were permitted in Soweto. It was much harder to hide someone who looked like me, and the government was watching much more closely. In the white areas you rarely saw the police, and if you did it was Officer Friendly in his collared shirt and pressed pants. In Soweto the police were an occupying army. They didn't wear collared shirts. They wore riot gear. They were militarized. They operated in teams known as flying squads, because they would swoop in out of nowhere, riding in armored personnel carriers—hippos, we called them—tanks with enormous tires and slotted holes in the side of the vehicle to fire their guns out of. You didn't mess with a hippo. You saw one, you ran. That was a fact of life. The township was in a constant state of insurrection; someone was always marching or protesting somewhere and had to be suppressed. Playing in my grandmother's house, I'd hear gunshots, screams, tear gas being fired into crowds.

My memories of the hippos and the flying squads come from when I was five or six, when apartheid was finally coming apart. I never saw the police before that, because we could never risk the police seeing me. Whenever we went to Soweto, my grandmother refused to let me outside. If she was watching me it was, "No, no, no. He doesn't leave the house." Behind the wall, in the yard, I could play, but not in the street. And that's where the rest of the boys and girls were playing, in the street. My cousins, the neighborhood kids, they'd open the gate and head out and roam free and come back at dusk. I'd beg my grandmother to go outside.

"Please. *Please,* can I go play with my cousins?"

"No! They're going to take you!"

For the longest time I thought she meant that the other kids were going to steal me, but she was talking about the police. Children could be taken. Children *were* taken. The wrong color kid in the wrong color area, and the government could come in, strip your parents of custody, haul you off to an orphanage. To police the townships, the government relied on its network of *impipis,* the anonymous snitches who'd inform on suspicious activity. There were also the blackjacks, black people who worked for the police. My grandmother's neighbor was a blackjack. She had to make sure he wasn't watching when she smuggled me in and out of the house.

My gran still tells the story of when I was three years old and, fed up with being a prisoner, I dug a hole under the gate in the driveway, wriggled through, and ran off. Everyone panicked. A search party went out and tracked me down. I had no idea how much danger I was putting everyone in. The family could have been deported, my gran could have been arrested, my mom might have gone to prison, and I probably would have been packed off to a home for colored kids.

So I was kept inside. Other than those few instances of walking in the park, the flashes of memory I have from when I was young are almost all indoors, me with my mom in her tiny flat, me by myself at my gran's. I didn't have any friends. I didn't know any kids besides my cousins. I wasn't a lonely kid—I was good at being alone. I'd read books, play with the toy that I had, make up imaginary worlds. I lived inside my head. I still live inside my head. To this day you can leave me alone for hours and I'm perfectly happy entertaining myself. I have to remember to be with people.

Obviously, I was not the only child born to black and white parents during apartheid. Traveling around the world today, I meet other mixed South Africans all the time. Our stories start off identically. We're around the same age. Their parents met at some underground party in Hillbrow or Cape Town. They lived in an illegal flat. The difference is that in virtually every other case they left. The white parent smuggled them out through Lesotho or Botswana, and they grew up in exile, in England or Germany or Switzerland, because being a mixed family under apartheid was just that unbearable.

Once Mandela was elected we could finally live freely. Exiles started to return. I met my first one when I was around seventeen. He told me his story, and I was like, "Wait, *what?* You mean we could have *left?*

That was an *option*?" Imagine being thrown out of an airplane. You hit the ground and break all your bones, you go to the hospital and you heal and you move on and finally put the whole thing behind you—and then one day somebody tells you about parachutes. That's how I felt. I couldn't understand why we'd stayed. I went straight home and asked my mom.

"Why? Why didn't we just leave? Why didn't we go to Switzerland?"

"Because I am not Swiss," she said, as stubborn as ever. "This is my country. Why should I leave?"

South Africa is a mix of the old and the new, the ancient and the modern, and South African Christianity is a perfect example of this. We adopted the religion of our colonizers, but most people held on to the old ancestral ways, too, just in case. In South Africa, faith in the Holy Trinity exists quite comfortably alongside belief in witchcraft, in casting spells and putting curses on one's enemies.

I come from a country where people are more likely to visit *sangomas*—shamans, traditional healers, pejoratively known as witch doctors—than they are to visit doctors of Western medicine. I come from a country where people have been arrested and tried for witchcraft—in a court of law. I'm not talking about the 1700s. I'm talking about five years ago. I remember a man being on trial for striking another person with lightning. That happens a lot in the homelands. There are no tall buildings, few tall trees, nothing between you and the sky, so people get hit by lightning all the time. And when someone gets killed by lightning, everyone knows it's because somebody used Mother Nature to take out a hit. So if you had a beef with the guy who got killed, someone will accuse you of murder and the police will come knocking.

"Mr. Noah, you've been accused of murder. You used witchcraft to kill David Kibuuka by causing him to be struck by lightning."

"What is the evidence?"

"The evidence is that David Kibuuka got struck by lightning and it wasn't even raining."

And you go to trial. The court is presided over by a judge. There is a docket. There is a prosecutor. Your defense attorney has to prove lack of motive, go through the crime-scene forensics, present a staunch defense. And your attorney's argument can't be "Witchcraft isn't real." No, no, no. You'll lose.

3

TREVOR, PRAY

I grew up in a world run by women. My father was loving and devoted, but I could only see him when and where apartheid allowed. My uncle Velile, my mom's younger brother, lived with my grandmother, but he spent most of his time at the local tavern getting into fights.

The only semi-regular male figure in my life was my grandfather, my mother's father, who was a force to be reckoned with. He was divorced from my grandmother and didn't live with us, but he was around. His name was Temperance Noah, which was odd since he was not a man of moderation at all. He was boisterous and loud. His nickname in the neighborhood was "Tat Shisha," which translates loosely to "the smokin' hot grandpa." And that's exactly who he was. He loved the ladies, and the ladies loved him. He'd put on his best suit and stroll through the streets of Soweto on random afternoons, making every-body laugh and charming all the women he'd meet. He had a big, daz-zling smile with bright white teeth—false teeth. At home, he'd take them out and I'd watch him do that thing where he looked like he was eating his own face.

We found out much later in life that he was bipolar, but before that we just thought he was eccentric. One time he borrowed my mother's car to go to the shop for milk and bread. He disappeared and didn't come home until late that night when we were way past the point of needing the milk or the bread. Turned out he'd passed a young woman at the bus stop and, believing no beautiful woman should have to wait for a bus, he offered her a ride to where she lived—three hours away. My mom was furious with him because he'd cost us a whole tank of petrol, which was enough to get us to work and school for two weeks.

When he was up you couldn't stop him, but his mood swings were wild. In his youth he'd been a boxer, and one day he said I'd disrespected him and now he wanted to box me. He was in his eighties. I was twelve. He had his fists up, circling me. "Let's go, Trevah! Come on! Put your fists up! Hit me! I'll show you I'm still a man! Let's go!" I couldn't hit him because I wasn't about to hit my elder. Plus I'd never been in a fight and I wasn't going to have my first one be with an eighty-year-old man. I ran to my mom, and she got him to stop. The day after his pugilistic rage, he sat in his chair and didn't move or say a word all day.

Temperance lived with his second family in the Meadowlands, and we visited them sparingly because my mom was always afraid of being poisoned. Which was a thing that would happen. The first family were the heirs, so there was always the chance they might get poisoned by the second family. It was like *Game of Thrones* with poor people. We'd go into that house and my mom would warn me.

"Trevor, don't eat the food."

"But I'm starving."

"No. They might poison us."

"Okay, then why don't I just pray to Jesus and Jesus will take the poison out of the food?"

"Trevor! *Sun'qhela!*"

So I only saw my grandfather now and then, and when he was gone the house was in the hands of women.

In addition to my mom there was my aunt Sibongile; she and her first husband, Dinky, had two kids, my cousins Mlungisi and Bulelwa. Sibongile was a powerhouse, a strong woman in every sense, big-chested, the mother hen. Dinky, as his name implies, was dinky. He was a small man. He was abusive, but not really. It was more like he tried to be abusive, but he wasn't very good at it. He was trying to live up to this image of what he thought a husband should be, dominant, controlling. I remember being told as a child, "If you don't hit your woman, you don't love her." That was the talk you'd hear from men in bars and in the streets.

Dinky was trying to masquerade as this patriarch that he wasn't. He'd slap my aunt and hit her and she'd take it and take it, and then eventually she'd snap and smack him down and put him back in his place. Dinky would always walk around like, "I control my woman." And you'd want to say, "Dinky, first of all, you don't. Second of all, you don't need to. Because she loves you." I can remember one day my aunt had really had enough. I was in the yard and Dinky came running out of the house screaming bloody murder. Sibongile was right behind him with a pot of boiling water, cursing at him and threatening to douse him with it. In Soweto you were always hearing about men getting doused with pots of boiling water—often a woman's only re-course. And men were lucky if it was water. Some women used hot cooking oil. Water was if the woman wanted to teach her man a lesson. Oil meant she wanted to end it.

My grandmother Frances Noah was the family matriarch. She ran the house, looked after the kids, did the cooking and the cleaning. She's barely five feet tall, hunched over from years in the factory, but rock hard and still to this day very active and very much alive. Where my grandfather was big and boisterous, my grandmother was calm, calcu-lating, with a mind as sharp as anything. If you need to know anything in the family history, going back to the 1930s, she can tell you what day it happened, where it happened, and why it happened. She remembers it all.

My great-grandmother lived with us as well. We called her Koko. She was super old, well into her nineties, stooped and frail, completely blind. Her eyes had gone white, clouded over by cataracts. She couldn't walk without someone holding her up. She'd sit in the kitchen next to the coal stove, bundled up in long skirts and head scarves, blankets over her shoulders. The coal stove was always on. It was for cooking, heating the house, heating water for baths. We put her there because it was the warmest spot in the house. In the morning someone would wake her and bring her to sit in the kitchen. At night someone would come take her to bed. That's all she did, all day, every day. Sit by the stove. She was fantastic and fully with it. She just couldn't see and didn't move.

Koko and my gran would sit and have long conversations, but as a five-year-old I didn't think of Koko as a real person. Since her body didn't move, she was like a brain with a mouth. Our relationship was nothing but command prompts and replies, like talking to a computer.

"Good morning, Koko."

"Good morning, Trevor."

"Koko, did you eat?"

"Yes, Trevor."

"Koko, I'm going out."

"Okay, be careful."

"Bye, Koko."

"Bye, Trevor."

The fact that I grew up in a world run by women was no accident. Apartheid kept me away from my father because he was white, but for almost all the kids I knew on my grandmother's block in Soweto, apartheid had taken away their fathers as well, just for different reasons. Their fathers were off working in a mine somewhere, able to come home only during the holidays. Their fathers had been sent to prison.

Their fathers were in exile, fighting for the cause. Women held the community together. *"Wathint'Abafazi Wathint'imbokodo!"* was the chant they would rally to during the freedom struggle. "When you strike a woman, you strike a rock." As a nation, we recognized the power of women, but in the home they were expected to submit and obey.

In Soweto, religion filled the void left by absent men. I used to ask my mom if it was hard for her to raise me alone without a husband. She'd reply, "Just because I live without a man doesn't mean I've never had a husband. God is my husband." For my mom, my aunt, my grandmother, and all the other women on our street, life centered on faith. Prayer meetings would rotate houses up and down the block based on the day. These groups were women and children only. My mom would always ask my uncle Velile to join, and he'd say, "I would join if there were more men, but I can't be the only one here." Then the singing and praying would start, and that was his cue to leave.

For these prayer meetings, we'd jam ourselves into the tiny living area of the host family's house and form a circle. Then we would go around the circle offering prayers. The grannies would talk about what was happening in their lives. "I'm happy to be here. I had a good week at work. I got a raise and I wanted to say thank you and praise Jesus." Sometimes they'd pull out their Bible and say, "This scripture spoke to me and maybe it will help you." Then there would be a bit of song. There was a leather pad called "the beat" that you'd strap to your palm, like a percussion instrument. Someone would clap along on that, keeping time while everyone sang, *"Masango vulekani singene eJerusalema. Masango vulekani singene eJerusalema."*

That's how it would go. Pray, sing, pray. Sing, pray, sing. Sing, sing, sing. Pray, pray, pray. Sometimes it would last for hours, always ending with an "amen," and they could keep that "amen" going on for five minutes at least. *"Ah-men. Ah-ah-ah-men. Ah-ah-ah-ah-men. Ahhhhhhhhah-hhhhhhhhhhhahhhhhhahhhhhhahhhhhhmen. Meni-meni-meni. Men-men-men. Ahhhhhhhhhhhhhhhhhhhhhhhhhhhhhhhhhhhhhhhhhhhhhhhmmmmmmmennn-nnnnnnnnnnnnnnnnnnnnnnnnnnnnnnnnnnnnnnnnnnnnnnnnnnnnnnnnnnnnn-*

nnnnnnnnnnnnnnnnnnnnnnnnnnnnnnnnnnnnnnnnnnnnnnnnnnnnnnnnnnnnnnnnnnnnn-nnnnnnnnnnnnnnn. "Then everyone would say goodbye and go home. Next night, different house, same thing.

Tuesday nights, the prayer meeting came to my grandmother's house, and I was always excited, for two reasons. One, I got to clap along on the beat for the singing. And two, I loved to pray. My grandmother always told me that she loved my prayers. She believed my prayers were more powerful, because I prayed in English. Everyone knows that Jesus, who's white, speaks English. The Bible is in English. Yes, the Bible was not *written* in English, but the Bible came to South Africa in English so to us it's in English. Which made my prayers the best prayers because English prayers get answered first. How do we know this? Look at white people. Clearly they're getting through to the right person. Add to that Matthew 19:14. "Suffer little children to come unto me," Jesus said, "for theirs is the kingdom of heaven." So if a child is praying in English? To White Jesus? That's a powerful combination right there. Whenever I prayed, my grandmother would say, "That prayer is going to get answered. I can *feel* it."

Women in the township always had something to pray for—money problems, a son who'd been arrested, a daughter who was sick, a husband who drank. Whenever the prayer meetings were at our house, because my prayers were so good, my grandmother would want me to pray for everyone. She would turn to me and say, "Trevor, pray." And I'd pray. I loved doing it. My grandmother had convinced me that my prayers got answered. I felt like I was helping people.

There is something magical about Soweto. Yes, it was a prison designed by our oppressors, but it also gave us a sense of self-determination and control. Soweto was ours. It had an aspirational quality that you don't find elsewhere. In America the dream is to make it out of the ghetto. In Soweto, because there was no leaving the ghetto, the dream was to transform the ghetto.

For the million people who lived in Soweto, there were no stores, no bars, no restaurants. There were no paved roads, minimal electricity, inadequate sewerage. But when you put one million people together in one place, they find a way to make a life for themselves. A black-market economy rose up, with every type of business being run out of someone's house: auto mechanics, day care, guys selling refurbished tires.

The most common were the *spaza* shops and the shebeens. The *spaza* shops were informal grocery stores. People would build a kiosk in their garage, buy wholesale bread and eggs, and then resell them piecemeal. Everyone in the township bought things in minute quantities because nobody had any money. You couldn't afford to buy a dozen eggs at a time, but you could buy two eggs because that's all you needed that morning. You could buy a quarter loaf of bread, a cup of sugar. The shebeens were unlawful bars in the back of someone's house. They'd put chairs in their backyard and hang out an awning and run a speakeasy. The shebeens were where men would go to drink after work and during prayer meetings and most any other time of day as well.

People built homes the way they bought eggs: a little at a time. Every family in the township was allocated a piece of land by the government. You'd first build a shanty on your plot, a makeshift structure of plywood and corrugated iron. Over time, you'd save up money and build a brick wall. One wall. Then you'd save up and build another wall. Then, years later, a third wall and eventually a fourth. Now you had a room, one room for everyone in your family to sleep, eat, do everything. Then you'd save up for a roof. Then windows. Then you'd plaster the thing. Then your daughter would start a family. There was nowhere for them to go, so they'd move in with you. You'd add another corrugated-iron structure onto your brick room and slowly, over years, turn that into a proper room for them as well. Now your house had two rooms. Then three. Maybe four. Slowly, over generations, you'd keep trying to get to the point where you had a home.

My grandmother lived in Orlando East. She had a two-room house. Not a two-bedroom house. A two-room house. There was a bedroom, and then there was basically a living room/kitchen/everything-else room. Some might say we lived like poor people. I prefer "open plan." My mom and I would stay there during school holidays. My aunt and cousins would be there whenever she was on the outs with Dinky. We all slept on the floor in one room, my mom and me, my aunt and my cousins, my uncle and my grandmother and my great-grandmother. The adults each had their own foam mattresses, and there was one big one that we'd roll out into the middle, and the kids slept on that.

We had two shanties in the backyard that my grandmother would rent out to migrants and seasonal workers. We had a small peach tree in a tiny patch on one side of the house and on the other side my grandmother had a driveway. I never understood why my grandmother had a driveway. She didn't have a car. She didn't know how to drive. Yet she had a driveway. All of our neighbors had driveways, some with fancy, cast-iron gates. None of them had cars, either. There was no future in which most of these families would ever have cars. There was maybe one car for every thousand people, yet almost everyone had a driveway. It was almost like building the driveway was a way of willing the car to happen. The story of Soweto is the story of the driveways. It's a hopeful place.

Sadly, no matter how fancy you made your house, there was one thing you could never aspire to improve: your toilet. There was no indoor running water, just one communal outdoor tap and one outdoor toilet shared by six or seven houses. Our toilet was in a corrugated-iron outhouse shared among the adjoining houses. Inside, there was a concrete slab with a hole in it and a plastic toilet seat on top; there had been a lid at some point, but it had broken and disappeared long ago. We couldn't afford toilet paper, so on the wall next to the seat was a wire hanger with old newspaper on it for you to wipe. The newspaper was uncomfortable, but at least I stayed informed while I handled my business.

The thing that I couldn't handle about the outhouse was the flies. It was a long drop to the bottom, and they were always down there, eating on the pile, and I had an irrational, all-consuming fear that they were going to fly up and into my bum.

One afternoon, when I was around five years old, my gran left me at home for a few hours to go run errands. I was lying on the floor in the bedroom, reading. I needed to go, but it was pouring down rain. I was dreading going outside to use the toilet, getting drenched running out there, water dripping on me from the leaky ceiling, wet newspaper, the flies attacking me from below. Then I had an idea. Why bother with the outhouse at all? Why not put some newspaper on the floor and do my business like a puppy? That seemed like a fantastic idea. So that's what I did. I took the newspaper, laid it out on the kitchen floor, pulled down my pants, and squatted and got to it.

When you shit, as you first sit down, you're not fully in the experience yet. You are not yet a shitting person. You're transitioning from a person about to shit to a person who is shitting. You don't whip out your smartphone or a newspaper right away. It takes a minute to get the first shit out of the way and get in the zone and get comfortable. Once you reach that moment, that's when it gets really nice.

It's a powerful experience, shitting. There's something magical about it, profound even. I think God made humans shit in the way we do because it brings us back down to earth and gives us humility. I don't care who you are, we all shit the same. Beyoncé shits. The pope shits. The Queen of England shits. When we shit we forget our airs and our graces, we forget how famous or how rich we are. All of that goes away.

You are never more yourself than when you're taking a shit. You have that moment where you realize, *This is me. This is who I am.* You can pee without giving it a second thought, but not so with shitting. Have you ever looked in a baby's eyes when it's shitting? It's having a moment of pure self-awareness. The outhouse ruins that for you. The rain, the flies, you are robbed of your moment, and nobody should be robbed of that. Squatting and shitting on the kitchen floor that day, I was like, *Wow. There are no flies. There's no stress. This is really great. I'm really enjoying this.* I knew I'd made an excellent choice, and I was very proud of myself for making it. I'd reached that moment where I could relax and be with myself. Then I casually looked around the room and I glanced to my left and there, just a few feet away, right next to the coal stove, was Koko.

It was like the scene in *Jurassic Park* when the children turn and the T. rex is right there. Her eyes were wide open, cloudy white and darting around the room. I knew she couldn't see me, but her nose was starting to crinkle—she could sense that something was wrong.

I panicked. I was mid-shit. All you can do when you're mid-shit is finish shitting. My only option was to finish as quietly and as slowly as I could, so that's what I decided to do. Then: the softest *plop* of a little-boy turd on the newspaper. Koko's head snapped toward the sound.

"Who's there? Hallo? *Hallo?!*"

I froze. I held my breath and waited.

"Who's there?! Hallo?!"

I kept quiet, waited, then started again.

"Is somebody there?! Trevor, is that you?! Frances? Hallo? Hallo?"

She started calling out the whole family. "Nombuyiselo? Sibongile? Mlungisi? Bulelwa? Who's there? What's happening?"

It was like a game, like I was trying to hide and a blind woman was trying to find me using sonar. Every time she called out, I froze. There would be complete silence. "Who's there?! Hallo?!" I'd pause, wait for her to settle back in her chair, and then I'd start up again.

Finally, after what felt like forever, I finished. I stood up, took the newspaper—which is not the quietest thing—and I slowwwwwly folded it over. It crinkled. "Who's there?" Again I paused, waited. Then I folded it over some more, walked over to the rubbish bin, placed my sin at the bottom, and gingerly covered it with the rest of the trash. Then I tiptoed back to the other room, curled up on the mattress on the floor, and pretended to be asleep. The shit was done, no outhouse involved, and Koko was none the wiser.

Mission accomplished.

An hour later the rain had stopped. My grandmother came home. The second she walked in, Koko called out to her.

"Frances! Thank God you're here. There's something in the house."

"What was it?"

"I don't know, but I could hear it, and there was a smell."

My gran started sniffing the air. "Dear Lord! Yes, I can smell it, too. Is it a rat? Did something die? It's definitely in the house."

They went back and forth about it, quite concerned, and then, as it was getting dark, my mother came home from work. The second she walked in, my gran called out to her.

"Oh, Nombuyiselo! Nombuyiselo! There's something in the house!"

"What?! What do you mean?"

Koko told her the story, the sounds, the smells.

Then my mom, who has a keen sense of smell, started going around the kitchen, sniffing. "Yes, I can smell it. I can find it . . . I can find it . . ." She went to the rubbish bin. "It's in here." She lifted out the rubbish, pulled out the folded newspaper underneath, and opened it up, and there was my little turd. She showed it to gran.

"Look!"

"What?! How did it get there?!"

Koko, still blind, still stuck in her chair, was dying to know what was happening.

"What's going on?!" she cried. "What's going on?! Did you find it?!"

"It's shit," Mom said. "There's shit in the bottom of the dustbin."

"But how?!" Koko said. "There was no one here!"

"Are you sure there was no one here?"

"Yes. I called out to everyone. Nobody came."

My mother gasped. "We've been bewitched! It's a demon!"

For my mother, this was the logical conclusion. Because that's how witchcraft works. If someone has put a curse on you or your home, there is always the talisman or totem, a tuft of hair or the head of a cat, the physical manifestation of the spiritual thing, proof of the demon's presence.

Once my mom found the turd, all hell broke loose. This was *serious*. They had *evidence*. She came into the bedroom.

"Trevor! Trevor! Wake up!"

"What?!" I said, playing dumb. "What's going on?!"

"Come! There's a demon in the house!"

She took my hand and dragged me out of bed. It was all hands on deck, time for action. The first thing we had to do was go outside and burn the shit. That's what you do with witchcraft; the only way to destroy it is to burn the physical thing. We went out to the yard, and my mom put the newspaper with my little turd on the driveway, lit a match, and set it on fire. Then my mom and my gran stood around the burning shit, praying and singing songs of praise.

The commotion didn't stop there because when there's a demon around, the whole community has to join together to drive it out. If you're not part of the prayer, the demon might leave our house and go to your house and curse you. So we needed everyone. The alarm was raised. The call went out. My tiny old gran was out the gate, going up and down the block, calling to all the other old grannies for an emergency prayer meeting. "Come! We've been bewitched!"

I stood there, my shit burning in the driveway, my poor aged grandmother tottering up and down the street in a panic, and I didn't know what to do. I knew there was no demon, but there was no way I could come clean. The hiding I would have to endure? Good Lord. Honesty was never the best policy when it came to a hiding. I kept quiet.

Moments later the grannies came streaming in with their Bibles, through the gate and up the driveway, a dozen or more at least. Everyone went inside. The house was packed. This was by far the biggest prayer meeting we'd ever had—the biggest thing that had ever happened in the history of our home, period. Everyone sat in the circle, praying and praying, and the prayers were strong. The grannies were chanting and murmuring and swaying back and forth, speaking in tongues. I was doing my best to keep my head low and stay out of it. Then my grandmother reached back and grabbed me, pulled me into the middle of the circle, and looked into my eyes.

"Trevor, pray."

"Yes!" my mother said. "Help us! Pray, Trevor. Pray to God to kill the demon!"

I was terrified. I believed in the power of prayer. I knew that my prayers *worked*. So if I prayed to God to kill the thing that left the shit, and the thing that left the shit was me, then God was going to kill me. I froze. I didn't know what to do. But all the grannies were looking at me, waiting for me to pray, so I prayed, stumbling through as best I could.

"Dear Lord, please protect us, um, you know, from whoever did this but, like, we don't know what happened exactly and maybe it was a big misunderstanding and, you know, maybe we shouldn't be quick to judge when we don't know the whole story and, I mean, of course you know best, Heavenly Father, but maybe this time it wasn't actually a demon, because who can say for certain, so maybe cut whoever it was a break . . ."

It was not my best performance. Eventually I wrapped it up and sat back down. The praying continued. It went on for some time. Pray, sing, pray. Sing, pray, sing. Sing, sing, sing. Pray, pray, pray. Then everyone finally felt that the demon was gone and life could continue, and we had the big "amen" and everyone said good night and went home.

That night I felt terrible. Before bed, I quietly prayed, "God, I am so sorry for all of this. I know this was not cool." Because I knew: God answers your prayers. God is your father. He's the man who's there for you, the man who takes care of you. When you pray, He stops and He takes His time and He listens, and I had subjected Him to two hours of old grannies praying when I knew that with all the pain and suffering in the world He had more important things to deal with than my shit.

When I was growing up we used to get American TV shows rebroadcast on our stations: *Doogie Howser, M.D.; Murder, She Wrote; Rescue 911* with William Shatner. Most of them were dubbed into African languages. *ALF* was in Afrikaans. *Transformers* was in Sotho. But if you wanted to watch them in English, the original American audio would be simulcast on the radio. You could mute your TV and listen to that. Watching those shows, I realized that whenever black people were on-screen speaking in African languages, they felt familiar to me. They sounded like they were supposed to sound. Then I'd listen to them in simulcast on the radio, and they would all have black American accents. My perception of them changed. They didn't feel familiar. They felt like foreigners.

Language brings with it an identity and a culture, or at least the perception of it. A shared language says "We're the same." A language barrier says "We're different." The architects of apartheid understood this. Part of the effort to divide black people was to make sure we were separated not just physically but by language as well. In the Bantu schools, children were only taught in their home language. Zulu kids learned in Zulu. Tswana kids learned in Tswana. Because of this, we'd fall into the trap the government had set for us and fight among ourselves, believing that we were different.

The great thing about language is that you can just as easily use it to do the opposite: convince people that they are the same. Racism teaches us that we are different because of the color of our skin. But because racism is stupid, it's easily tricked. If you're racist and you meet someone who doesn't look like you, the fact that he can't speak like you reinforces your racist preconceptions: He's different, less intelligent. A brilliant scientist can come over the border from Mexico to live in America, but if he speaks in broken English, people say, "Eh, I don't trust this guy."

"But he's a scientist."

"In Mexican science, maybe. I don't trust him."

However, if the person who doesn't look like you speaks like you, your brain short-circuits because your racism program has none of those instructions in the code. "Wait, wait," your mind says, "the racism code says if he doesn't look like me he isn't like me, but the language code says if he speaks like me he . . . is like me? Something is off here. I can't figure this out."

4

CHAMELEON

One afternoon I was playing with my cousins. I was a doctor and they were my patients. I was operating on my cousin Bulelwa's ear with a set of matches when I accidentally perforated her eardrum. All hell broke loose. My grandmother came running in from the kitchen. *"Kwenzeka ntoni?!"* "What's happening?!" There was blood coming out of my cousin's head. We were all crying. My grandmother patched up Bulelwa's ear and made sure to stop the bleeding. But we kept crying. Because clearly we'd done something we were not supposed to do, and we knew we were going to be punished. My grandmother finished up with Bulelwa's ear and whipped out a belt and she beat the shit out of Bulelwa. Then she beat the shit out of Mlungisi, too. She didn't touch me.

Later that night my mother came home from work. She found my cousin with a bandage over her ear and my gran crying at the kitchen table.

"What's going on?" my mom said.

"Oh, Nombuyiselo," she said. "Trevor is so naughty. He's the naughtiest child I've ever come across in my life."

"Then you should hit him."

"I can't hit him."

"Why not?"

"Because I don't know how to hit a white child," she said. "A black child, I understand. A black child, you hit them and they stay black. Trevor, when you hit him he turns blue and green and yellow and red. I've never seen those colors before. I'm scared I'm going to break him. I don't want to kill a white person. I'm so afraid. I'm not going to touch him." And she never did.

My grandmother treated me like I was white. My grandfather did, too, only he was even more extreme. He called me "Mastah." In the car, he insisted on driving me as if he were my chauffeur. "Mastah must always sit in the backseat." I never challenged him on it. What was I going to say? "I believe your perception of race is flawed, Grand-father." No. I was five. I sat in the back.

There were so many perks to being "white" in a black family, I can't even front. I was having a great time. My own family basically did what the American justice system does: I was given more lenient treatment than the black kids. Misbehavior that my cousins would have been pun-ished for, I was given a warning and let off. And I was way naughtier than either of my cousins. It wasn't even close. If something got broken or if someone was stealing granny's cookies, it was me. I was trouble.

My mom was the only force I truly feared. She believed if you spare the rod, you spoil the child. But everyone else said, "No, he's differ-ent," and they gave me a pass. Growing up the way I did, I learned how easy it is for white people to get comfortable with a system that awards them all the perks. I knew my cousins were getting beaten for things that I'd done, but I wasn't interested in changing my grandmother's perspective, because that would mean I'd get beaten, too. Why would I do that? So that I'd *feel* better? Being beaten didn't make me feel better. I had a choice. I could champion racial justice in our home, or I could enjoy granny's cookies. I went with the cookies.

At that point I didn't think of the special treatment as having to do with color. I thought of it as having to do with Trevor. It wasn't, "Trevor doesn't get beaten because Trevor is white." It was, "Trevor doesn't get beaten because Trevor is Trevor." Trevor can't go outside. Trevor can't walk without supervision. It's because I'm me; that's why this is happening. I had no other points of reference. There were no other mixed kids around so that I could say, "Oh, this happens to *us*."

Nearly one million people lived in Soweto. Ninety-nine point nine percent of them were black—and then there was me. I was famous in my neighborhood just because of the color of my skin. I was so unique people would give directions using me as a landmark. "The house on Makhalima Street. At the corner you'll see a light-skinned boy. Take a right there."

Whenever the kids in the street saw me they'd yell, *"Indoda yom-lungu!"* "The white man!" Some of them would run away. Others would call out to their parents to come look. Others would run up and try to touch me to see if I was real. It was pandemonium. What I didn't understand at the time was that the other kids genuinely had no clue what a white person was. Black kids in the township didn't leave the township. Few people had televisions. They'd seen the white police roll through, but they'd never dealt with a white person face-to-face, ever.

I'd go to funerals and I'd walk in and the bereaved would look up and see me and they'd stop crying. They'd start whispering. Then they'd wave and say, "Oh!" like they were more shocked by me walking in than by the death of their loved ones. I think people felt like the dead person was more important because a white person had come to the funeral.

After a funeral, the mourners all go to the house of the surviving family to eat. A hundred people might show up, and you've got to feed them. Usually you get a cow and slaughter it and your neighbors come over and help you cook. Neighbors and acquaintances eat outside in the yard and in the street, and the family eats indoors. Every funeral I ever went to, I ate indoors. It didn't matter if we knew the deceased or not. The family would see me and invite me in. *"Awunakuvumela umntana womlungu ame ngaphandle. Yiza naye apha ngaphakathi,"* they'd say. "You can't let the white child stand outside. Bring him in here."

As a kid I understood that people were different colors, but in my head white and black and brown were like types of chocolate. Dad was the white chocolate, mom was the dark chocolate, and I was the milk chocolate. But we were all just chocolate. I didn't know any of it had anything to do with "race." I didn't know what race was. My mother never referred to my dad as white or to me as mixed. So when the other kids in Soweto called me "white," even though I was light brown, I just thought they had their colors mixed up, like they hadn't learned them properly. "Ah, yes, my friend. You've confused aqua with turquoise. I can see how you made that mistake. You're not the first."

I soon learned that the quickest way to bridge the race gap was through language. Soweto was a melting pot: families from different tribes and homelands. Most kids in the township spoke only their home language, but I learned several languages because I grew up in a house where there was no option but to learn them. My mom made sure English was the first language I spoke. If you're black in South Africa, speaking English is the one thing that can give you a leg up. English is the language of money. English comprehension is equated with intelligence. If you're looking for a job, English is the difference between getting the job or staying unemployed. If you're standing in the dock, English is the difference between getting off with a fine or going to prison.

After English, Xhosa was what we spoke around the house. When my mother was angry she'd fall back on her home language. As a naughty child, I was well versed in Xhosa threats. They were the first phrases I picked up, mostly for my own safety—phrases like *"Ndiza kubetha entloko."* "I'll knock you upside the head." Or *"Sidenge ndini somntwana."* "You idiot of a child." It's a very passionate language. Outside of that, my mother picked up different languages here and there. She learned Zulu because it's similar to Xhosa. She spoke German because of my father. She spoke Afrikaans because it is useful to know the language of your oppressor. Sotho she learned in the streets.

Living with my mom, I saw how she used language to cross boundaries, handle situations, navigate the world. We were in a shop once, and the shopkeeper, right in front of us, turned to his security guard and said, in Afrikaans, *"Volg daai swartes, netnou steel hulle iets."* "Follow those blacks in case they steal something."

My mother turned around and said, in beautiful, fluent Afrikaans, *"Hoekom volg jy nie daai swartes sodat jy hulle kan help kry waarna hulle soek nie?"* "Why don't you follow these blacks so you can help them find what they're looking for?"

"Ag, jammer!" he said, apologizing in Afrikaans. Then—and this was the funny thing—he didn't apologize for being racist; he merely apologized for aiming his racism at us. "Oh, I'm so sorry," he said. "I thought you were like the other blacks. You know how they love to steal."

I learned to use language like my mother did. I would simulcast—give you the program in your own tongue. I'd get suspicious looks from people just walking down the street. "Where are you from?" they'd ask. I'd reply in whatever language they'd addressed me in, using the same accent that they used. There would be a brief moment of confusion, and then the suspicious look would disappear. "Oh, okay. I thought you were a stranger. We're good then."

It became a tool that served me my whole life. One day as a young man I was walking down the street, and a group of Zulu guys was walking behind me, closing in on me, and I could hear them talking to one another about how they were going to mug me. *"Asibambe le autie yomlungu. Phuma ngapha mina ngizoqhamuka ngemuva kwakhe."* "Let's get this white guy. You go to his left, and I'll come up behind him." I didn't know what to do. I couldn't run, so I just spun around real quick and said, *"Kodwa bafwethu yingani singavele sibambe umuntu inkunzi? Asenzeni. Mina ngikulindele."* "Yo, guys, why don't we just mug someone together? I'm ready. Let's do it."

They looked shocked for a moment, and then they started laughing.

"Oh, sorry, dude. We thought you were something else. We weren't trying to take anything from you. We were trying to steal from white people. Have a good day, man." They were ready to do me violent harm, until they felt we were part of the same tribe, and then we were cool. That, and so many other smaller incidents in my life, made me realize that language, even more than color, defines who you are to people.

I became a chameleon. My color didn't change, but I could change your perception of my color. If you spoke to me in Zulu, I replied to you in Zulu. If you spoke to me in Tswana, I replied to you in Tswana. Maybe I didn't look like you, but if I spoke like you, I was you.

As apartheid was coming to an end, South Africa's elite private schools started accepting children of all colors. My mother's company offered bursaries, scholarships, for underprivileged families, and she managed to get me into Maryvale College, an expensive private Catholic school. Classes taught by nuns. Mass on Fridays. The whole bit. I started pre-school there when I was three, primary school when I was five.

In my class we had all kinds of kids. Black kids, white kids, Indian kids, colored kids. Most of the white kids were pretty well off. Every child of color pretty much wasn't. But because of scholarships we all sat at the same table. We wore the same maroon blazers, the same gray slacks and skirts. We had the same books. We had the same teachers. There was no racial separation. Every clique was racially mixed.

Kids still got teased and bullied, but it was over usual kid stuff: being fat or being skinny, being tall or being short, being smart or being dumb. I don't remember anybody being teased about their race. I didn't learn to put limits on what I was supposed to like or not like. I had a wide berth to explore myself. I had crushes on white girls. I had crushes on black girls. Nobody asked me what I was. I was Trevor.

It was a wonderful experience to have, but the downside was that it sheltered me from reality. Maryvale was an oasis that kept me from the truth, a comfortable place where I could avoid making a tough decision. But the real world doesn't go away. Racism exists. People are getting hurt, and just because it's not happening to you doesn't mean it's not happening. And at some point, you have to choose. Black or white. Pick a side. You can try to hide from it. You can say, "Oh, I don't pick sides," but at some point life will force you to pick a side.

At the end of grade six I left Maryvale to go to H. A. Jack Primary, a government school. I had to take an aptitude test before I started, and, based on the results of the test, the school counselor told me, "You're going to be in the smart classes, the A classes." I showed up for the first day of school and went to my classroom. Of the thirty or so kids in my class, almost all of them were white. There was one Indian kid, maybe one or two black kids, and me.

Then recess came. We went out on the playground, and black kids were *everywhere*. It was an ocean of black, like someone had opened a tap and all the black had come pouring out. I was like, *Where were they all hiding?* The white kids I'd met that morning, they went in one direction, the black kids went in another direction, and I was left standing in the middle, totally confused. Were we going to meet up later on? I did not understand what was happening.

I was eleven years old, and it was like I was seeing my country for the first time. In the townships you don't see segregation, because everyone is black. In the white world, any time my mother took me to a white church, we were the only black people there, and my mom didn't separate herself from anyone. She didn't care. She'd go right up and sit with the white people. And at Maryvale, the kids were mixed up and hanging out together. Before that day, I had never seen people being together and yet not together, occupying the same space yet choosing not to associate with each other in any way. In an instant I could see, I could feel, how the boundaries were drawn. Groups moved in color patterns across the yard, up the stairs, down the hall. It was insane. I looked over at the white kids I'd met that morning. Ten minutes earlier I'd thought I was at a school where they were a majority. Now I realized how few of them there actually were compared to everyone else.

I stood there awkwardly by myself in this no-man's-land in the middle of the playground. Luckily, I was rescued by the Indian kid from my class, a guy named Theesan Pillay. Theesan was one of the few Indian kids in school, so he'd noticed me, another obvious out-sider, right away. He ran over to introduce himself. "Hello, fellow anomaly! You're in my class. Who are you? What's your story?" We started talking and hit it off. He took me under his wing, the Artful Dodger to my bewildered Oliver.

Through our conversation it came up that I spoke several African languages, and Theesan thought a colored kid speaking black languages was the most amazing trick. He brought me over to a group of black kids. "Say something," he told them, "and he'll show you he under-stands you." One kid said something in Zulu, and I replied to him in Zulu. Everyone cheered. Another kid said something in Xhosa, and I replied to him in Xhosa. Everyone cheered. For the rest of recess Theesan took me around to different black kids on the playground. "Show them your trick. Do your language thing."

The black kids were fascinated. In South Africa back then, it wasn't common to find a white person or a colored person who spoke African languages; during apartheid white people were always taught that those languages were beneath them. So the fact that I did speak African lan-guages immediately endeared me to the black kids.

"How come you speak our languages?" they asked.

"Because I'm black," I said, "like you."

"You're not black."

"Yes, I am."

"No, you're not. Have you not seen yourself?"

They were confused at first. Because of my color, they thought I was a colored person, but speaking the same languages meant that I belonged to their tribe. It just took them a moment to figure it out. It took me a moment, too.

At some point I turned to one of them and said, "Hey, how come I don't see you guys in any of my classes?" It turned out they were in the B classes, which also happened to be the black classes. That same after-noon, I went back to the A classes, and by the end of the day I realized that they weren't for me. Suddenly, I knew who my people were, and I wanted to be with them. I went to see the school counselor.

"I'd like to switch over," I told her. "I'd like to go to the B classes."

She was confused. "Oh, no," she said. "I don't think you want to do that."

"Why not?"

"Because those kids are . . . you know."

"No, I don't know. What do you mean?"

"Look," she said, "you're a smart kid. You don't want to be in that class."

"But aren't the classes the same? English is English. Math is math."

"Yeah, but that class is . . . those kids are gonna hold you back. You want to be in the smart class."

"But surely there must be some smart kids in the B class."

"No, there aren't."

"But all my friends are there."

"You don't want to be friends with those kids."

"Yes, I do."

We went back and forth. Finally she gave me a stern warning.

"You do realize the effect this will have on your future? You do understand what you're giving up? This will impact the opportunities you'll have open to you for the rest of your life."

"I'll take that chance."

I moved to the B classes with the black kids. I decided I'd rather be held back with people I liked than move ahead with people I didn't know.

Being at H. A. Jack made me realize I was black. Before that recess I'd never had to choose, but when I was forced to choose, I chose black. The world saw me as colored, but I didn't spend my life looking at myself. I spent my life looking at other people. I saw myself as the people around me, and the people around me were black. My cousins are black, my mom is black, my gran is black. I grew up black. Because I had a white father, because I'd been in white Sunday school, I got along with the white kids, but I didn't *be*long with the white kids. I wasn't a part of their tribe. But the black kids embraced me. "Come along," they said. "You're rolling with us." With the black kids, I wasn't constantly trying to be. With the black kids, I just was.

Before apartheid, any black South African who received a formal education was likely taught by European missionaries, foreign enthusiasts eager to Christianize and Westernize the natives. In the mission schools, black people learned English, European literature, medicine, the law. It's no coincidence that nearly every major black leader of the anti-apartheid movement, from Nelson Mandela to Steve Biko, was educated by the missionaries—a knowledgeable man is a free man, or at least a man who longs for freedom.

The only way to make apartheid work, therefore, was to cripple the black mind. Under apartheid, the government built what became known as Bantu schools. Bantu schools taught no science, no history, no civics. They taught metrics and agriculture: how to count potatoes, how to pave roads, chop wood, till the soil. "It does not serve the Bantu to learn history and science because he is primitive," the government said. "This will only mislead him, showing him pastures in which he is not allowed to graze." To their credit, they were simply being honest. Why educate a slave? Why teach someone Latin when his only purpose is to dig holes in the ground?

Mission schools were told to conform to the new curriculum or shut down. Most of them shut down, and black children were forced into crowded classrooms in dilapidated schools, often with teachers who were barely literate themselves. Our parents and grandparents were taught with little singsong lessons, the way you'd teach a preschooler shapes and colors. My grandfather used to sing the songs and laugh about how silly they were. *Two times two is four. Three times two is six. La la la la la.* We're talking about fully grown teenagers being taught this way, for generations.

What happened with education in South Africa, with the mission schools and the Bantu schools, offers a neat comparison of the two groups of whites who oppressed us, the British and the Afrikaners. The difference between British racism and Afrikaner racism was that at least the British gave the natives something to aspire to. If they could learn to speak correct English and dress in proper clothes, if they could Anglicize and civilize themselves, one day they *might* be welcome in society. The Afrikaners never gave us that option. British racism said, "If the monkey can walk like a man and talk like a man, then perhaps he is a man." Afrikaner racism said, "Why give a book to a monkey?"

———————

5

THE SECOND GIRL

My mother used to tell me, "I chose to have you because I wanted something to love and something that would love me unconditionally in return." I was a product of her search for belonging. She never felt like she belonged anywhere. She didn't belong to her mother, didn't belong to her father, didn't belong with her siblings. She grew up with nothing and wanted something to call her own.

My grandparents' marriage was an unhappy one. They met and married in Sophiatown, but one year later the army came in and drove them out. The government seized their home and bulldozed the whole area to build a fancy, new white suburb, *Triomf*. Triumph. Along with tens of thousands of other black people, my grandparents were forcibly relocated to Soweto, to a neighborhood called the Meadowlands. They divorced not long after that, and my grandmother moved to Orlando with my mom, my aunt, and my uncle.

My mom was the problem child, a tomboy, stubborn, defiant. My gran had no idea how to raise her. Whatever love they had was lost in the constant fighting that went on between them. But my mom adored her father, the charming, charismatic Temperance. She went gallivanting with him on his manic misadventures. She'd tag along when he'd go drinking in the shebeens. All she wanted in life was to please him and be with him. She was always being swatted away by his girlfriends, who didn't like having a reminder of his first marriage hanging around, but that only made her want to be with him all the more.

When my mother was nine years old, she told my gran that she didn't want to live with her anymore. She wanted to live with her father. "If that's what you want," Gran said, "then go." Temperance came to pick my mom up, and she happily bounded up into his car, ready to go and be with the man she loved. But instead of taking her to live with him in the Meadowlands, without even telling her why, he packed her off and sent her to live with his sister in the Xhosa homeland, Transkei—he didn't want her, either. My mom was the middle child. Her sister was the eldest and firstborn. Her brother was the only son, bearer of the family name. They both stayed in Soweto, were both raised and cared for by their parents. But my mom was unwanted. She was the second girl. The only place she would have less value would be China.

My mother didn't see her family again for twelve years. She lived in a hut with fourteen cousins—fourteen children from fourteen different mothers and fathers. All the husbands and uncles had gone off to the cities to find work, and the children who weren't wanted, or whom no one could afford to feed, had been sent back to the homeland to live on this aunt's farm.

The homelands were, ostensibly, the original homes of South Africa's tribes, sovereign and semi-sovereign "nations" where black people would be "free." Of course, this was a lie. For starters, despite the fact that black people made up over 80 percent of South Africa's population, the territory allocated for the homelands was about 13 percent of the country's land. There was no running water, no electricity. People lived in huts.

Where South Africa's white countryside was lush and irrigated and green, the black lands were overpopulated and overgrazed, the soil depleted and eroding. Other than the menial wages sent home from the cities, families scraped by with little beyond subsistence-level farming. My mother's aunt hadn't taken her in out of charity. She was there to work. "I was one of the cows," my mother would later say, "one of the oxen." She and her cousins were up at half past four, plowing fields and herding animals before the sun baked the soil as hard as cement and made it too hot to be anywhere but in the shade.

For dinner there might be one chicken to feed fourteen children. My mom would have to fight with the bigger kids to get a handful of meat or a sip of the gravy or even a bone from which to suck out some marrow. And that's when there was food for dinner at all. When there wasn't, she'd steal food from the pigs. She'd steal food from the dogs. The farmers would put out scraps for the animals, and she'd jump for it. She was hungry; let the animals fend for themselves. There were times when she literally ate dirt. She would go down to the river, take the clay from the riverbank, and mix it with the water to make a grayish kind of milk. She'd drink that to feel full.

But my mother was blessed that her village was one of the places where a mission school had contrived to stay open in spite of the government's Bantu education policies. There she had a white pastor who taught her English. She didn't have food or shoes or even a pair of underwear, but she had English. She could read and write. When she was old enough she stopped working on the farm and got a job at a factory in a nearby town. She worked on a sewing machine making school uniforms. Her pay at the end of each day was a plate of food. She used to say it was the best food she'd ever eaten, because it was something she had earned on her own. She wasn't a burden to anyone and didn't owe anything to anyone.

When my mom turned twenty-one, her aunt fell ill and that family could no longer keep her in Transkei. My mom wrote to my gran, asking her to send the price of a train ticket, about thirty rand, to bring her home. Back in Soweto, my mom enrolled in the secretarial course that allowed her to grab hold of the bottom rung of the white-collar world. She worked and worked and worked but, living under my grandmother's roof, she wasn't allowed to keep her own wages. As a secretary, my mom was bringing home more money than anyone else, and my grandmother insisted it all go to the family. The family needed a radio, an oven, a refrigerator, and it was now my mom's job to provide it.

So many black families spend all of their time trying to fix the problems of the past. That is the curse of being black and poor, and it is a curse that follows you from generation to generation. My mother calls it "the black tax." Because the generations who came before you have been pillaged, rather than being free to use your skills and education to move forward, you lose everything just trying to bring everyone behind you back up to zero. Working for the family in Soweto, my mom had no more freedom than she'd had in Transkei, so she ran away. She ran all the way down to the train station and jumped on a train and disappeared into the city, determined to sleep in public restrooms and rely on the kindness of prostitutes until she could make her own way in the world.

My mother never sat me down and told me the whole story of her life in Transkei. She'd give me little bursts, random details, stories of having to keep her wits about her to avoid getting raped by strange men in the village. She'd tell me these things and I'd be like, *Lady, clearly you do not know what kind of stories to be telling a ten-year-old.*

My mom told me these things so that I'd never take for granted how we got to where we were, but none of it ever came from a place of self-pity. "Learn from your past and be better because of your past," she would say, "but don't cry about your past. Life is full of pain. Let the pain sharpen you, but don't hold on to it. Don't be bitter." And she never was. The deprivations of her youth, the betrayals of her parents, she never complained about any of it.

Just as she let the past go, she was determined not to repeat it: my childhood would bear no resemblance to hers. She started with my name. The names Xhosa families give their children always have a meaning, and that meaning has a way of becoming self-fulfilling. You have my cousin, Mlungisi. "The Fixer." That's who he is. Whenever I got into trouble he was the one trying to help me fix it. He was always the good kid, doing chores, helping around the house. You have my uncle, the unplanned pregnancy, Velile. "He Who Popped Out of Nowhere." And that's all he's done his whole life, disappear and reappear. He'll go off on a drinking binge and then pop back up out of nowhere a week later.

Then you have my mother, Patricia Nombuyiselo Noah. "She Who Gives Back." That's what she does. She gives and gives and gives. She did it even as a girl in Soweto. Playing in the streets she would find toddlers, three- and four-year-olds, running around unsupervised all day long. Their fathers were gone and their mothers were drunks. My mom, who was only six or seven herself, used to round up the abandoned kids and form a troop and take them around to the shebeens. They'd collect empties from the men who were passed out and take the bottles to where you could turn them in for a deposit. Then my mom would take that money, buy food in the *spaza* shops, and feed the kids. She was a child taking care of children.

When it was time to pick my name, she chose Trevor, a name with no meaning whatsoever in South Africa, no precedent in my family. It's not even a Biblical name. It's just a name. My mother wanted her child beholden to no fate. She wanted me to be free to go anywhere, do anything, be anyone.

She gave me the tools to do it as well. She taught me English as my first language. She read to me constantly. The first book I learned to read was *the* book. The Bible. Church was where we got most of our other books, too. My mom would bring home boxes that white people had donated—picture books, chapter books, any book she could get her hands on. Then she signed up for a subscription program where we got books in the mail. It was a series of how-to books. *How to Be a*

Good Friend. How to Be Honest. She bought a set of encyclopedias, too; it was fifteen years old and way out of date, but I would sit and pore through those.

My books were my prized possessions. I had a bookshelf where I put them, and I was so proud of it. I loved my books and kept them in pristine condition. I read them over and over, but I did not bend the pages or the spines. I treasured every single one. As I grew older I started buying my own books. I loved fantasy, loved to get lost in worlds that didn't exist. I remember there was some book about white boys who solved mysteries or some shit. I had no time for that. Give me Roald Dahl. *James and the Giant Peach*, *The BFG*, *Charlie and the Chocolate Factory*, *The Wonderful Story of Henry Sugar*. That was my fix.

I had to fight to convince my mom to get the Narnia books for me. She didn't like them.

"This lion," she said, "he is a false God—a false idol! You remember what happened when Moses came down from the mountain after he got the tablets . . ."

"Yes, Mom," I explained, "but the lion is a Christ *figure*. Technically, he is Jesus. It's a story to explain Jesus."

She wasn't comfortable with that. "No, no. No false idols, my friend."

Eventually I wore her down. That was a big win.

If my mother had one goal, it was to free my mind. My mother spoke to me like an adult, which was unusual. In South Africa, kids play with kids and adults talk to adults. The adults supervise you, but they don't get down on your level and talk to you. My mom did. All the time. I was like her best friend. She was always telling me stories, giving me lessons, Bible lessons especially. She was big into Psalms. I had to read Psalms every day. She would quiz me on it. "What does the passage mean? What does it mean to *you*? How do you apply it to your life?" That was every day of my life. My mom did what school didn't. She taught me how to think.

• • •

The end of apartheid was a gradual thing. It wasn't like the Berlin Wall where one day it just came down. Apartheid's walls cracked and crumbled over many years. Concessions were made here and there, some laws were repealed, others simply weren't enforced. There came a point, in the months before Mandela's release, when we could live less furtively. It was then that my mother decided we needed to move. She felt we had grown as much as we could hiding in our tiny flat in town.

The country was open now. Where would we go? Soweto came with its burdens. My mother still wanted to get out from the shadow of her family. My mother also couldn't walk with me through Soweto without people saying, "There goes that prostitute with a white man's child." In a black area she would always be seen as that. So, since my mom didn't want to move to a black area and couldn't afford to move to a white area, she decided to move to a colored area.

Eden Park was a colored neighborhood adjacent to several black townships on the East Rand. Half-colored and half-black, she figured, like us. We'd be camouflaged there. It didn't work out that way; we never fit in at all. But that was her thinking when we made the move. Plus it was a chance to buy a home—our own home. Eden Park was one of those "suburbs" that are actually out on the edge of civilization, the kind of place where property developers have said, "Hey, poor people. You can live the good life, too. Here's a house. In the middle of nowhere. But look, you have a yard!" For some reason the streets in Eden Park were named after cars: Jaguar Street. Ferrari Street. Honda Street. I don't know if that was a coincidence or not, but it's funny because colored people in South Africa are known for loving fancy cars. It was like living in a white neighborhood with all the streets named after varietals of fine wine.

I remember moving out there in flashbacks, snippets, driving to a place I'd never seen, seeing people I'd never seen. It was flat, not many trees, the same dusty red-clay dirt and grass as Soweto but with proper houses and paved roads and a sense of suburbia to it. Ours was a tiny house at the bend in the road right off Toyota Street. It was modest and cramped inside, but walking in I thought, *Wow. We are really living*. It was crazy to have my own room. I didn't like it. My whole life I'd slept in a room with my mom or on the floor with my cousins. I was used to having other human beings right next to me, so I slept in my mom's bed most nights.

There was no stepfather in the picture yet, no baby brother crying in the night. It was me and her, alone. There was this sense of the two of us embarking on a grand adventure. She'd say things to me like, "It's you and me against the world." I understood even from an early age that we weren't just mother and son. We were a team.

It was when we moved to Eden Park that we finally got a car, the beat-up, tangerine Volkswagen my mother bought secondhand for next to nothing. One out of five times it wouldn't start. There was no AC. Anytime I made the mistake of turning on the fan the vent would fart bits of leaves and dust all over me. Whenever it broke down we'd catch minibuses, or sometimes we'd hitchhike. She'd make me hide in the bushes because she knew men would stop for a woman but not a woman with a child. She'd stand by the road, the driver would pull over, she'd open the door and then whistle, and I'd come running up to the car. I would watch their faces drop as they realized they weren't picking up an attractive single woman but an attractive single woman with a fat little kid.

When the car did work, we had the windows down, sputtering along and baking in the heat. For my entire life the dial on that car's radio stayed on one station. It was called Radio Pulpit, and as the name suggests it was nothing but preaching and praise. I wasn't allowed to touch that dial. Anytime the radio wasn't getting reception, my mom would pop in a cassette of Jimmy Swaggart sermons. (When we finally found out about the scandal? Oh, man. That was rough.)

But as shitty as our car was, it was a *car*. It was freedom. We weren't black people stuck in the townships, waiting for public transport. We were black people who were out in the world. We were black people who could wake up and say, "Where do we choose to go today?" On the commute to work and school, there was a long stretch of the road into town that was completely deserted. That's where Mom would let me drive. On the highway. I was six. She'd put me on her lap and let me steer and work the indicators while she worked the pedals and the stick shift. After a few months of that, she taught me how to work the stick. She was still working the clutch, but I'd climb onto her lap and take the stick, and she'd call out the gears as we drove. There was this one part of the road that ran deep into a valley and then back up the other side. We'd get up a head of speed, and we'd stick it into neutral and let go of the brake and the clutch, and, *woo-hoo!*, we'd race down the hill and then, *zoom!*, we'd shoot up the other side. We were flying.

If we weren't at school or work or church, we were out exploring. My mom's attitude was "I chose you, kid. I brought you into this world, and I'm going to give you everything I never had." She poured herself into me. She would find places for us to go where we didn't have to spend money. We must have gone to every park in Johannesburg. My mom would sit under a tree and read the Bible, and I'd run and play and play and play. On Sunday afternoons after church, we'd go for drives out in the country. My mom would find places with beautiful views for us to sit and have a picnic. There was none of the fanfare of a picnic basket or plates or anything like that, only baloney and brown bread and margarine sandwiches wrapped up in butcher paper. To this day, baloney and brown bread and margarine will instantly take me back. You can come with all the Michelin stars in the world, just give me baloney and brown bread and margarine and I'm in heaven.

Food, or the access to food, was always the measure of how good or bad things were going in our lives. My mom would always say, "My job is to feed your body, feed your spirit, and feed your mind." That's exactly what she did, and the way she found money for food and books was to spend absolutely nothing on anything else. Her frugality was the stuff of legend. Our car was a tin can on wheels, and we lived in the middle of nowhere. We had threadbare furniture, busted old sofas with holes worn through the fabric. Our TV was a tiny black-and-white with a bunny aerial on top. We changed the channels using a pair of pliers because the buttons didn't work. Most of the time you had to squint to see what was going on.

We always wore secondhand clothes, from Goodwill stores or that were giveaways from white people at church. All the other kids at school got brands, Nike and Adidas. I never got brands. One time I asked my mom for Adidas sneakers. She came home with some knock-off brand, Abidas.

"Mom, these are fake," I said.

"I don't see the difference."

"Look at the logo. There are four stripes instead of three."

"Lucky you," she said. "You got one extra."

We got by with next to nothing, but we always had church and we always had books and we always had food. Mind you, it wasn't necessarily *good* food. Meat was a luxury. When things were going well we'd have chicken. My mom was an expert at cracking open a chicken bone and getting out every last bit of marrow inside. We didn't eat chickens. We obliterated them. Our family was an archaeologist's nightmare. We left no bones behind. When we were done with a chicken there was nothing left but the head. Sometimes the only meat we had was a packaged meat you could buy at the butcher called "sawdust." It was literally the dust of the meat, the bits that fell off the cuts being packaged for the shop, the bits of fat and whatever's left. They'd sweep it up and put it into bags. It was meant for dogs, but my mom bought it for us. There were many months where that was all we ate.

The butcher sold bones, too. We called them "soup bones," but they were actually labeled "dog bones" in the store; people would cook them for their dogs as a treat. Whenever times were really tough we'd fall back on dog bones. My mom would boil them for soup. We'd suck the marrow out of them. Sucking marrow out of bones is a skill poor people learn early. I'll never forget the first time I went to a fancy restaurant as a grown man and someone told me, "You have to try the bone marrow. It's such a delicacy. It's *divine*." They ordered it, the waiter brought it out, and I was like, "Dog bones, motherfucker!" I was not impressed.

As modestly as we lived at home, I never felt poor because our lives were so rich with experience. We were always out doing something, going somewhere. My mom used to take me on drives through fancy white neighborhoods. We'd go look at people's houses, look at their mansions. We'd look at their walls, mostly, because that's all we could see from the road. We'd look at a wall that ran from one end of the block to the other and go, "Wow. That's only *one* house. All of that is for *one* family." Sometimes we'd pull over and go up to the wall, and she'd put me up on her shoulders like I was a little periscope. I would look into the yards and describe everything I was seeing. "It's a big white house! They have two dogs! There's a lemon tree! They have a swimming pool! And a tennis court!"

My mother took me places black people never went. She refused to be bound by ridiculous ideas of what black people couldn't or shouldn't do. She'd take me to the ice rink to go skating. Johannesburg used to have this epic drive-in movie theater, Top Star Drive-In, on top of a massive mine dump outside the city. She'd take me to movies there; we'd get snacks, hang the speaker on our car window. Top Star had a 360-degree view of the city, the suburbs, Soweto. Up there I could see for miles in every direction. I felt like I was on top of the world.

My mom raised me as if there were no limitations on where I could go or what I could do. When I look back I realize she raised me like a white kid—not white culturally, but in the sense of believing that the world was my oyster, that I should speak up for myself, that my ideas and thoughts and decisions mattered.

We tell people to follow their dreams, but you can only dream of what you can imagine, and, depending on where you come from, your imagination can be quite limited. Growing up in Soweto, our dream was to put another room on our house. Maybe have a driveway. Maybe, someday, a cast-iron gate at the end of the driveway. Because that is all we knew. But the highest rung of what's possible is far beyond the world you can see. My mother showed me what was possible. The thing that always amazed me about her life was that no one showed her. No one chose her. She did it on her own. She found her way through sheer force of will.

Perhaps even more amazing is the fact that my mother started her little project, me, at a time when she could not have known that apartheid would end. There was no reason to think it would end; it had seen generations come and go. I was nearly six when Mandela was released, ten before democracy finally came, yet she was preparing me to live a life of freedom long before we knew freedom would exist. A hard life in the township or a trip to the colored orphanage were the far more likely options on the table. But we never lived that way. We only moved forward and we always moved fast, and by the time the law and everyone else came around we were already miles down the road, flying across the freeway in a bright-orange, piece-of-shit Volkswagen with the windows down and Jimmy Swaggart praising Jesus at the top of his lungs.

People thought my mom was crazy. Ice rinks and drive-ins and suburbs, these things were *izinto zabelungu*—the things of white people. So many black people had internalized the logic of apartheid and made it their own. Why teach a black child white things? Neighbors and relatives used to pester my mom. "Why do all this? Why show him the world when he's never going to leave the ghetto?"

"Because," she would say, "even if he never leaves the ghetto, he will know that the ghetto is not the world. If that is all I accomplish, I've done enough."

Apartheid, for all its power, had fatal flaws baked in, starting with the fact that it never made any sense. Racism is not logical. Consider this: Chinese people were classified as black in South Africa. I don't mean they were running around acting black. They were still Chinese. But, unlike Indians, there weren't enough Chinese people to warrant devising a whole separate classification. Apartheid, despite its intricacies and precision, didn't know what to do with them, so the government said, "Eh, we'll just call 'em black. It's simpler that way."

Interestingly, at the same time, Japanese people were labeled as white. The reason for this was that the South African government wanted to establish good relations with the Japanese in order to import their fancy cars and electronics. So Japanese people were given honorary white status while Chinese people stayed black. I always like to imagine being a South African policeman who likely couldn't tell the difference between Chinese and Japanese but whose job was to make sure that people of the wrong color weren't doing the wrong thing. If he saw an Asian person sitting on a whites-only bench, what would he say?

"Hey, get off that bench, you Chinaman!"

"Excuse me. I'm Japanese."

"Oh, I apologize, sir. I didn't mean to be racist. Have a lovely afternoon."

6

LOOPHOLES

My mother used to tell me, "I chose to have you because I wanted something to love and something that would love me unconditionally in return—and then I gave birth to the most selfish piece of shit on earth and all it ever did was cry and eat and shit and say, 'Me, me, me, me me.'"

My mom thought having a child was going to be like having a partner, but every child is born the center of its own universe, incapable of understanding the world beyond its own wants and needs, and I was no different. I was a voracious kid. I consumed boxes of books and wanted more, more, more. I ate like a pig. The way I ate I should have been obese. At a certain point the family thought I had worms. Whenever I went to my cousins' house for the holidays, my mom would drop me off with a bag of tomatoes, onions, and potatoes and a large sack of cornmeal. That was her way of preempting any complaints about my visit. At my gran's house I always got seconds, which none of the other kids got. My grandmother would give me the pot and say, "Finish it." If you didn't want to wash the dishes, you called Trevor. They called me the rubbish bin of the family. I ate and ate and ate.

I was hyperactive, too. I craved constant stimulation and activity. When I walked down the sidewalk as a toddler, if you didn't have my arm in a death grip, I was off, running full-speed toward the traffic. I loved to be chased. I thought it was a game. The old grannies my mom hired to look after me while she was at work? I would leave them in tears. My mom would come home and they'd be crying. "I quit. I can't do this. Your son is a tyrant." It was the same with my schoolteachers, with Sunday school teachers. If you weren't engaging me, you were in trouble. I wasn't a shit to people. I wasn't whiny and spoiled. I had good manners. I was just high-energy and knew what I wanted to do.

My mom used to take me to the park so she could run me to death to burn off the energy. She'd take a Frisbee and throw it, and I'd run and catch it and bring it back. Over and over and over. Sometimes she'd throw a tennis ball. Black people's dogs don't play fetch; you don't throw anything to a black person's dog unless it's food. So it was only when I started spending time in parks with white people and their pets that I realized my mom was training me like a dog.

Anytime my extra energy wasn't burned off, it would find its way into general naughtiness and misbehavior. I prided myself on being the ultimate prankster. Every teacher at school used overhead projectors to put their notes up on the wall during class. One day I went around and took the magnifying glass out of every projector in every classroom. Another time I emptied a fire extinguisher into the school piano, because I knew we were going to have a performance at assembly the next day. The pianist sat down and played the first note and, *foomp!*, all this foam exploded out of the piano.

The two things I loved most were fire and knives. I was endlessly fascinated by them. Knives were just cool. I collected them from pawnshops and garage sales: flick knives, butterfly knives, the Rambo knife, the Crocodile Dundee knife. Fire was the ultimate, though. I loved fire and I especially loved fireworks. We celebrated Guy Fawkes Day in November, and every year my mom would buy us a ton of fireworks, like a mini-arsenal. I realized that I could take the gunpowder out of all the fireworks and create one massive firework of my own. One afternoon I was doing precisely that, goofing around with my cousin and filling an empty plant pot with a huge pile of gunpowder, when I got distracted by some Black Cat firecrackers. The cool thing you could do with a Black Cat was, instead of lighting it to make it explode, you could break it in half and light it and it would turn into a mini-flamethrower. I stopped midway through building my gunpowder pile to play with the Black Cats and somehow dropped a match into the pile. The whole thing exploded, throwing a massive ball of flame up in my face. Mlungisi screamed, and my mom came running into the yard in a panic.

"What happened?!"

I played it cool, even though I could still feel the heat of the fireball on my face. "Oh, nothing. Nothing happened."

"Were you playing with fire?!"

"No."

She shook her head. "You know what? I would beat you, but Jesus has already exposed your lies."

"Huh?"

"Go to the bathroom and look at yourself."

I went to the toilet and looked in the mirror. My eyebrows were gone and the front inch or so of my hair was completely burned off.

From an adult's point of view, I was destructive and out of control, but as a child I didn't think of it that way. I never wanted to destroy. I wanted to create. I wasn't burning my eyebrows. I was creating fire. I wasn't breaking overhead projectors. I was creating chaos, to see how people reacted.

And I couldn't help it. There's a condition kids suffer from, a compulsive disorder that makes them do things they themselves don't understand. You can tell a child, "Whatever you do, don't draw on the wall. You can draw on this paper. You can draw in this book. You can draw on any surface you want. But do not draw or write or color on the wall." The child will look you dead in the eye and say, "Got it." Ten minutes later the child is drawing on the wall. You start screaming. "Why the hell are you drawing on the wall?!" The child looks at you, and he genuinely has no idea why he drew on the wall. As a kid, I remember having that feeling all the time. Every time I got punished, as my mom was whooping my ass, I'd be thinking, *Why did I just do that? I knew not to do that. She told me not to do that.* Then once the hiding was over I'd say to myself, *I'm going to be so good from here on. I'm never ever going to do a bad thing in my life ever ever ever ever ever—and to remember not to do anything bad, let me write something on the wall to remind myself . . .* and then I would pick up a crayon and get straight back into it, and I never understood why.

My relationship with my mom was like the relationship between a cop and a criminal in the movies—the relentless detective and the devious mastermind she's determined to catch. They're bitter rivals, but, damn, they respect the hell out of each other, and somehow they even grow to like each other. Sometimes my mom would catch me, but she was usually one step behind, and she was always giving me the eye. *Someday, kid. Someday I'm going to catch you and put you away for the rest of your life.* Then I would give her a nod in return. *Have a good evening, Officer.* That was my whole childhood.

My mom was forever trying to rein me in. Over the years, her tactics grew more and more sophisticated. Where I had youth and energy on my side, she had cunning, and she figured out different ways to keep me in line. One Sunday we were at the shops and there was a big display of toffee apples. I loved toffee apples, and I kept nagging her the whole way through the shop. "*Please* can I have a toffee apple? *Please* can I have a toffee apple? *Please* can I have a toffee apple? *Please* can I have a toffee apple?"

Finally, once we had our groceries and my mom was heading to the front to pay, I succeeded in wearing her down. "Fine," she said. "Go and get a toffee apple." I ran, got a toffee apple, came back, and put it on the counter at the checkout.

"Add this toffee apple, please," I said.

The cashier looked at me skeptically. "Wait your turn, boy. I'm still helping this lady."

"No," I said. "She's buying it for me."

My mother turned to me. "Who's buying it for you?"

"You're buying it for me."

"No, no. Why doesn't your mother buy it for you?"

"What? My mother? You are my mother."

"I'm your mother? No, I'm not your mother. Where's your mother?"

I was so confused. "*You're* my mother."

The cashier looked at her, looked back at me, looked at her again. She shrugged, like, *I have no idea what that kid's talking about.* Then she looked at me like she'd never seen me before in her life.

"Are you lost, little boy? Where's your mother?"

"Yeah," the cashier said. "Where's your mother?"

I pointed at my mother. "She's my mother."

"What? She can't be your mother, boy. She's black. Can't you see?"

My mom shook her head. "Poor little colored boy lost his mother. What a shame."

I panicked. Was I crazy? Is she not my mother? I started bawling. "*You're* my mother. *You're* my mother. *She's* my mother. *She's* my mother."

She shrugged again. "So sad. I hope he finds his mother."

The cashier nodded. She paid him, took our groceries, and walked out of the shop. I dropped the toffee apple, ran out behind her in tears, and caught up to her at the car. She turned around, laughing hysterically, like she'd really got me good.

"Why are you crying?" she asked.

"Because you said you weren't my mother. Why did you say you weren't my mother?"

"Because you wouldn't shut up about the toffee apple. Now get in the car. Let's go."

By the time I was seven or eight, I was too smart to be tricked, so she changed tactics. Our life turned into a courtroom drama with two lawyers constantly debating over loopholes and technicalities. My mom was smart and had a sharp tongue, but I was quicker in an argument. She'd get flustered because she couldn't keep up. So she started writing me letters. That way she could make her points and there could be no verbal sparring back and forth. If I had chores to do, I'd come home to find an envelope slipped under the door, like from the landlord.

Dear Trevor,

"Children, obey your parents in everything, for this pleases the Lord."
—Colossians 3:20

There are certain things I expect from you as my child and as a young man. You need to clean your room. You need to keep the house clean. You need to look after your school uniform. Please, my child, I ask you. Respect my rules so that I may also respect you. I ask you now, please go and do the dishes and do the weeds in the garden.

Yours sincerely,
Mom

I would do my chores, and if I had anything to say I would write back. Because my mom was a secretary and I spent hours at her office every day after school, I'd learned a great deal about business correspondence. I was extremely proud of my letter-writing abilities.

To Whom It May Concern:
Dear Mom,

I have received your correspondence earlier. I am delighted to say that I am ahead of schedule on the dishes and I will continue to wash them in an hour or so. Please note that the garden is wet and so I cannot do the weeds at this time, but please be assured this task

will be completed by the end of the weekend. Also, I completely
agree with what you are saying with regard to my respect levels and
I will maintain my room to a satisfactory standard.

Yours sincerely,
Trevor

Those were the polite letters. If we were having a real, full-on argument or if I'd gotten in trouble at school, I'd find more accusatory missives waiting for me when I got home.

Dear Trevor,

"Foolishness is bound up in the heart of a child; the rod of discipline will remove it far from him."
—Proverbs 22:15

Your school marks this term have been very disappointing, and
your behavior in class continues to be disruptive and disrespectful.
It is clear from your actions that you do not respect me. You do
not respect your teachers. Learn to respect the women in your life.
The way you treat me and the way you treat your teachers will
be the way you treat other women in the world. Learn to buck that
trend now and you will be a better man because of it. Because of
your behavior I am grounding you for one week. There will be no
television and no videogames.

Yours sincerely,
Mom

I, of course, would find this punishment completely unfair. I'd take the letter and confront her.
"Can I speak to you about this?"
"No. If you want to reply, you have to write a letter."
I'd go to my room, get out my pen and paper, sit at my little desk, and go after her arguments one by one.

To Whom It May Concern:
Dear Mom,

First of all, this has been a particularly tough time in school, and for you to say that my marks are bad is extremely unfair, especially considering the fact that you yourself were not very good in school and I am, after all, a product of yours, and so in part you are to blame because if you were not good in school, why would I be good in school because genetically we are the same. Gran always talks about how naughty you were, so obviously my naughtiness comes from you, so I don't think it is right or just for you to say any of this.

Yours sincerely,
Trevor

I'd bring her the letter and stand there while she read it. Invariably she'd tear it up and throw it in the dustbin. "Rubbish! This is rubbish!" Then she'd start to launch into me and I'd say, "Ah-ah-ah. No. You have to write a letter." Then I'd go to my room and wait for her reply. This sometimes went back and forth for days.

The letter writing was for minor disputes. For major infractions, my mom went with the ass-whooping. Like most black South African parents, when it came to discipline my mom was old school. If I pushed her too far, she'd go for the belt or switch. That's just how it was in those days. Pretty much all of my friends had it the same.

My mom would have given me proper sit-down hidings if I'd given her the opportunity, but she could never catch me. My gran called me "Springbok," after the second-fastest land mammal on earth, the deer that the cheetah hunts. My mom had to become a guerrilla fighter. She got her licks in where she could, her belt or maybe a shoe, administered on the fly.

One thing I respected about my mom was that she never left me in any doubt as to why I was receiving the hiding. It wasn't rage or anger. It was discipline from a place of love. My mom was on her own with a crazy child. I destroyed pianos. I shat on floors. I would screw up, she'd beat the shit out of me and give me time to cry, and then she'd pop back into my room with a big smile and go, "Are you ready for dinner? We need to hurry and eat if we want to watch *Rescue 911*. Are you coming?"

"What? What kind of psychopath are you? You just beat me!"

"Yes. Because you did something wrong. It doesn't mean I don't love you anymore."

"What?"

"Look, did you or did you not do something wrong?"

"I did."

"And then? I hit you. And now that's over. So why sit there and cry? It's time for *Rescue 911*. William Shatner is waiting. Are you coming or not?"

When it came to discipline, Catholic school was no joke. Whenever I got into trouble with the nuns at Maryvale they'd rap me on the knuckles with the edge of a metal ruler. For cursing they'd wash my mouth out with soap. For serious offenses I'd get sent to the principal's office. Only the principal could give you an official hiding. You'd have to bend over and he'd hit your ass with this flat rubber thing, like the sole of a shoe.

Whenever the principal would hit me, it was like he was afraid to do it too hard. One day I was getting a hiding and I thought, *Man, if only my mom hit me like this*, and I started laughing. I couldn't help it. The principal was quite disturbed. "If you're laughing while you're getting beaten," he said, "then something is definitely wrong with you."

That was the first of three times the school made my mom take me to a psychologist to be evaluated. Every psychologist who examined me came back and said, "There's nothing wrong with this kid." I wasn't ADD. I wasn't a sociopath. I was just creative and independent and full of energy. The therapists did give me a series of tests, and they came to the conclusion that I was either going to make an excellent criminal or be very good at catching criminals, because I could always find loopholes in the law. Whenever I thought a rule wasn't logical, I'd find my way around it.

The rules about communion at Friday mass, for example, made absolutely no sense. We'd be in there for an hour of kneeling, standing, sitting, kneeling, standing, sitting, kneeling, standing, sitting, and by the end of it I'd be starving, but I was never allowed to take communion, because I wasn't Catholic. The other kids could eat Jesus's body and drink Jesus's blood, but I couldn't. And Jesus's blood was grape juice. I loved grape juice. Grape juice and crackers—what more could a kid want? And they wouldn't let me have any. I'd argue with the nuns and the priest all the time.

"Only Catholics can eat Jesus's body and drink Jesus's blood, right?"

"Yes."

"But Jesus wasn't Catholic."

"No."

"Jesus was Jewish."

"Well, yes."

"So you're telling me that if Jesus walked into your church right now, Jesus would not be allowed to have the body and blood of Jesus?"

"Well . . . uh . . . um . . ."

They never had a satisfactory reply.

One morning before mass I decided, *I'm going to get me some Jesus blood and Jesus body.* I snuck behind the altar and I drank the entire bottle of grape juice and I ate the entire bag of Eucharist to make up for all the other times that I couldn't.

In my mind, I wasn't breaking the rules, because the rules didn't make any sense. And I got caught only because they broke their own rules. Another kid ratted me out in confession, and the priest turned me in.

"No, no," I protested. "*You've* broken the rules. That's confidential information. The priest isn't supposed to repeat what you say in confession."

They didn't care. The school could break whatever rules it wanted. The principal laid into me.

"What kind of a sick person would eat all of Jesus's body and drink all of Jesus's blood?"

"A hungry person."

I got another hiding and a second trip to the psychologist for that one. The third visit to the shrink, and the last straw, came in grade six. A kid was bullying me. He said he was going to beat me up, and I brought one of my knives to school. I wasn't going to use it; I just wanted to have it. The school didn't care. That was the last straw for them. I wasn't expelled, exactly. The principal sat me down and said, "Trevor, we can expel you. You need to think hard about whether you really want to be at Maryvale next year." I think he thought he was giving me an ultimatum that would get me to shape up. But I felt like he was offering me an out, and I took it. "No," I told him, "I don't want to be here." And that was the end of Catholic school.

Funnily enough, I didn't get into trouble with my mom when it happened. There was no ass-whooping waiting for me at home. She'd lost the bursary when she'd left her job at ICI, and paying for private school was becoming a burden. But more than that, she thought the school was overreacting. The truth is she probably took my side against Maryvale more often than not. She agreed with me 100 percent about the Eucharist thing. "Let me get this straight," she told the principal. "You're punishing a child because he *wants* Jesus's body and Jesus's blood? Why shouldn't he have those things? Of course he should have them." When they made me see a therapist for laughing while the principal hit me, she told the school that was ridiculous, too.

"Ms. Noah, your son was laughing while we were hitting him."

"Well, clearly you don't know how to hit a kid. That's your problem, not mine. Trevor's never laughed when I've hit him, I can tell you."

That was the weird and kind of amazing thing about my mom. If she agreed with me that a rule was stupid, she wouldn't punish me for breaking it. Both she and the psychologists agreed that the school was the one with the problem, not me. Catholic school is not the place to be creative and independent.

Catholic school is similar to apartheid in that it's ruthlessly authoritarian, and its authority rests on a bunch of rules that don't make any sense. My mother grew up with these rules and she questioned them. When they didn't hold up, she simply went around them. The only authority my mother recognized was God's. God is love and the Bible is truth—everything else was up for debate. She taught me to challenge authority and question the system. The only way it backfired on her was that I constantly challenged and questioned her.

When I was seven years old, my mother had been dating her new boyfriend, Abel, for a year maybe, but at that point I was too young to know who they were to each other. It was just "Hey, that's mom's friend who's around a lot." I liked Abel; he was a really nice guy.

As a black person back then, if you wanted to live in the suburbs you'd have to find a white family renting out their servants' quarters or sometimes their garage, which was what Abel had done. He lived in a neighborhood called Orange Grove in a white family's garage, which he'd turned into a cottage-type thing with a hot plate and a bed. Sometimes he'd come and sleep at our house, and sometimes we'd go stay with him. Staying in a garage when we owned our own house wasn't ideal, but Orange Grove was close to my school and my mom's work so it had its benefits.

This white family also had a black maid who lived in the servants' quarters in the backyard, and I'd play with her son whenever we stayed there. At that age my love of fire was in full bloom. One afternoon everyone was at work—my mom and Abel and both of the white parents—and the kid and I were playing together while his mom was inside the house cleaning. One thing I loved doing at the time was using a magnifying glass to burn my name into pieces of wood. You had to aim the lens and get the focus just right and then you got the flame and then you moved it slowly and you could burn shapes and letters and patterns. I was fascinated by it.

That afternoon I was teaching this kid how to do it. We were inside the servants' quarters, which was really more of a toolshed added on to the back of the house, full of wooden ladders, buckets of old paint, turpentine. I had a box of matches with me, too—all my usual fire-making tools. We were sitting on an old mattress that they used to sleep on the floor, basically a sack stuffed with dried straw. The sun was beaming in through the window, and I was showing the kid how to burn his name into a piece of plywood.

At one point we took a break to go get a snack. I set the magnifying glass and the matches on the mattress and we left. When we came back a few minutes later we found the shed had one of those doors that self-locks from the inside. We couldn't get back in without going to get his mother, so we decided to run around and play in the yard. After a while I noticed smoke coming out of the cracks in the window frame. I ran over and looked inside. A small fire was burning in the middle of the straw mattress where we'd left the matches and the magnifying glass. We ran and called the maid. She came, but she didn't know what to do. The door was locked, and before we could figure out how to get into the shed the whole thing caught—the mattress, the ladders, the paint, the turpentine, everything.

The flames moved quickly. Soon the roof was on fire, and from there the blaze spread to the main house, and the whole thing burned and burned and burned. Smoke was billowing into the sky. A neighbor had called the fire brigade, and the sirens were on their way. Me and this kid and the maid, we ran out to the road and watched as the firemen tried to put it out, but by the time they did, it was too late. There was nothing left but a charred brick-and-mortar shell, roof gone, and gutted from the inside.

The white family came home and stood on the street, staring at the ruins of their house. They asked the maid what happened and she asked her son and the kid totally snitched. "Trevor had matches," he said. The family said nothing to me. I don't think they knew what to say.

They were completely dumbfounded. They didn't call the police, didn't threaten to sue. What were they going to do, arrest a seven-year-old for arson? And we were so poor you couldn't actually sue us for anything. Plus they had insurance, so that was the end of it.

They kicked Abel out of the garage, which I thought was hilarious because the garage, which was freestanding, was the only piece of the property left unscathed. I saw no reason for Abel to have to leave, but they made him. We packed up his stuff, put it into our car, and drove home to Eden Park; Abel basically lived with us from then on. He and my mom got into a huge fight. "Your son has burned down my life!" But there was no punishment for me that day. My mom was too much in shock. There's naughty, and then there's burning down a white person's house. She didn't know what to do.

I didn't feel bad about it at all. I still don't. The lawyer in me maintains that I am completely innocent. There were matches and there was a magnifying glass and there was a mattress and then, clearly, a series of unfortunate events. Things catch fire sometimes. That's why there's a fire brigade. But everyone in my family will tell you, "Trevor burned down a house." If people thought I was naughty before, after the fire I was notorious. One of my uncles stopped calling me Trevor. He called me "Terror" instead. "Don't leave that kid alone in your home," he'd say. "He'll burn it to the ground."

My cousin Mlungisi, to this day, cannot comprehend how I survived being as naughty as I was for as long as I did, how I withstood the number of hidings that I got. Why did I keep misbehaving? How did I never learn my lesson? Both of my cousins were supergood kids. Mlungisi got maybe one hiding in his life. After that he said he never wanted to experience anything like it ever again, and from that day he always followed the rules. But I was blessed with another trait I inherited from my mother: her ability to forget the pain in life. I remember the thing that caused the trauma, but I don't hold on to the trauma. I never let the memory of something painful prevent me from trying something new. If you think too much about the ass-kicking your mom gave you, or the ass-kicking that life gave you, you'll stop pushing the boundaries and breaking the rules. It's better to take it, spend some time crying, then wake up the next day and move on. You'll have a few bruises and they'll remind you of what happened and that's okay. But after a while the bruises fade, and they fade for a reason—because now it's time to get up to some shit again.

I grew up in a black family in a black neighborhood in a black country. I've traveled to other black cities in black countries all over the black continent. And in all of that time I've yet to find a place where black people like cats. One of the biggest reasons for that, as we know in South Africa, is that only witches have cats, and all cats are witches.

There was a famous incident during an Orlando Pirates soccer match a few years ago. A cat got into the stadium and ran through the crowd and out onto the pitch in the middle of the game. A security guard, seeing the cat, did what any sensible black person would do. He said to himself, "That cat is a witch." He caught the cat and—live on TV—he kicked it and stomped it and beat it to death with a *sjambok,* a hard leather whip.

It was front-page news all over the country. White people lost their shit. Oh my word, it was insane. The security guard was arrested and put on trial and found guilty of animal abuse. He had to pay some enormous fine to avoid spending several months in jail. What was ironic to me was that white people had spent years seeing video of black people being beaten to death by other white people, but this one video of a black man kicking a cat, that's what sent them over the edge. Black people were just confused. They didn't see any problem with what the man did. They were like, "Obviously that cat was a witch. How else would a cat know how to get out onto a soccer pitch? Somebody sent it to jinx one of the teams. That man had to kill the cat. He was protecting the players."

In South Africa, black people have dogs.

7

FUFI

A month after we moved to Eden Park, my mother brought home two cats. Black cats. Beautiful creatures. Some woman from her work had a litter of kittens she was trying to get rid of, and my mom ended up with two. I was excited because I'd never had a pet before. My mom was excited because she loves animals. She didn't believe in any nonsense about cats. It was just another way in which she was a rebel, refusing to conform to ideas about what black people did and didn't do.

In a black neighborhood, you wouldn't dare own a cat, especially a black cat. That would be like wearing a sign that said, "Hello, I am a witch." That would be suicide. Since we'd moved to a colored neighborhood, my mom thought the cats would be okay. Once they were grown we let them out during the day to roam the neighborhood. Then we came home one evening and found the cats strung up by their tails from our front gate, gutted and skinned and bleeding out, their heads chopped off. On our front wall someone had written in Afrikaans, "*Heks*"—"Witch."

Colored people, apparently, were no more progressive than black people on the issue of cats.

I wasn't exactly devastated about the cats. I don't think we'd had them long enough for me to get attached; I don't even remember their names. And cats are dicks for the most part. As much as I tried they never felt like real pets. They never showed me affection nor did they accept any of mine. Had the cats made more of an effort, I might have felt like I had lost something. But even as a kid, looking at these dead, mutilated animals, I was like, "Well, there you have it. Maybe if they'd been nicer, they could have avoided this."

After the cats were killed, we took a break from pets for a while. Then we got dogs. Dogs are cool. Almost every black family I knew had a dog. No matter how poor you were, you had a dog. White people treat dogs like children or members of the family. Black people's dogs are more for protection, a poor-man's alarm system. You buy a dog and you keep it out in the yard. Black people name dogs by their traits. If it has stripes, you call it Tiger. If it's vicious, you call it Danger. If it has spots, you call it Spotty. Given the finite number of traits a dog can have, pretty much everyone's dogs have the same names; people just recycle them.

We'd never had dogs in Soweto. Then one day some lady at my mom's work offered us two puppies. They weren't planned puppies. This woman's Maltese poodle had been impregnated by the bull terrier from next door, a strange mix. My mom said she'd take them both. She brought them home, and I was the happiest kid on earth.

My mom named them Fufi and Panther. Fufi, I don't know where her name came from. Panther had a pink nose, so she was Pink Panther and eventually just Panther. They were two sisters who loved and hated each other. They would look out for each other, but they would also fight all the time. Like, blood fights. Biting. Clawing. It was a strange, gruesome relationship.

Panther was my mom's dog; Fufi was mine. Fufi was beautiful. Clean lines, happy face. She looked like a perfect bull terrier, only skinnier because of the Maltese mixed in. Panther, who was more half-and-half, came out weird and scruffy-looking. Panther was smart. Fufi was dumb as shit. At least we always thought she was dumb as shit. Whenever we called them, Panther would come right away, but Fufi wouldn't do anything. Panther would run back and get Fufi and then they'd both come. It turned out that Fufi was deaf. Years later Fufi died when a burglar was trying to break into our house. He pushed the gate over and it fell on her back and broke her spine. We took her to the vet and she had to be put down. After examining her, the vet came over and gave us the news.

"It must have been strange for your family living with a dog that was deaf," he said.

"What?"

"You didn't know your dog was deaf?"

"No, we thought it was stupid."

That's when we realized that their whole lives the one dog had been telling the other dog what to do somehow. The smart, hearing one was helping the dumb, deaf one.

Fufi was the love of my life. Beautiful but stupid. I raised her. I potty-trained her. She slept in my bed. A dog is a great thing for a kid to have. It's like a bicycle but with emotions.

Fufi could do all sorts of tricks. She could jump super high. I mean, Fufi could *jump*. I could hold a piece of food out above my own head and she'd leap up and grab it like it was nothing. If YouTube had been around, Fufi would have been a star.

Fufi was a little rascal as well. During the day we kept the dogs in the backyard, which was enclosed by a wall at least five feet high. After a while, every day we'd come home and Fufi would be sitting outside the gate, waiting for us. We were always confused. Was someone opening the gate? What was going on? It never occurred to us that she could actually scale a five-foot wall, but that was exactly what was happening. Every morning, Fufi would wait for us to leave, jump over the wall, and go roaming around the neighborhood.

I caught her one day when I was home for the school holidays. My mom had left for work and I was in the living room. Fufi didn't know I was there; she thought I was gone because the car was gone. I heard Panther barking in the backyard, looked out, and there was Fufi, scaling the wall. She'd jumped, scampered up the last couple of feet, and then she was gone.

I couldn't believe this was happening. I ran out front, grabbed my bicycle, and followed her to see where she was going. She went a long way, many streets over, to another part of the neighborhood. Then she went up to this other house and jumped over their wall and into their backyard. What the hell was she doing? I went up to the gate and rang the doorbell. This colored kid answered.

"May I help you?" he said.

"Yeah. My dog is in your yard."

"What?"

"My dog. She's in your yard."

Fufi walked up and stood between us.

"Fufi, come!" I said. "Let's go!"

This kid looked at Fufi and called her by some other stupid name, Spotty or some bullshit like that.

"Spotty, go back inside the house."

"Whoa, whoa," I said. "Spotty? That's Fufi!"

"No, that's my dog, Spotty."

"No, that's Fufi, my friend."

"No, this is Spotty."

"How could this be Spotty? She doesn't even have spots. You don't know what you're talking about."

"This is Spotty!"

"Fufi!"

"Spotty!"

"Fufi!"

Of course, since Fufi was deaf she didn't respond to "Spotty" or "Fufi." She just stood there. I started cursing the kid out.

"Give me back my dog!"

"I don't know who you are," he said, "but you better get out of here."

Then he went into the house and got his mom and she came out.

"What do you want?" she said.

"That's my dog!"

"This is our dog. Go away."

I started crying. "Why are you stealing my dog?!" I turned to Fufi and begged her. "Fufi, why are you doing this to me?! Why, Fufi?! Why?!" I called to her. I begged her to come. Fufi was deaf to my pleas. And everything else.

I jumped onto my bike and raced home, tears running down my face. I loved Fufi so much. To see her with another boy, acting like she didn't know me, after I raised her, after all the nights we spent together. I was heartbroken.

That evening Fufi didn't come home. Because the other family thought I was coming to steal their dog, they had decided to lock her inside, so she couldn't make it back the way she normally did to wait for us outside the fence. My mom got home from work. I was in tears. I told her Fufi had been kidnapped. We went back to the house. My mom rang the bell and confronted the mom.

"Look, this is our dog."

This lady lied to my mom's face. "This is not your dog. We bought this dog."

"You didn't buy the dog. It's our dog."

They went back and forth. This woman wasn't budging, so we went home to get evidence: pictures of us with the dogs, certificates from the vet. I was crying the whole time, and my mom was losing her patience with me. "Stop crying! We'll get the dog! Calm down!"

We gathered up our documentation and went back to the house. This time we brought Panther with us, as part of the proof. My mom showed this lady the pictures and the information from the vet. She still wouldn't give us Fufi. My mom threatened to call the police. It turned into a whole thing. Finally my mom said, "Okay, I'll give you a hundred rand."

"Fine," the lady said.

My mom gave her some money and she brought Fufi out. The other kid, who thought Fufi was Spotty, had to watch his mother sell the dog he thought was his. Now he started crying. "Spotty! No! Mom, you can't sell Spotty!" I didn't care. I just wanted Fufi back.

Once Fufi saw Panther she came right away. The dogs left with us and we walked. I sobbed the whole way home, still heartbroken. My mom had no time for my whining.

"Why are you crying?!"

"Because Fufi loves another boy."

"So? Why would that hurt you? It didn't cost you anything. Fufi's here. She still loves you. She's still your dog. So get over it."

Fufi was my first heartbreak. No one has ever betrayed me more than Fufi. It was a valuable lesson to me. The hard thing was understanding that Fufi wasn't cheating on me with another boy. She was merely living her life to the fullest. Until I knew that she was going out on her own during the day, her other relationship hadn't affected me at all. Fufi had no malicious intent.

I believed that Fufi was *my* dog, but of course that wasn't true. Fufi was *a* dog. I was *a* boy. We got along well. She happened to live in my house. That experience shaped what I've felt about relationships for the rest of my life: You do not own the thing that you love. I was lucky to learn that lesson at such a young age. I have so many friends who still, as adults, wrestle with feelings of betrayal. They'll come to me angry and crying and talking about how they've been cheated on and lied to, and I feel for them. I understand what they're going through. I sit with them and buy them a drink and I say, "Friend, let me tell you the story of Fufi."

When I was twenty-four years old, one day out of the blue my mother said to me, "You need to find your father."

"Why?" I asked. At that point I hadn't seen him in over ten years and didn't think I'd ever see him again.

"Because he's a piece of you," she said, "and if you don't find him you won't find yourself."

"I don't need him for that," I said. "I know who I am."

"It's not about knowing who you are. It's about him knowing who you are, and you knowing who he is. Too many men grow up without their fathers, so they spend their lives with a false impression of who their father is and what a father should be. You need to find your father. You need to show him what you've become. You need to finish that story."

8

ROBERT

My father is a complete mystery. There are so many questions about his life that I still cannot even begin to answer.

Where'd he grow up? Somewhere in Switzerland.

Where'd he go to university? I don't know if he did.

How'd he end up in South Africa? I haven't a clue.

I've never met my Swiss grandparents. I don't know their names or anything about them. I do know my dad has an older sister, but I've never met her, either. I know that he worked as a chef in Montreal and New York for a while before moving to South Africa in the late 1970s. I know that he worked for an industrial food-service company and that he opened a couple of bars and restaurants here and there. That's about it.

I never called my dad "Dad." I never addressed him "Daddy" or "Father," either. I couldn't. I was instructed not to. If we were out in public or anywhere people might overhear us and I called him "Dad," someone might have asked questions or called the police. So for as long as I can remember I always called him Robert.

While I know nothing of my dad's life before me, thanks to my mom and just from the time I have been able to spend with him, I do have a sense of who he is as a person. He's very Swiss, clean and particular and precise. He's the only person I know who checks into a hotel room and leaves it cleaner than when he arrived. He doesn't like anyone waiting on him. No servants, no housekeepers. He cleans up after himself. He likes his space. He lives in his own world and does his own everything.

I know that he never married. He used to say that most people marry because they want to control another person, and he never wanted to be controlled. I know that he loves traveling, loves entertaining, having people over. But at the same time his privacy is everything to him. Wherever he lives he's never listed in the phone book. I'm sure my parents would have been caught in their time together if he hadn't been as private as he is. My mom was wild and impulsive. My father was reserved and rational. She was fire, he was ice. They were opposites that attracted, and I am a mix of them both.

One thing I do know about my dad is that he hates racism and homogeneity more than anything, and not because of any feelings of self-righteousness or moral superiority. He just never understood how white people could be racist in South Africa. "Africa is full of black people," he would say. "So why would you come all the way to Africa if you hate black people? If you hate black people so much, why did you move into their house?" To him it was insane.

Because racism never made sense to my father, he never subscribed to any of the rules of apartheid. In the early eighties, before I was born, he opened one of the first integrated restaurants in Johannesburg, a steakhouse. He applied for a special license that allowed businesses to serve both black and white patrons. These licenses existed because hotels and restaurants needed them to serve black travelers and diplomats from other countries, who in theory weren't subject to the same restrictions as black South Africans; black South Africans with money in turn exploited that loophole to frequent those hotels and restaurants.

My dad's restaurant was an instant, booming success. Black people came because there were few upscale establishments where they could eat, and they wanted to come and sit in a nice restaurant and see what that was like. White people came because they wanted to see what it was like to sit with black people. The white people would sit and watch the black people eat, and the black people would sit and eat and watch the white people watching them eat. The curiosity of being together overwhelmed the animosity keeping people apart. The place had a great vibe.

The restaurant closed only because a few people in the neighborhood took it upon themselves to complain. They filed petitions, and the government started looking for ways to shut my dad down. At first the inspectors came and tried to get him on cleanliness and health-code violations. Clearly they had never heard of the Swiss. That failed dismally. Then they decided to go after him by imposing additional and arbitrary restrictions.

"Since you've got the license you can keep the restaurant open," they said, "but you'll need to have separate toilets for every racial category. You'll need white toilets, black toilets, colored toilets, and Indian toilets."

"But then it will be a whole restaurant of nothing but toilets."

"Well, if you don't want to do that, your other option is to make it a normal restaurant and only serve whites."

He closed the restaurant.

After apartheid fell, my father moved from Hillbrow to Yeoville, a formerly quiet, residential neighborhood that had transformed into this vibrant melting pot of black and white and every other hue. Immigrants were pouring in from Nigeria and Ghana and all over the continent, bringing different food and exciting music. Rockey Street was the main strip, and its sidewalks were filled with street vendors and restaurants and bars. It was an explosion of culture.

My dad lived two blocks over from Rockey, on Yeo Street, right next to this incredible park where I loved to go because kids of all races and different countries were running around and playing there. My dad's house was simple. Nice, but nothing fancy. I feel like my dad had enough money to be comfortable and travel, but he never spent lavishly on things. He's extremely frugal, the kind of guy who drives the same car for twenty years.

My father and I lived on a schedule. I visited him every Sunday afternoon. Even though apartheid had ended, my mom had made her decision: She didn't want to get married. So we had our house, and he had his. I'd made a deal with my mom that if I went with her to mixed church and white church in the morning, after that I'd get to skip black church and go to my dad's, where we'd watch Formula 1 racing instead of casting out demons.

I celebrated my birthday with my dad every year, and we spent Christmas with him as well. I loved Christmas with my dad because my dad celebrated European Christmas. European Christmas was the best Christmas ever. My dad went all out. He had Christmas lights and a Christmas tree. He had fake snow and snow globes and stockings hung by the fireplace and lots of wrapped presents from Santa Claus. African Christmas was a lot more practical. We'd go to church, come home, have a nice meal with good meat and lots of custard and jelly. But there was no tree. You'd get a present, but it was usually just clothes, a new outfit. You might get a toy, but it wasn't wrapped and it was never from Santa Claus. The whole issue of Santa Claus is a rather contentious one when it comes to African Christmas, a matter of pride. When an African dad buys his kid a present, the last thing he's going to do is give some fat white man credit for it. African Dad will tell you straight up, "No, no, no. *I* bought you that."

Outside of birthdays and special occasions, all we had were our Sunday afternoons. He would cook for me. He'd ask me what I wanted, and I'd always request the exact same meal, a German dish called *Rösti*, which is basically a pancake made out of potatoes and some sort of meat with a gravy. I'd have that and a bottle of Sprite, and for dessert a plastic container of custard with caramel on top.

A good chunk of those afternoons would pass in silence. My dad didn't talk much. He was caring and devoted, attentive to detail, always a card on my birthday, always my favorite food and toys when I came for a visit. But at the same time he was a closed book. We'd talk about the food he was making, talk about the F1 racing we'd watched. Every now and then he'd drop a tidbit of information, about a place he'd visited or his steakhouse. But that was it. Being with my dad was like watching a web series. I'd get a few minutes of information a few minutes at a time, then I'd have to wait a week for the next installment.

When I was thirteen my dad moved to Cape Town, and we lost touch. We'd been losing touch for a while, for a couple of reasons. I was a teenager. I had a whole other world I was dealing with now. Video-games and computers meant more to me than spending time with my parents. Also, my mom had married Abel. He was incensed by the idea of my mom being in contact with her previous love, and she decided it was safer for everyone involved not to test his anger. I went from seeing my dad every Sunday to seeing him every other Sunday, maybe once a month, whenever my mom could sneak me over, same as she'd done back in Hillbrow. We'd gone from living under apartheid to living under another kind of tyranny, that of an abusive, alcoholic man.

At the same time, Yeoville had started to suffer from white flight, neglect, general decline. Most of my dad's German friends had left for Cape Town. If he wasn't seeing me, he had no reason to stay, so he left. His leaving wasn't anything traumatic, because it never registered that we might lose touch and never see each other again. In my mind it was just *Dad's moving to Cape Town for a bit. Whatever.*

Then he was gone. I stayed busy living my life, surviving high school, surviving my early twenties, becoming a comedian. My career took off quickly. I got a radio DJ gig and hosted a kids' adventure reality show on television. I was headlining at clubs all over the country. But even as my life was moving forward, the questions about my dad were always there in the back of my mind, bubbling up to the surface now and then. "I wonder where he is. Does he think about me? Does he know what I'm doing? Is he proud of me?" When a parent is absent, you're left in the lurch of not knowing, and it's so easy to fill that space with negative thoughts. "They don't care." "They're selfish." My one saving grace was that my mom never spoke ill of him. She would always compliment him. "You're good with your money. You get that from your dad." "You have your dad's smile." "You're clean and tidy like your father." I never turned to bitterness, because she made sure I knew his absence was because of circumstance and not a lack of love. She always told me the story of her coming home from the hospital and my dad saying, "Where's my kid? I want that kid in my life." She'd say to me, "Don't ever forget: He chose you." And, ultimately, when I turned twenty-four, it was my mom who made me track him down.

Because my father is so private, finding him was hard work. We didn't have an address. He wasn't in the phone book. I started by reaching out to some of his old connections, German expats in Johannesburg, a woman who used to date one of his friends who knew somebody who knew the last place he stayed. I got nowhere. Finally my mom suggested the Swiss embassy. "They have to know where he is," she said, "because he has to be in touch with them."

I wrote to the Swiss embassy asking them where my father was, but because my father is not on my birth certificate I had no proof that my father is my father. The embassy wrote back and said they couldn't give me any information, because they didn't know who I was. I tried calling them, and I got the runaround there as well. "Look, kid," they said. "We can't help you. We're the *Swiss* embassy. Do you know nothing about the Swiss? Discretion is kind of our thing. That's what we do. Tough luck." I kept pestering them and finally they said, "Okay, we'll take your letter and, if a man such as you're describing exists, we might forward your letter to him. If he doesn't, maybe we won't. Let's see what happens."

A few months later, a letter came back in the post: "Great to hear from you. How are you? Love, Dad." He gave me his address in Cape

Town, in a neighborhood called Camps Bay, and a few months later I went down to visit.

I'll never forget that day. It was probably one of the weirdest days of my life, going to meet a person I knew and yet did not know at all. My memories of him felt just out of reach. I was trying to remember how he spoke, how he laughed, what his manner was. I parked on his street and started looking for his address. Camps Bay is full of older, semiretired white people, and as I walked down the road all these old white men were walking toward me and past me. My father was pushing seventy by that point, and I was so afraid I'd forgotten what he looked like. I was looking in the face of every old white man who passed me, like, *Are* you *my daddy?* Basically it looked like I was cruising old white dudes in a beachfront retirement community. Then finally I got to the address I'd been given and rang the bell, and the second he opened the door I recognized him. *Hey! It's you,* I thought. *Of course it's you. You're the guy. I know you.*

We picked up right where we'd left off, which was him treating me exactly the way he'd treated me as a thirteen-year-old boy. Like the creature of habit he was, my father went straight back into it. "Right! So where were we? Here, I've got all your favorites. Potato *Rösti.* A bottle of Sprite. Custard with caramel." Luckily my tastes hadn't matured much since the age of thirteen, so I tucked right in.

While I was eating he got up and went and picked up this book, an oversized photo album, and brought it back to the table. "I've been following you," he said, and he opened it up. It was a scrapbook of everything I had ever done, every time my name was mentioned in a newspaper, everything from magazine covers to the tiniest club listings, from the beginning of my career all the way through to that week. He was smiling so big as he took me through it, looking at the headlines. "Trevor Noah Appearing This Saturday at the Blues Room." "Trevor Noah Hosting New TV Show."

I felt a flood of emotions rushing through me. It was everything I could do not to start crying. It felt like this ten-year gap in my life closed right up in an instant, like only a day had passed since I'd last seen him.

For years I'd had so many questions. Is he thinking about me? Does he know what I'm doing? Is he proud of me? But he'd been with me the whole time. He'd always been proud of me. Circumstance had pulled us apart, but he was never not my father.

I walked out of his house that day an inch taller. Seeing him had reaffirmed his choosing of me. He chose to have me in his life. He chose to answer my letter. I was wanted. Being chosen is the greatest gift you can give to another human being.

Once we reconnected, I was overcome by this drive to make up for all the years we'd missed. I decided the best way to do it was to interview him. I realized very quickly that that was a mistake. Interviews will give you facts and information, but facts and information weren't really what I was after. What I wanted was a relationship, and an interview is not a relationship. Relationships are built in the silences. You spend time with people, you observe them and interact with them, and you come to know them—and that is what apartheid stole from us: time. You can't make up for that with an interview, but I had to figure that out for myself.

I went down to spend a few days with my father, and I made it my mission: This weekend I will get to know my father. As soon as I arrived I started peppering him with questions. "Where are you from? Where did you go to school? Why did you do this? How did you do that?" He started getting visibly irritated.

"What is this?" he said. "Why are you interrogating me? What's going on here?"

"I want to get to know you."

"Is this how you normally get to know people, by interrogating them?"

"Well . . . not really."

"So how do you get to know people?"

"I dunno. By spending time with them, I guess."

"Okay. So spend time with me. See what you find out."

So we spent the weekend together. We had dinner and talked about politics. We watched F1 racing and talked about sports. We sat quietly in his backyard and listened to old Elvis Presley records. The whole time he said not one word about himself. Then, as I was packing up to leave, he walked over to me and sat down.

"So," he said, "in the time we've spent together, what would you say you've learned about your dad?"

"Nothing. All I know is that you're extremely secretive."

"You see? You're getting to know me already."

PART II

PART II

When Dutch colonists landed at the southern tip of Africa over three hundred years ago, they encountered an indigenous people known as the Khoisan. The Khoisan are the Native Americans of South Africa, a lost tribe of bushmen, nomadic hunter-gatherers distinct from the darker, Bantu-speaking peoples who later migrated south to become the Zulu, Xhosa, and Sotho tribes of modern South Africa. While settling in Cape Town and the surrounding frontier, the white colonists had their way with the Khoisan women, and the first mixed people of South Africa were born.

To work the colonists' farms, slaves were soon imported from different corners of the Dutch empire, from West Africa, Madagascar, and the East Indies. The slaves and the Khoisan intermarried, and the white colonists continued to dip in and take their liberties, and over time the Khoisan all but disappeared from South Africa. While most were killed off through disease, famine, and war, the rest of their bloodline was bred out of existence, mixed in with the descendants of whites and slaves to form an entirely new race of people: coloreds. Colored people are a hybrid, a complete mix. Some are light and some are dark. Some have Asian features, some have white features, some have black features. It's not uncommon for a colored man and a colored woman to have a child that looks nothing like either parent.

The curse that colored people carry is having no clearly defined heritage to go back to. If they trace their lineage back far enough, at a certain point it splits into white and native and a tangled web of "other." Since their native mothers are gone, their strongest affinity has always been with their white fathers, the Afrikaners. Most colored people don't speak African languages. They speak Afrikaans. Their religion, their institutions, all of the things that shaped their culture came from Afrikaners.

The history of colored people in South Africa is, in this respect, worse than the history of black people in South Africa. For all that black people have suffered, they know who they are. Colored people don't.

———

9

THE MULBERRY TREE

At the end of our street in Eden Park, right in a bend at the top of the road, stood a giant mulberry tree growing out of someone's front yard. Every year when it bore fruit the neighborhood kids would go and pick berries from it, eating as many as they could and filling up bags to take home. They would all play under the tree together. I had to play under the tree by myself. I didn't have any friends in Eden Park.

I was the anomaly wherever we lived. In Hillbrow, we lived in a white area, and nobody looked like me. In Soweto, we lived in a black area, and nobody looked like me. Eden Park was a colored area. In Eden Park, *everyone* looked like me, but we couldn't have been more different. It was the biggest mindfuck I've ever experienced.

The animosity I felt from the colored people I encountered growing up was one of the hardest things I've ever had to deal with. It taught me that it is easier to be an insider as an outsider than to be an outsider as an insider. If a white guy chooses to immerse himself in hip-hop culture and only hang out with black people, black people will say, "Cool, white guy. Do what you need to do." If a black guy chooses to button up his blackness to live among white people and play lots of golf, white people will say, "Fine. I like Brian. He's safe." But try being a black person who immerses himself in white culture while still living in the black community. Try being a white person who adopts the trappings of black culture while still living in the white community. You will face more hate and ridicule and ostracism than you can even begin to fathom. People are willing to accept you if they see you as an outsider trying to assimilate into their world. But when they see you as a fellow tribe member attempting to disavow the tribe, that is something they will never forgive. That is what happened to me in Eden Park.

When apartheid came, colored people defied easy categorization, so the system used them—quite brilliantly—to sow confusion, hatred, and mistrust. For the purposes of the state, colored people became the almost-whites. They were second-class citizens, denied the rights of white people but given special privileges that black people didn't have, just to keep them holding out for more. Afrikaners used to call them *amperbaas:* "the almost-boss." The almost-master. "You're *almost* there. You're *so close.* You're *this close* to being white. Pity your grandfather couldn't keep his hands off the chocolate, eh? But it's not your fault you're colored, so keep trying. Because if you work hard enough you can erase this taint from your bloodline. Keep on marrying lighter and whiter and don't touch the chocolate and maybe, *maybe,* someday, if you're lucky, you can become white."

Which seems ridiculous, but it would happen. Every year under apartheid, some colored people would get promoted to white. It wasn't a myth; it was real. People could submit applications to the government. Your hair might become straight enough, your skin might become light enough, your accent might become polished enough—and you'd be reclassified as white. All you had to do was denounce your people, denounce your history, and leave your darker-skinned friends and family behind.

The legal definition of a white person under apartheid was "one who in appearance is obviously a white person who is generally not accepted as a coloured person; or is generally accepted as a white person and is not in appearance obviously a white person." It was completely arbitrary, in other words. That's where the government came up with things like the pencil test. If you were applying to be white, the pencil went into your hair. If it fell out, you were white. If it stayed in, you were colored. You were what the government said you were. Sometimes that came down to a lone clerk eyeballing your face and making a snap decision. Depending on how high your cheekbones were or how broad your nose was, he could tick whatever box made sense to him, thereby deciding where you could live, whom you could marry, what jobs and rights and privileges you were allowed.

And colored people didn't just get promoted to white. Sometimes colored people became Indian. Sometimes Indian people became colored. Sometimes blacks were promoted to colored, and sometimes coloreds were demoted to black. And of course whites could be demoted to colored as well. That was key. Those mixed bloodlines were always lurking, waiting to peek out, and fear of losing their status kept white people in line. If two white parents had a child and the government decided that child was too dark, even if both parents produced documentation proving they were white, the child could be classified as colored, and the family had to make a decision. Do they give up their white status to go and live as colored people in a colored area? Or would they split up, the mother taking the colored child to live in the ghetto while the father stayed white to make a living to support them?

Many colored people lived in this limbo, a true purgatory, always yearning for the white fathers who disowned them, and they could be horribly racist to one another as a result. The most common colored slur was *boesman*. "Bushman." "Bushie." Because it called out their blackness, their primitiveness. The worst way to insult a colored person was to infer that they were in some way black. One of the most sinister things about apartheid was that it taught colored people that it was black people who were holding them back. Apartheid said that the only reason colored people couldn't have first-class status was because black people might use coloredness to sneak past the gates to enjoy the benefits of whiteness.

That's what apartheid did: It convinced every group that it was because of the other race that they didn't get into the club. It's basically the bouncer at the door telling you, "We can't let you in because of your friend Darren and his ugly shoes." So you look at Darren and say, "Screw you, Black Darren. You're holding me back." Then when Darren goes up, the bouncer says, "No, it's actually your friend Sizwe and his weird hair." So Darren says, "Screw you, Sizwe," and now everyone hates everyone. But the truth is that none of you were ever getting into that club.

Colored people had it rough. Imagine: You've been brainwashed into believing that your blood is tainted. You've spent all your time assimilating and aspiring to whiteness. Then, just as you think you're closing in on the finish line, some fucking guy named Nelson Mandela comes along and flips the country on its head. Now the finish line is back where the starting line was, and the benchmark is black. Black is in charge. Black is beautiful. Black is powerful. For centuries colored people were told: Blacks are monkeys. Don't swing from the trees like them. Learn to walk upright like the white man. Then all of a sudden it's *Planet of the Apes,* and the monkeys have taken over.

So you can imagine how weird it was for me. I was mixed but not colored—colored by complexion but not by culture. Because of that I was seen as a colored person who didn't want to be colored.

In Eden Park, I encountered two types of colored people. Some colored people hated me because of my blackness. My hair was curly and I was proud of my Afro. I spoke African languages and loved speaking them. People would hear me speaking Xhosa or Zulu and they'd say, *"Wat is jy? 'n Boesman?"* "What are you, a Bushman?" Why are you trying to be black? Why do you speak that click-click language? Look at your light skin. You're almost there and you're throwing it away.

Other colored people hated me because of my whiteness. Even though I identified as being black, I had a white father. I went to an English private school. I'd learned to get along with white people at church. I could speak perfect English, and I barely spoke Afrikaans, the language colored people were supposed to speak. So colored people thought that I thought I was better than them. They would mock my accent, like I was putting on airs. *"Dink jy, jy is grênd?"* "You think you're high class?"—uppity, people would say in America.

Even when I thought I was liked, I wasn't. One year I got a brand-new bike during the summer holidays. My cousin Mlungisi and I were taking turns riding around the block. I was riding up our street when this cute colored girl came out to the road and stopped me. She smiled and waved to me sweetly.

"Hey," she said, "can I ride your bike?"

I was completely shocked. *Oh, wow,* I thought, *I made a friend.*

"Yeah, of course," I said.

I got off and she got on and rode about twenty or thirty feet. Some random older kid came running up to the street, she stopped and got off, and he climbed on and rode away. I was so happy that a girl had spoken to me that it didn't fully sink in that they'd stolen my bicycle. I ran back home, smiling and skipping along. My cousin asked where the bicycle was. I told him.

"Trevor, you've been robbed," he said. "Why didn't you chase them?"

"I thought they were being nice. I thought I'd made a friend."

Mlungisi was older, my protector. He ran off and found the kids, and thirty minutes later he came back with my bike.

Things like that happened a lot. I was bullied all the time. The incident at the mulberry tree was probably the worst of them. Late one afternoon I was playing by myself like I always did, running around the neighborhood. This group of five or six colored boys was up the street picking berries off the mulberry tree and eating them. I went over and started picking some to take home for myself. The boys were a few years older than me, around twelve or thirteen. They didn't talk to me, and I didn't talk to them. They were speaking to one another in Afrikaans, and I could understand what they were saying. Then one of them, this kid who was the ringleader of the group, walked over. *"Mag ek jou moerbeie sien?"* "Can I see your mulberries?" My first thought, again, was, *Oh, cool. I made a friend.* I held up my hand and showed him my mulberries. Then he knocked them out of my hand and smushed them into the ground. The other kids started laughing. I stood there and looked at him a moment. By that point I'd developed thick skin. I was used to being bullied. I shrugged it off and went back to picking berries.

Clearly not getting the reaction he wanted, this kid started cursing me out. *"Fok weg, jou onnosele Boesman!"* "Get the fuck out of here! Go away, you stupid Bushie! Bushman!" I ignored him and went on about my business. Then I felt a *splat!* on the back of my head. He'd hit me with a mulberry. It wasn't painful, just startling. I turned to look at him and, *splat!*, he hit me again, right in my face.

Then, in a split second, before I could even react, all of these kids started pelting me with berries, pelting the shit out of me. Some of the berries weren't ripe, and they stung like rocks. I tried to cover my face with my hands, but there was a barrage coming at me from all sides. They were laughing and pelting me and calling me names. "Bushie! Bushman!" I was terrified. Just the suddenness of it, I didn't know what to do. I started crying, and I ran. I ran for my life, all the way back down the road to our house.

When I ran inside I looked like I'd been beaten to a pulp because I was bawling my eyes out and was covered in red-purple berry juice. My mother looked at me, horrified.

"What happened?"

In between sobs I told her the story. "These kids . . . the mulberry tree . . . they threw berries at me . . ." When I finished, she burst out laughing. "It's not funny!" I said.

"No, no, Trevor," she said. "I'm not laughing because it's funny. I'm laughing out of relief. I thought you'd been beaten up. I thought this was blood. I'm laughing because it's only berry juice."

My mom thought everything was funny. There was no subject too dark or too painful for her to tackle with humor. "Look on the bright side," she said, laughing and pointing to the half of me covered in dark berry juice. "Now you really are half black and half white."

"It's not funny!"

"Trevor, you're okay," she said. "Go and wash up. You're not hurt. You're hurt emotionally. But you're not hurt."

Half an hour later, Abel showed up. At that point Abel was still my mom's boyfriend. He wasn't trying to be my father or even a stepfather, really. He was more like a big brother than anything. He'd joke around with me, have fun. I didn't know him that well, but one thing I did know about him was that he had a temper. Very charming when he wanted to be, incredibly funny, but fuck he could be mean. He'd grown up in the homelands, where you had to fight to survive. Abel was big, too, around six-foot-three, long and lean. He hadn't hit my mom yet. He hadn't hit me yet, either. But I knew he was dangerous. I'd seen it. Someone would cut us off in traffic. Abel would yell out the window. The other guy would honk and yell back. In a flash Abel would be out of our car, over to theirs, grabbing the guy through the driver's-side window, screaming in his face, raising a fist. You'd see the other guy panic. "Whoa, whoa, whoa. I'm sorry, I'm sorry."

When Abel walked in that night, he sat down on the couch and saw that I'd been crying.

"What happened?" he said.

I started to explain. My mother cut me off. "Don't tell him," she said. She knew what would happen. She knew better than me.

"Don't tell me what?" Abel said.

"It's nothing," she said.

"It's not nothing," I said.

She glared at me. "Don't tell him."

Abel was getting frustrated. "What? Don't tell me what?"

He'd been drinking; he never came home from work sober, and the drinking always made his temper worse. It was strange, but in that moment I realized that if I said the right things I could get him to step in and do something. We were almost family, and I knew if I made him feel like his family had been insulted, he'd help me get back at the boys. I knew he had a demon inside him, and I hated that; it terrified me how violent and dangerous he was when he snapped. But in that moment I knew exactly what I had to say to get the monster on my side.

I told him the story, the names they called me, the way they attacked me. My mother kept laughing it off, telling me to get over it, that it was kids being kids, no big deal. She was trying to defuse the situation, but I couldn't see that. I was just mad at her. "You think it's a joke, but it's not funny! It's not *funny*!"

Abel wasn't laughing. As I told him what the bullies had done, I could see the anger building up inside him. With Abel's anger, there was no ranting and raving, no clenched fists. He sat there on the couch listening to me, not saying a word. Then, very calm and deliberate, he stood up.

"Take me to these boys," he said.

Yes, I thought, *this is it. Big brother is going to get my revenge for me.*

We got into his car and drove up the road, stopping a few houses down from the tree. It was dark now except for the light from the streetlamps, but we could see the boys were still there, playing under the tree. I pointed to the ringleader. "That one. He was the main one." Abel slammed his foot on the gas and shot up onto the grass and straight toward the bottom of the tree. He jumped out. I jumped out. As soon as the kids saw me they knew exactly what was happening. They scattered and ran like hell.

Abel was quick. Good Lord, he was fast. The ringleader had made a dash for it and was trying to climb over a wall. Abel grabbed him, pulled him down, and dragged him back. Then he stripped a branch off the tree, a switch, and started whipping him. He whipped the *shit* out of him, and I loved it. I have never enjoyed anything as much as I enjoyed that moment. Revenge truly is sweet. It takes you to a dark place, but, man, it satisfies a thirst.

Then there was the strangest moment where it flipped. I caught a glimpse of the look of terror in the boy's face, and I realized that Abel had gone past getting revenge for me. He wasn't doing this to teach the kid a lesson. He was just beating him. He was a grown man venting his rage on a twelve-year-old boy. In an instant I went from *Yes, I got my revenge* to *No, no, no. Too much. Too much. Oh shit. Oh shit. Oh shit. Dear God, what have I done?*

Once this kid was beat to shit, Abel dragged him over to the car and held him up in front of me. "Say you're sorry." The kid was whimpering, trembling. He looked me in the eye, and I had never seen fear in someone's eyes like I saw in his. He'd been beaten by a stranger in a way I don't think he'd ever been beaten before. He said he was sorry, but it was like his apology wasn't for what he'd done to me. It was like he was sorry for every bad thing he'd ever done in his life, because he didn't know there could be a punishment like this.

Looking in that boy's eyes, I realized how much he and I had in common. He was a kid. I was a kid. He was crying. I was crying. He was a colored boy in South Africa, taught how to hate and how to hate himself. Who had bullied him that he needed to bully me? He'd made me feel fear, and to get my revenge I'd unleashed my own hell on his world. But I knew I'd done a terrible thing.

Once the kid apologized, Abel shoved him away and kicked him. "Go." The kid ran off, and we drove back to the house in silence. At home Abel and my mom got in a huge fight. She was always on him about his temper. "You can't go around hitting other people's children! You're not the law! This anger, this is no way to live!"

A couple of hours later this kid's dad drove over to our house to confront Abel. Abel went out to the gate, and I watched from inside the house. By that point Abel was truly drunk. This kid's dad had no idea what he was walking into. He was some mild-mannered, middle-aged guy. I don't remember much about him, because I was watching Abel the whole time. I never took my eyes off him. I knew that's where the danger was.

Abel didn't have a gun yet; he bought that later. But Abel didn't need a gun to put the fear of God in you. I watched as he got right in this guy's face. I couldn't hear what the other man was saying, but I heard Abel. "Don't fuck with me. I will kill you." The guy turned quickly and got back in his car and drove away. He thought he was coming to defend the honor of his family. He left happy to escape with his life.

When I was growing up, my mom spent a lot of time trying to teach me about women. She was always giving me lessons, little talks, pieces of advice. It was never a full-blown, sit-down lecture about relationships. It was more like tidbits along the way. And I never understood why, because I was a kid. The only women in my life were my mom and my grandmother and my aunt and my cousin. I had no love interest whatsoever, yet my mom insisted. She would go off on a whole range of things.

"Trevor, remember a man is not determined by how much he earns. You can still be the man of the house and earn less than your woman. Being a man is not what you have, it's who you are. Being more of a man doesn't mean your woman has to be less than you."

"Trevor, make sure your woman is the woman in your life. Don't be one of these men who makes his wife compete with his mother. A man with a wife cannot be beholden to his mother."

The smallest thing could prompt her. I'd walk through the house on the way to my room and say, "Hey, Mom" without glancing up. She'd say, "No, Trevor! You look at me. You acknowledge me. Show me that I exist to you, because the way you treat me is the way you will treat your woman. Women like to be noticed. Come and acknowledge me and let me know that you see me. Don't just see me when you need something."

These little lessons were always about grown-up relationships, funnily enough. She was so preoccupied with teaching me how to be a man that she never taught me how to be a boy. How to talk to a girl or pass a girl a note in class—there was none of that. She only told me about adult things. She would even lecture me about sex. As I was a kid, that would get very awkward.

"Trevor, don't forget: You're having sex with a woman in her mind before you're having sex with her in her vagina."

"Trevor, foreplay begins during the day. It doesn't begin in the bedroom."

I'd be like, "What? What is foreplay? What does that even mean?"

————

10

A YOUNG MAN'S LONG, AWKWARD, OCCASIONALLY TRAGIC, AND FREQUENTLY HUMILIATING EDUCATION IN AFFAIRS OF THE HEART, PART I: VALENTINE'S DAY

It was my first year at H. A. Jack, the primary school I transferred to after leaving Maryvale. Valentine's Day was approaching fast. I was twelve years old, and I'd never done Valentine's Day before. We didn't celebrate it in Catholic school. I understood Valentine's Day, as a concept. The naked baby shoots you with an arrow and you fall in love. I got that part. But this was my first time being introduced to it as an activity. At H. A. Jack, Valentine's Day was used as a fundraiser. Pupils were going around selling flowers and cards, and I had to go ask a friend what was happening.

"What is this?" I said. "What are we doing?"

"Oh, you know," she said, "it's Valentine's Day. You pick a special person and you tell them that you love them, and they love you back."

Wow, I thought, *that seems intense*. But I hadn't been shot by Cupid's arrow, and I didn't know of anyone getting shot on my behalf. I had no clue what was going on. All week, the girls in school kept saying, "Who's your valentine? Who's your valentine?" I didn't know what I was supposed to do. Finally one of the girls, a white girl, said, "You should ask Maylene." The other kids agreed. "Yes, Maylene. You should definitely ask Maylene. You have to ask Maylene. You guys are *perfect* for each other."

Maylene was a girl I used to walk home from school with. We lived in the city now, me, my mom and Abel, who was now my stepfather, and my new baby brother, Andrew. We'd sold our house in Eden Park to invest in Abel's new garage. Then that fell apart, and we ended up moving to a neighborhood called Highlands North, a thirty-minute walk from H. A. Jack. A group of us would leave school together every afternoon, each kid peeling off and going their separate way when we reached their house. Maylene and I lived the farthest, so we'd always be the last two. We'd walk together until we got where we needed to go, and then we'd part ways.

Maylene was cool. She was good at tennis, smart, cute. I liked her. I didn't have a crush on her; I wasn't even thinking about girls that way yet. I just liked hanging out with her. Maylene was also the only colored girl in school. I was the only mixed kid in school. We were the only two people who looked like each other. The white girls were insistent about me asking Maylene to be my valentine. They were like, "Trevor, you *have* to ask her. You're the *only two*. It's your *responsibility*." It was like our species was going to die out if we didn't mate and carry on. Which I've learned in life is something that white people do without even realizing it. "You two look the same, therefore we must arrange for you to have sex."

I honestly hadn't thought of asking Maylene, but when the girls brought it up, that thing happened where someone plants the idea in your head and it changes your perception.

"Maylene's totally got a thing for you."

"*Does* she?"

"Yeah, you guys are great together!"

"*Are* we?"

"Totally."

"Well, okay. If you say so."

I liked Maylene as much as I liked anyone, I suppose. Mostly I think I liked the idea of being liked. I decided I'd ask her to be my valentine, but I had no idea how to do it. I didn't know the first thing about having a girlfriend. I had to be taught the whole love bureaucracy of the school. There was the thing where you don't actually talk straight to the person. You have your group of friends and she has her group of friends, and your group of friends has to go to her group of friends and say, "Okay, Trevor likes Maylene. He wants her to be his valentine. We're in favor. We're ready to sign off with your approval." Her friends say, "Okay. Sounds good. We have to run it by Maylene." They go to Maylene. They consult. They tell her what they think. "Trevor says he likes you. We're in favor. We think you'd be good together. What do you say?" Maylene says, "I like Trevor." They say, "Okay. Let's move forward." They come back to us. "Maylene says she approves and she's waiting for Trevor's Valentine's Day advance."

The girls told me this process was what needed to happen. I said, "Cool. Let's do it." The friends sorted it out, Maylene got on board, and I was all set.

The week before Valentine's, Maylene and I were walking home together, and I was trying to get up the courage to ask her. I was so nervous. I'd never done anything like it. I already knew the answer; her friends had told me she'd say yes. It's like being in Congress. You know you have the votes before you go to the floor, but it's still difficult because anything could happen. I didn't know how to do it, all I knew was I wanted it to be perfect, so I waited until we were standing outside McDonald's. Then I mustered up all of my courage and turned to her.

"Hey, Valentine's Day is coming up, and I was wondering, would you be my valentine?"

"Yes. I'll be your valentine."

And then, under the golden arches, we kissed. It was my first time ever kissing a girl. It was just a peck, our lips touched for only a few seconds, but it set off explosions in my head. *Yes! Oh, yes. This. I don't know what this is, but I like it.* Something had awakened. And it was right outside McDonald's, so it was extra special.

Now I was truly excited. I had a valentine. I had a girlfriend. I spent the whole week thinking about Maylene, wanting to make her Valentine's Day as memorable as I could. I saved up my pocket money and bought her flowers and a teddy bear and a card. I wrote a poem with her name in the card, which was really hard because there aren't many good words that rhyme with Maylene. (Machine? Ravine? Sardine?) Then the big day came. I got my Valentine's card and the flowers and the teddy bear and got them ready and took them to school. I was the happiest boy on earth.

The teachers had set aside a period before recess for everyone to exchange valentines. There was a corridor outside our classrooms where I knew Maylene would be, and I waited for her there. All around me, love was in bloom. Boys and girls exchanging cards and gifts, laughing and giggling and stealing kisses. I waited and waited. Finally Maylene showed up and walked over to me. I was about to say "Happy Valentine's Day!" when she stopped me and said, "Oh, hi, Trevor. Um, listen, I can't be your girlfriend anymore. Lorenzo asked me to be his valentine and I can't have two valentines, so I'm his girlfriend now and not yours."

She said it so matter-of-factly that I had no idea how to process it. This was my first time having a girlfriend, so at first I thought, *Huh, maybe this is just how it goes.*

"Oh, okay," I said. "Well, um . . . happy Valentine's Day."

I held out the card and the flowers and the teddy bear. She took them and said thanks, and she was gone.

I felt like someone had taken a gun and shot holes in every part of me. But at the same time some part of me said, "Well, this makes sense." Lorenzo was everything I wasn't. He was popular. He was *white*. He'd upset the balance of everything by asking out the only colored girl in school. Girls loved him, and he was dumb as rocks. A nice guy, but kind of a bad boy. Girls did his homework for him; he was that guy. He was really good-looking, too. It was like when he was creating his character he traded in all his intelligence points for beauty points. I stood no chance.

As devastated as I was, I understood why Maylene made the choice that she did. I would have picked Lorenzo over me, too. All the other kids were running up and down the corridors and out on the playground, laughing and smiling with their red and pink cards and flowers, and I went back to the classroom and sat by myself and waited for the bell to ring.

Petrol for the car, like food, was an expense we could not avoid, but my mom could get more mileage out of a tank of petrol than any human who has ever been on a road in the history of automobiles. She knew every trick. Driving around Johannesburg in our rusty old Volkswagen, every time she stopped in traffic, she'd turn off the car. Then the traffic would start and she'd turn the car on again. That stop-start technology that they use in hybrid cars now? That was my mom. She was a hybrid car before hybrid cars came out. She was the master of coasting. She knew every downhill between work and school, between school and home. She knew exactly where the gradient shifted to put it into neutral. She could time the traffic lights so we could coast through intersections without using the brakes or losing momentum.

There were times when we would be in traffic and we had so little money for petrol that I would have to push the car. If we were stuck in gridlock, my mom would turn the car off and it was my job to get out and push it forward six inches at a time. People would pitch up and offer to help.

"Are you stuck?"

"Nope. We're fine."

"You sure?"

"Yep."

"Can we help you?"

"Nope."

"Do you need a tow?"

And what do you say? The truth? "Thanks, but we're just so poor my mom makes her kid push the car"?

That was some of the most embarrassing shit in my life, pushing the car to school like the fucking Flintstones. Because the other kids were coming in on that same road to go to school. I'd take my blazer off so that no one could tell what school I went to, and I would bury my head and push the car, hoping no one would recognize me.

———

OUTSIDER

After finishing primary school at H. A. Jack, I started grade eight at Sandringham High School. Even after apartheid, most black people still lived in the townships and the areas formerly designated as homelands, where the only available government schools were the broken remnants of the Bantu system. Wealthy white kids—along with the few black people and colored people and Indians who had money or could get scholarships—were holed up in private schools, which were super-expensive but virtually guaranteed entry into university. Sandringham was what we call a Model C school, which meant it was a mix of government and private, similar to charter schools in America. The place was huge, a thousand kids on sprawling grounds with tennis courts, sports fields, and a swimming pool.

Being a Model C school and not a government school, Sandringham drew kids from all over, making it a near-perfect microcosm of post-apartheid South Africa as a whole—a perfect example of what South Africa has the potential to be. We had rich white kids, a bunch of middle-class white kids, and some working-class white kids. We had black kids who were newly rich, black kids who were middle-class, and black kids from the townships. We had colored kids and Indian kids, and even a handful of Chinese kids, too. The pupils were as integrated as they could be given that apartheid had just ended. At H. A. Jack, race was broken up into blocks. Sandringham was more like a spectrum.

South African schools don't have cafeterias. At Sandringham we'd buy our lunch at what we call the tuck shop, a little canteen, and then have free rein to go wherever we wanted on the school grounds to eat—the quad, the courtyard, the playground, wherever. Kids would break off and cluster into their cliques and groups. People were still grouped by color in most cases, but you could see how they all blended and shaded into one another. The kids who played soccer were mostly black. The kids who played tennis were mostly white. The kids who played cricket were a mix. The Chinese kids would hang out next to the prefab buildings. The matrics, what South Africans call seniors, would hang out on the quad. The popular, pretty girls would hang out over here, and computer geeks would hang out over there. To the extent that the groupings were racial, it was because of the ways race overlapped class and geography out in the real world. Suburban kids hung out with suburban kids. Township kids hung out with township kids.

At break, as the only mixed kid out of a thousand, I faced the same predicament I had on the playground at H. A. Jack: Where was I supposed to go? Even with so many different groups to choose from, I wasn't a natural constituent of any particular one. I obviously wasn't Indian or Chinese. The colored kids would shit on me all the time for being too black. So I wasn't welcome there. As always, I was adept enough with white kids not to get bullied by them, but the white kids were always going shopping, going to the movies, going on trips—things that required money. We didn't have any money, so I was out of the mix there, too. The group I felt the most affinity for was the poor black kids. I hung out with them and got along with them, but most of them took minibuses to school from way out in the townships, from Soweto, from Tembisa, from Alexandra. They rode to school as friends and went home as friends. They had their own groups. Weekends and school holidays, they were hanging out with one another and I couldn't visit. Soweto was a forty-minute drive from my house. We didn't have money for petrol. After school I was on my own. Weekends I was on my own. Ever the outsider, I created my own strange little world. I did it out of necessity. I needed a way to fit in. I also needed money, a way to buy the same snacks and do the things that the other kids were doing. Which is how I became the tuck-shop guy.

Thanks to my long walk to school, I was late every single day. I'd have to stop off in the prefect's office to write my name down for detention. I was the patron saint of detention. Already late, I'd run to join my morning classes—math, English, biology, whatever. The last period before break was assembly. The pupils would come together in the assembly hall, each grade seated row by row, and the teachers and the prefects would get up onstage and go over the business of what was happening in the school—announcements, awards, that sort of thing. The names of the kids with detention were announced at every assembly, and I was always one of them. Always. Every single day. It was a running joke. The prefect would say, "Detentions for today . . ." and I would stand up automatically. It was like the Oscars and I was Meryl Streep. There was one time I stood up and then the prefect named the five people and I wasn't one of them. Everyone burst out laughing. Somebody yelled out, "Where's Trevor?!" The prefect looked at the paper and shook his head. "Nope." The entire hall erupted with cheers and applause. *"Yay!!!!"*

Then, immediately after assembly, there would be a race to the tuck shop because the queue to buy food was so long. Every minute you spent in the queue was working against your break time. The sooner you got your food, the longer you had to eat, play a game of soccer, or hang out. Also, if you got there late, the best food was gone.

Two things were true about me at that age. One, I was still the fastest kid in school. And two, I had no pride. The second we were dismissed from assembly I would run like a bat out of hell to the tuck shop so I could be the first one there. I was *always* first in line. I became notorious for being that guy, so much so that people started coming up to me in line. "Hey, can you buy this for me?" Which would piss off the kids behind me because it was basically cutting the line. So people started approaching me during assembly. They'd say, "Hey, I've got ten rand. If you buy my food for me, I'll give you two." That's when I learned: time is money. I realized people would pay me to buy their food because I was willing to run for it. I started telling everyone at assembly, "Place your orders. Give me a list of what you want, give me a percentage of what you're going to spend, and I'll buy your food for you."

I was an overnight success. Fat guys were my number-one customers. They loved food, but couldn't run. I had all these rich, fat white kids who were like, "This is fantastic! My parents spoil me, I've got money, and now I've got a way I can get food without having to work for it—and I still get my break." I had so many customers I was turning kids away. I had a rule: I would take five orders a day, high bidders only. I'd make so much that I could buy my lunch using other kids' money and keep the lunch money my mom gave me for pocket cash. Then I could afford to catch a bus home instead of walking or save up to buy whatever. Every day I'd take orders, assembly would end, and I'd make my mad dash and buy everybody's hot dogs and Cokes and muffins. If you paid me extra you could even tell me where you'd be and I'd deliver it to you.

I'd found my niche. Since I belonged to no group I learned to move seamlessly between groups. I floated. I was a chameleon, still, a cultural chameleon. I learned how to blend. I could play sports with the jocks. I could talk computers with the nerds. I could jump in the circle and dance with the township kids. I popped around to everyone, working, chatting, telling jokes, making deliveries.

I was like a weed dealer, but of food. The weed guy is always welcome at the party. He's not a part of the circle, but he's invited into the circle temporarily because of what he can offer. That's who I was. Always an outsider. As the outsider, you can retreat into a shell, be anonymous, be invisible. Or you can go the other way. You protect yourself by opening up. You don't ask to be accepted for everything you are, just the one part of yourself that you're willing to share. For me it was humor. I learned that even though I didn't belong to one group, I could be a part of any group that was laughing. I'd drop in, pass out the snacks, tell a few jokes. I'd perform for them. I'd catch a bit of their conversation, learn more about their group, and then leave. I never overstayed my welcome. I wasn't popular, but I wasn't an outcast. I was everywhere with everybody, and at the same time I was all by myself.

I don't regret anything I've ever done in life, any choice that I've made. But I'm consumed with regret for the things I didn't do, the choices I didn't make, the things I didn't say. We spend so much time being afraid of failure, afraid of rejection. But regret is the thing we should fear most. Failure is an answer. Rejection is an answer. Regret is an eternal question you will never have the answer to. "What if . . ." "If only . . ." "I wonder what would have . . ." You will never, never know, and it will haunt you for the rest of your days.

A YOUNG MAN'S LONG, AWKWARD, OCCASIONALLY TRAGIC, AND FREQUENTLY HUMILIATING EDUCATION IN AFFAIRS OF THE HEART, PART II: THE CRUSH

In high school, the attention of girls was not an affliction I suffered from. I wasn't the hot guy in class. I wasn't even the cute guy in class. I was ugly. Puberty was not kind to me. My acne was so bad that people used to ask what was wrong with me, like I'd had an allergic reaction to something. It was the kind of acne that qualifies as a medical condition. *Acne vulgaris*, the doctor called it. We're not talking about pimples, kids. We're talking pustules—big, pus-filled blackheads and white-heads. They started on my forehead, spread down the sides of my face, and covered my cheeks and neck and ravaged me everywhere.

Being poor didn't help. Not only could I not afford a decent haircut, leaving me with a huge, unruly Afro, but my mother also used to get angry at the fact that I grew out of my school uniforms too fast, so to save money she started buying my clothes three sizes too big. My blazer was too long and my pants were too baggy and my shoes flopped around. I was a clown. And of course, Murphy's Law, the year my mom started buying my clothes too big was the year that I stopped growing. So now I was never going to grow into my clown clothes and I was stuck being a clown. The only thing I had going for me was the fact that I was tall, but even there I was gangly and awkward-looking. Duck feet. High ass. Nothing worked.

After suffering my Valentine's Day heartbreak at the hands of Maylene and the handsome, charming Lorenzo, I learned a valuable lesson about dating. What I learned was that cool guys get girls, and funny guys get to hang out with the cool guys with their girls. I was not a cool guy; therefore I did not have girls. I understood that formula very quickly and I knew my place. I didn't ask girls out. I didn't have a girlfriend. I didn't even try.

For me to try to get a girl would have upset the natural order of things. Part of my success as the tuck-shop guy was that I was welcome everywhere, and I was welcome everywhere because I was nobody. I was the acne-ridden clown with duck feet in floppy shoes. I wasn't a threat to the guys. I wasn't a threat to the girls. The minute I became somebody, I risked no longer being welcomed as nobody. The pretty girls were already spoken for. The popular guys had staked their claim. They would say, "I like Zuleika," and you knew that meant if you tried anything with Zuleika there'd be a fight. In the interest of survival, the smart move was to stay on the fringe, stay out of trouble.

At Sandringham, the only time girls in class looked at me was when they wanted me to pass a letter to the hot guy in class. But there was one girl I knew named Johanna. Johanna and I had been at the same school intermittently our whole lives. We were in preschool at Maryvale together. Then she left and went to another school. Then we were in primary school at H. A. Jack together. Then she left and went to another school. Then finally we were at Sandringham together. Because of that we became friends.

Johanna was one of the popular girls. Her best friend was Zaheera. Johanna was beautiful. Zaheera was stunning. Zaheera was colored, Cape Malay. She looked like Salma Hayek. Johanna was out and about and kissing boys, so the guys were all into her. Zaheera, as beautiful as she was, was extremely shy, so there weren't as many guys after her.

Johanna and Zaheera were always together. They were one grade below me, but in terms of popularity they were three grades above me. Still I got to hang out with them because I knew Johanna and we had this thing from being in different schools together. Dating girls may have been out of the question for me, but talking to them was not, because I could make them laugh. Human beings like to laugh, and lucky for me pretty girls are human beings. So I could relate to them in that way, but never in the other way. I knew this because whenever they stopped laughing at my jokes and stories they'd say, "So how do you think I can get Daniel to ask me out?" I always had a clear idea of where I stood.

Outwardly, I had carefully cultivated my status as the funny, nonthreatening guy, but secretly I had the hugest crush on Zaheera. She was *so* pretty and *so* funny. We'd hang out and have great conversations. I thought about her constantly, but for the life of me I never considered myself worthy of dating her. I told myself, *I'm going to have a crush on her forever, and that's all that's ever going to happen.*

At a certain point I decided to map out a strategy. I decided I'd be best friends with Zaheera and stay friends with her long enough to ask her to the matric dance, what we call our senior prom. Mind you, we were in grade nine at this point. The matric dance was three years away. But I decided to play the long game. I was like, *Yep, just gonna take my time.* Because that's what happens in the movies, right? I'd seen my American high school movies. You hang around long enough as the friendly good guy and the girl dates a bunch of handsome jerks, and then one day she turns around and goes, "Oh, it's you. It was always you. You're the guy I was supposed to be with all along."

That was my plan. It was foolproof.

I hung out with Zaheera every chance I got. We'd talk about boys, which ones she liked and which ones liked her. I'd give her advice. At one point she got set up with this guy Gary. They started dating. Gary was in the popular group but kind of shy and Zaheera was in the popular group but kind of shy, so his friends and her friends set them up together, like an arranged marriage. But Zaheera didn't like Gary at all. She told me. We talked about everything.

One day, I don't know how, but I plucked up the courage to ask Zaheera for her phone number, which was a big deal back then because it wasn't like cellphone numbers where everybody has everyone's number for texting and everything. This was the landline. To her house. Where her parents might answer. We were talking one afternoon at school and I asked, "Can I get your phone number? Maybe I can call you and we can talk at home sometime." She said yes, and my mind exploded. *What???!!!! A girl is giving me her phone number???!!! This is insane!!! What do I do??!!* I was so nervous. I'll never forget her telling me the digits one by one as I wrote them down, trying to keep my hand from shaking. We said goodbye and went our separate ways to class, and I was like, *Okay, Trevor. Play it cool. Don't call her right away.* I called her that night. At seven. She'd given me her number at two. That was me being cool. *Dude, don't call her at five. That's too obvious. Call her at seven.*

I phoned her house that night. Her mom answered. I said, "May I speak to Zaheera, please?" Her mom called her, and she came to the phone and we talked. For like an hour. After that we started talking more, at school, on the phone. I never told her how I felt. Never made a move. Nothing. I was always too scared.

Zaheera and Gary broke up. Then they got back together. Then they broke up. Then they got back together. They kissed once, but she didn't like it, so they never kissed again. Then they broke up for real. I bided my time through it all. I watched Popular Gary go down in flames, and I was still the good friend. *Yep, the plan is working. Matric dance, here we come. Only two and a half years to go . . .*

Then we had the mid-year school holidays. The day we came back, Zaheera wasn't at school. Then she wasn't at school the next day. Then she wasn't at school the day after that. Eventually I went and tracked down Johanna on the quad.

"Hey, where's Zaheera?" I said. "She hasn't been around for a while. Is she sick?"

"No," she said. "Didn't anyone tell you? She left the school. She doesn't go here anymore."

"What?"

"Yeah, she left."

My first thought was, *Wow, okay. That's news. I should give her a call to catch up.*

"What school did she move to?" I asked.

"She didn't. Her dad got a job in America. During the break they moved there. They've emigrated."

"What?"

"Yeah. She's gone. She was such a good friend, too. I'm really sad. Are you as sad as I am?"

"Uh . . . yeah," I said, still trying to process everything. "I liked Zaheera. She was really cool."

"Yeah, she was super sad, too, because she had such a huge crush on you. She was always waiting for you to ask her out. Okay, I gotta go to class! Bye!"

She ran off and left me standing there, stunned. She'd hit me with so much information at once, first that Zaheera was gone, then that she had left for America, and then that she'd liked me all along. It was like I'd been hit by three successive waves of heartbreak, each one bigger than the last. My mind raced through all the hours we'd spent talking on the quad, on the phone, all the times I could have said, "Hey, Zaheera, I like you. Will you be my girlfriend?" Ten words that might have changed my life if I'd had the courage to say them. But I hadn't, and now she was gone.

In every nice neighborhood there's one white family that Does Not Give a Fuck. You know the family I'm talking about. They don't do their lawn, don't paint the fence, don't fix the roof. Their house is shit. My mom found that house and bought it, which is how she snuck a black family into a place as white as Highlands North.

Most black people integrating into white suburbs were moving to places like Bramley and Lombardy East. But for some reason my mom chose Highlands North. It was a suburban area, lots of shopping. Working people, mostly. Not wealthy but stable and middle-class. Older houses, but still a nice place to live. In Soweto I was the only white kid in the black township. In Eden Park I was the only mixed kid in the colored area. In Highlands North I was the only black kid in the white suburb—and by "only" I mean only. In Highlands North the white never took flight. It was a largely Jewish neighborhood, and Jewish people don't flee. They're done fleeing. They've already fled. They get to a place, build their shul, and hold it down. Since the white people around us weren't leaving, there weren't a lot of families like ours moving in behind us.

I didn't make any friends in Highlands North for the longest time. I had an easier time making friends in Eden Park, to be honest. In the suburbs, everyone lived behind walls. The white neighborhoods of Johannesburg were built on white fear—fear of black crime, fear of black uprisings and reprisals—and as a result virtually every house sits behind a six-foot wall, and on top of that wall is electric wire. Everyone lives in a plush, fancy maximum-security prison. There is no sitting on the front porch, no saying hi to the neighbors, no kids running back and forth between houses. I'd ride my bike around the neighborhood for hours without seeing a single kid. I'd hear them, though. They were all meeting up behind brick walls for play-dates I wasn't invited to. I'd hear people laughing and playing and I'd get off my bike and creep up and peek over the wall and see a bunch of white kids splashing around in someone's swimming pool. I was like a Peeping Tom, but for friendship.

It was only after a year or so that I figured out the key to making black friends in the suburbs: the children of domestics. Many domestic workers in South Africa, when they get pregnant they get fired. Or, if they're lucky, the family they work for lets them stay on and they can have the baby, but then the baby goes to live with relatives in the homelands. Then the black mother raises the white children, seeing her own child only once a year at the holidays. But a handful of families would let their domestics keep their children with them, living in little maids' quarters or flatlets in the back-yard.

For a long time, those kids were my only friends.

———

13

COLORBLIND

At Sandringham I got to know this one kid, Teddy. Funny guy, charming as hell. My mom used to call him Bugs Bunny; he had a cheeky smile with two big teeth that stuck out the front of his mouth. Teddy and I got along like a house on fire, one of those friends where you start hanging out and from that day forward you're never apart. We were both naughty as shit, too. With Teddy, I'd finally met someone who made me feel normal. I was the terror in my family. He was the terror in his family. When you put us together it was mayhem. Walking home from school we'd throw rocks through windows, just to see them shatter, and then we'd run away. We got detention together all the time. The teachers, the pupils, the principal, everyone at school knew: Teddy and Trevor, thick as thieves.

Teddy's mom worked as a domestic for a family in Linksfield, a wealthy suburb near school. Linksfield was a long walk from my house, nearly forty minutes, but still doable. Walking around was pretty much all I did back then, anyway. I couldn't afford to do anything else, and I couldn't afford to get around any other way. If you liked walking, you were my friend. Teddy and I walked all over Johannesburg together. I'd walk to Teddy's house and we'd hang out there. Then we'd walk back to my house and hang out there. We'd walk from my house down to the city center, which was like a three-hour hike, just to hang out, and then we'd walk all the way back.

Friday and Saturday nights we'd walk to the mall and hang out. The Balfour Park Shopping Mall was a few blocks from my house. It's not a big mall, but it has everything—an arcade, a cinema, restaurants, South Africa's version of Target, South Africa's version of the Gap. Then, once we were at the mall, since we never had any money to shop or watch movies or buy food, we'd just wander around inside.

One night we were at the mall and most of the shops were closed, but the cinema was still showing movies so the building was still open. There was this stationery shop that sold greeting cards and magazines, and it didn't have a door, so when it closed at night there was only a metal gate, like a trellis, that was pulled across the entrance and pad-locked. Walking past this shop, Teddy and I realized that if we put our arms through the trellis we could reach this rack of chocolates just in-side. And these weren't just any chocolates—they were alcohol-filled chocolates. I loved alcohol. Loved loved loved it. My whole life I'd steal sips of grown-ups' drinks whenever I could.

We reached in, grabbed a few, drank the liquor inside, and then gobbled down the chocolates. We'd hit the jackpot. We started going back again and again to steal more. We'd wait for the shops to start to close, then we'd go and sit against the gate, acting like we were just hanging out. We'd check to make sure the coast was clear, and then one of us would reach in, grab a chocolate, and drink the whiskey. Reach in, grab a chocolate, drink the rum. Reach in, grab a chocolate, drink the brandy. We did this every weekend for at least a month, having the best time. Then we pushed our luck too far.

It was a Saturday night. We were hanging out at the entrance to the stationery shop, leaning up against the gate. I reached in to grab a chocolate, and at that exact moment a mall cop came around the corner and saw me with my arm in up to my shoulder. I brought my hand out with a bunch of chocolates in it. It was almost like a movie. I saw him. He saw me. His eyes went wide. I tried to walk away, acting natural. Then he shouted out, "*Hey! Stop!*"

And the chase was on. We bolted, heading for the doors. I knew if a guard cut us off at the exit we'd be trapped, so we were hauling ass as fast as we could. We cleared the exit. The second we hit the parking lot, mall cops were coming at us from every direction, a dozen of them at least. I was running with my head down. These guards knew me. I was in that mall all the time. The guards knew my mom, too. She did her banking at that mall. If they even caught a glimpse of who I was, I was dead.

We ran straight across the parking lot, ducking and weaving between parked cars, the guards right behind us, yelling. We made it to the petrol station out at the road, ran through there, and hooked left up the main road. They chased and chased and we ran and ran, and it was *awesome*. The risk of getting caught was half the fun of being naughty, and now the chase was on. I was loving it. I was shitting myself, but also loving it. This was my turf. This was my neighborhood. You couldn't catch me in my neighborhood. I knew every alley and every street, every back wall to climb over, every fence with a gap big enough to slip through. I knew every shortcut you could possibly imagine. As a kid, wherever I went, whatever building I was in, I was always plotting my escape. You know, in case shit went down. In reality I was a nerdy kid with almost no friends, but in my mind I was an important and dangerous man who needed to know where every camera was and where all the exit points were.

I knew we couldn't run forever. We needed a plan. As Teddy and I booked past the fire station there was a road off to the left, a dead end that ran into a metal fence. I knew that there was a hole in the fence to squeeze through and on the far side was an empty field behind the mall that took you back to the main road and back to my house. A grown-up couldn't fit through the hole, but a kid could. All my years of imagining the life of a secret agent for myself finally paid off. Now that I needed an escape, I had one.

"Teddy, this way!" I yelled.

"No, it's a dead end!"

"We can get through! Follow me!"

He didn't. I turned and ran into the dead end. Teddy broke the other way. Half the mall cops followed him, half followed me. I got to the fence and knew exactly how to squirm through. Head, then shoulder, one leg, then twist, then the other leg—done. I was through. The guards hit the fence behind me and couldn't follow. I ran across the field to a fence on the far side, popped through there, and then I was right on the road, three blocks from my house. I slipped my hands into my pockets and casually walked home, another harmless pedestrian out for a stroll.

Once I got back to my house I waited for Teddy. He didn't show up. I waited thirty minutes, forty minutes, an hour. No Teddy.

Fuck.

I ran to Teddy's house in Linksfield. No Teddy. Monday morning I went to school. Still no Teddy.

Fuck.

Now I was worried. After school I went home and checked at my house again, nothing. Teddy's house again, nothing. Then I ran back home.

An hour later Teddy's parents showed up. My mom greeted them at the door.

"Teddy's been arrested for shoplifting," they said.

Fuuuck.

I eavesdropped on their whole conversation from the other room. From the start my mom was certain I was involved.

"Well, where was Trevor?" she asked.

"Teddy said he wasn't with Trevor," they said.

My mom was skeptical. "Hmm. Are you *sure* Trevor wasn't involved?"

"No, apparently not. The cops said there was another kid, but he got away."

"So it *was* Trevor."

"No, we asked Teddy, and he said it wasn't Trevor. He said it was some other kid."

"Huh . . . okay." My mom called me in. "Do you know about this thing?"

"What thing?"

"Teddy was caught shoplifting."

"Whhaaat?" I played dumb. "Noooo. That's crazy. I can't believe it. *Teddy?* No."

"Where were you?" my mom asked.

"I was at home."

"But you're always with Teddy."

I shrugged. "Not on this occasion, I suppose."

For a moment my mom thought she'd caught me red-handed, but Teddy'd given me a solid alibi. I went back to my room, thinking I was in the clear.

The next day I was in class and my name was called over the PA system. "Trevor Noah, report to the principal's office." All the kids were like, "Ooooohhh." The announcements could be heard in every classroom, so now, collectively, the whole school knew I was in trouble. I got up and walked to the office and waited anxiously on an uncomfortable wooden bench outside the door.

Finally the principal, Mr. Friedman, walked out. "Trevor, come in." Waiting inside his office was the head of mall security, two uniformed police officers, and my and Teddy's homeroom teacher, Mrs. Vorster. A roomful of silent, stone-faced white authority figures stood over me, the guilty young black man. My heart was pounding. I took a seat.

"Trevor, I don't know if you know this," Mr. Friedman said, "but Teddy was arrested the other day."

"*What?*" I played the whole thing again. "Teddy? Oh, no. What for?"

"For shoplifting. He's been expelled, and he won't be coming back to school. We know there was another boy involved, and these officers are going around to the schools in the area to investigate. We called you here because Mrs. Vorster tells us you're Teddy's best friend, and we want to know: Do you know anything about this?"

I shook my head. "No, I don't know anything."

"Do you know who Teddy was with?"

"No."

"Okay." He stood up and walked over to a television in the corner of the room. "Trevor, the police have video footage of the whole thing. We'd like you to take a look at it."

Fuuuuuuuuuuuuuuuuuuck.

My heart was pounding in my chest. *Well, life, it's been fun,* I thought. *I'm going to get expelled. I'm going to go to jail. This is it.*

Mr. Friedman pressed Play on the VCR. The tape started. It was grainy, black-and-white security-camera footage, but you could see what was happening plain as day. They even had it from multiple angles: Me and Teddy reaching through the gate. Me and Teddy racing for the door. They had the whole thing. After a few seconds, Mr. Friedman reached up and paused it with me, from a few meters out, freeze-framed in the middle of the screen. In my mind, this was when he was going to turn to me and say, "Now would you like to confess?" He didn't.

"Trevor," he said, "do you know of any white kids that Teddy hangs out with?"

I nearly shat myself. "*What?!*"

I looked at the screen and I realized: Teddy was dark. I am light; I have olive skin. But the camera can't expose for light and dark at the same time. So when you put me on a black-and-white screen next to a black person, the camera doesn't know what to do. If the camera has to pick, it picks me as white. My color gets blown out. In this video, there was a black person and a white person. But still: It was me. The picture wasn't great, and my facial features were a bit blurry, but if you looked closely: It was me. I was Teddy's best friend. I was Teddy's only friend. I was the *single most likely accomplice*. You had to at least *suspect* that it was me. They didn't. They grilled me for a good ten minutes, but only because they were so sure that I had to know who this white kid was.

"Trevor, you're Teddy's best friend. Tell us the truth. Who is this kid?"

"I don't know."

"You don't recognize him at all?"

"No."

"Teddy never mentioned him to you?"

"Never."

At a certain point Mrs. Vorster just started running through a list of all the white kids she thought it could be.

"Is it David?"

"No."

"Rian?"

"No."

"Frederik?"

"No."

I kept waiting for it to be a trick, for them to turn and say, "It's *you*!" They didn't. At a certain point, I felt so invisible I almost wanted to take credit. I wanted to jump up and point at the TV and say, "Are you people blind?! That's me! Can you not see that that's me?!" But of course I didn't. And they couldn't. These people had been so fucked by their own construct of race that they could not see that the white person they were looking for was sitting right in front of them.

Eventually they sent me back to class. I spent the rest of the day and the next couple of weeks waiting for the other shoe to drop, waiting for my mom to get the call. "We've got him! We figured it out!" But the call never came.

South Africa has eleven official languages. After democracy came, people said, "Okay, how do we create order without having different groups feel like they've been left out of power again?" English is the international language and the language of money and of the media, so we had to keep that. Most people were forced to learn at least some Afrikaans, so it's useful to keep that, too. Plus we didn't want the white minority to feel ostracized in the new South Africa, or else they'd take all their money and leave.

Of the African languages, Zulu has the largest number of native speakers, but we couldn't keep that without also having Xhosa and Tswana and Ndebele. Then there's Swazi, Tsonga, Venda, Sotho, and Pedi. We tried to keep all the major groups happy, so the next thing we knew we'd made eleven languages official languages. And those are just the languages big enough to demand recognition; there are dozens more.

It's the Tower of Babel in South Africa. Every single day. Every day you see people completely lost, trying to have conversations and having no idea what the other person is saying. Zulu and Tswana are fairly common. Tsonga and Pedi are pretty fringe. The more common your tongue, the less likely you are to learn others. The more fringe, the more likely you are to pick up two or three. In the cities most people speak at least some English and usually a bit of Afrikaans, enough to get around. You'll be at a party with a dozen people where bits of conversation are flying by in two or three different languages. You'll miss part of it, someone might translate on the fly to give you the gist, you pick up the rest from the context, and you just figure it out. The crazy thing is that, somehow, it works. Society functions. Except when it doesn't.

14

A YOUNG MAN'S LONG, AWKWARD, OCCASIONALLY TRAGIC, AND FREQUENTLY HUMILIATING EDUCATION IN AFFAIRS OF THE HEART, PART III: THE DANCE

By the end of high school I'd become a mogul. My tuck-shop business had evolved into a mini-empire that included selling pirated CDs I made at home. I'd convinced my mother, as frugal as she was, that I needed a computer for school. I didn't. I wanted it so I could surf the Internet and play *Leisure Suit Larry*. But I was very convincing, and she broke down and got it for me. Thanks to the computer, the Internet, and the fortunate gift of a CD writer from a friend, I was in business.

I had carved out my niche, and was having a great time; life was so good as an outsider that I didn't even think about dating. The only girls in my life were the naked ones on my computer. While I downloaded music and messed around in chat rooms, I'd dabble in porn sites here and there. No video, of course, only pictures. With online porn today you just drop straight into the madness, but with dial-up it took so long for the images to load. It was almost gentlemanly compared to now. You'd spend a good five minutes looking at her face, getting to know her as a person. Then a few minutes later you'd get some boobs. By the time you got to her vagina, you'd spent a lot of quality time together.

In September of grade twelve, the matric dance was coming up. Senior prom. This was the big one. I was again faced with the dilemma of Valentine's Day, confronting another strange ritual I did not understand. All I knew about prom was that, according to my American movies, prom is where *it* happens. You lose your virginity. You go and you ride in the limousine, and then you and the girl do the thing. That was literally my only reference. But I knew the rule: Cool guys get girls, and funny guys get to hang out with the cool guys with their girls. So I'd assumed I wouldn't be going, or if I did go it wouldn't be with a date.

I had two middlemen working for me in my CD business, Bongani and Tom. They sold the CDs that I copied in exchange for a cut. I met Tom at the arcade at the Balfour Park mall. Like Teddy, he lived nearby because his mom was a domestic worker. Tom was in my grade but went to a government school, Northview, a proper ghetto school. Tom handled my CD sales over there.

Tom was a chatterbox, hyperactive and go-go-go. He was a real hustler, too, always trying to cut a deal, work an angle. He could get people to do anything. A great guy, but fucking crazy and a complete liar as well. I went with him once to Hammanskraal, a settlement that was like a homeland, but not really. Hammanskraal, as its Afrikaans name suggests, was the kraal of Hamman, what used to be a white man's farm. The proper homelands, Venda and Gazankulu and Transkei, were places where black people actually lived, and the government drew a border around them and said, "Stay there." Hammanskraal and settlements like it were empty places on the map where deported black people had been relocated. That's what the government did. They would find some patch of arid, dusty, useless land, and dig row after row of holes in the ground—a thousand latrines to serve four thousand families. Then they'd forcibly remove people from illegally occupying some white area and drop them off in the middle of nowhere with some pallets of plywood and corrugated iron. "Here. This is your new home. Build some houses. Good luck." We'd watch it on the news. It was like some heartless, survival-based reality TV show, only nobody won any money.

One afternoon in Hammanskraal, Tom told me we were going to see a talent show. At the time, I had a pair of Timberland boots I'd bought. They were the only decent piece of clothing I owned. Back then, almost no one in South Africa had Timberlands. They were impossible to get, but everyone wanted them because American rappers wore them. I'd scrimped and saved my tuck-shop money and my CD money to buy them. As we were leaving, Tom told me, "Be sure to wear your Timberlands."

The talent show was in this little community hall attached to nothing in the middle of nowhere. When we got there, Tom was going around, shaking hands, chatting with everybody. There was singing, dancing, some poetry. Then the host got up onstage and said, *"Re na le modiragatsi yo o kgethegileng. Ka kopo amogelang . . . Spliff Star!"* "We've got a special performer, a rapper all the way from America. Please welcome . . . Spliff Star!"

Spliff Star was Busta Rhymes's hype man at the time. I sat there, confused. *What? Spliff Star? In Hammanskraal?* Then everyone in the room turned and looked at me. Tom walked over and whispered in my ear.

"Dude, come up onstage."

"What?"

"Come onstage."

"Dude, what are you talking about?"

"Dude, please, you're gonna get me in so much shit. They've already paid me the money."

"*Money?* What money?"

Of course, what Tom had failed to tell me was that he'd told these people he was bringing a famous rapper from America to come and rap in their talent show. He had demanded to be paid up front for doing so, and I, in my Timberlands, was that famous American rapper.

"Screw you," I said. "I'm not going anywhere."

"Please, dude, I'm begging you. Please do me this favor. Please. There's this girl here, and I wanna get with her, and I told her I know all these rappers . . . Please. I'm begging you."

"Dude, I'm not Spliff Star. What am I gonna do?!"

"Just rap Busta Rhymes songs."

"But I don't know any of the lyrics."

"It doesn't matter. These people don't speak English."

"Aw, fuck."

I got up onstage and Tom did some terrible beat-boxing—"*Bff ba-dff, bff bff ba-dff*"—while I stumbled through some Busta Rhymes lyrics that I made up as I went along. The audience erupted with cheers and applause. An American rapper had come to Hammanskraal, and it was the most epic thing they had ever seen.

So that's Tom.

One afternoon Tom came by my house and we started talking about the dance. I told him I didn't have a date, couldn't get a date, and wasn't going to get a date.

"I can get you a girl to go with you to the dance," he said.

"No, you can't."

"Yes, I can. Let's make a deal."

"I don't want one of your deals, Tom."

"No, listen, here's the deal. If you give me a better cut on the CDs I'm selling, plus a bunch of free music for myself, I'll come back with the most beautiful girl you've ever seen in your life, and she'll be your date for the dance."

"Okay, I'll take that deal because it's never going to happen."

"Do we have a deal?"

"We have a deal, but it's not going to happen."

"But do we have a *deal*?"

"It's a deal."

"Okay, I'm going to find you a date. She's going to be the most beautiful girl you've ever seen, and you're going to take her to the matric dance and you're going to be a superstar."

The dance was still two months away. I promptly forgot about Tom and his ridiculous deal. Then he came over to my house one afternoon and popped his head into my room.

"I found the girl."

"Really?"

"Yeah. You have to come and meet her."

I knew Tom was full of shit, but the thing that makes a con man successful is that he never gives you nothing. He delivers just enough to keep you believing. Tom had introduced me to many beautiful women. He was never dating them, but he talked a good game, and was always around them. So when he said he had a girl, I didn't doubt him. The two of us jumped on a bus and headed into the city.

The girl lived in a run-down block of flats downtown. We found her building, and a girl leaned over the balcony and waved us inside. That was the girl's sister Lerato, Tom said. Come to find out, he'd been trying to get with Lerato, and setting me up with the sister was his way in—of course, Tom was working an angle.

It was dark in the lobby. The elevator was busted, so we walked up several flights. This girl Lerato brought us into the flat. In the living room was this giant, but I mean really, really enormous, fat woman. I was like, *Oh, Tom. I see what you've done here. Nicely played.* Tom was a big joker as well.

"Is this my date?" I asked.

"No, no, no," he said. "This is not your date. This is her older sister. Your date is Babiki. Babiki has three older sisters, and Lerato is her younger sister. Babiki's gone to the store to buy groceries. She'll be back in a moment."

We waited, chatted with the older sister. Ten minutes later the door opened and the most beautiful girl I have ever seen in my life walked in. She was . . . good Lord. Beautiful eyes, beautiful golden yellow-brown skin. It was like she glowed. No girl at my high school looked anything like her.

"Hi," she said.

"Hi," I replied.

I was dumbfounded. I had no idea how to talk to a girl that beautiful. She was shy and didn't speak much, either. There was a bit of an awkward pause. Luckily Tom's a guy who just talks and talks. He jumped right in and smoothed everything over. "Trevor, this is Babiki. Babiki, Trevor." He went on and on about how great I was, how much she was looking forward to the dance, when I would pick her up for the dance, all the details. We hung out for a few, and then Tom needed to get going so we headed out the door. Babiki turned and smiled at me and waved as we left.

"Bye."

"Bye."

We walked out of that building and I was the happiest man on earth. I couldn't believe it. I was the guy at school who couldn't get a date. I'd resigned myself to never getting a date, didn't consider myself worthy of having a date. But now I was going to the matric dance with the most beautiful girl in the world.

Over the following weeks we went down to Hillbrow a few more times to hang out with Babiki and her sisters and her friends. Babiki's family was Pedi, one of South Africa's smaller tribes. I liked getting to know people of different backgrounds, so that was fun. Babiki and her friends were what we call *amabhujua*. They're as poor as most other black people, but they try to act like they're not. They dress fashionably and act rich. *Amabhujua* will put a shirt on layaway, one shirt, and spend seven months paying it off. They'll live in shacks wearing Italian leather shoes that cost thousands. An interesting crowd.

Babiki and I never went on a date alone. It was always the two of us in a group. She was shy, and I was a nervous wreck most of the time, but we had fun. Tom kept everyone loose and having a good time. Whenever we'd say goodbye, Babiki would give me a hug, and once she even gave me a little kiss. I was in heaven. I was like, *Yeah, I've got a girlfriend. Cool.*

As the dance approached, I started getting nervous. I didn't have a car. I didn't have any decent clothes. This was my first time taking out a beautiful girl, and I wanted it to be perfect.

We'd moved to Highlands North when my stepfather's garage went out of business, and he moved his workshop to the house. We had a big yard and a garage in the back, and that became his new workshop, essentially. At any given time, we had at least ten or fifteen cars in the driveway, in the yard, and out on the street, clients' cars being worked on and old junkers Abel kept around to tinker with. One afternoon Tom and I were at the house. Tom was telling Abel about my date, and Abel decided to be generous. He said I could take a car for the dance.

There was a red Mazda that we'd had for a while, a complete piece of shit but it worked well enough. I'd borrowed it before, but the car I really wanted was Abel's BMW. It was old and beat-up like the Mazda, but a shit BMW is still a BMW. I begged him to let me take it.

"Please, please, can I use the BMW?"

"Not a fucking chance."

"Please. This is the greatest moment in my life. Please. I'm begging you."

"No."

"Please."

"No. You can take the Mazda."

Tom, always the hustler and the dealmaker, stepped in.

"Bra Abie," he said. "I don't think you understand. If you saw the girl Trevor is taking to the dance, you would see why this is so important. Let's make a deal. If we bring her here and she's the most beautiful girl you've ever seen in your life, you'll let him take the BMW."

Abel thought about it.

"Okay. Deal."

We went to Babiki's flat, told her my parents wanted to meet her, and brought her back to my house. Then we brought her around to the garage in the back where Abel and his guys were working. Tom and I went over and introduced them.

"Abel, this is Babiki. Babiki, this is Abel."

Abel smiled big, was charming as always.

"Nice to meet you," he said.

They chatted for a few minutes. Tom and Babiki left. Abel turned to me.

"Is that the girl?"

"Yes."

"You can take the BMW."

Once I had the car, I desperately needed something to wear. I was taking out this girl who was really into fashion, and, except for my Timberlands, everything I owned was shit. I was limited in my wardrobe choices because I was stuck buying in the shops my mother let me go to, and my mother did not believe in spending money on clothes. She'd take me to some bargain clothing store and tell me what our budget was, and I'd have to find something to wear.

At the time I had no clue about clothes. My idea of fashion was a brand of clothing called Powerhouse. It was the kind of stuff weight lifters wear down in Miami or out at Venice Beach, baggy track pants with baggy sweatshirts. The logo was a cartoon of this giant body-building bulldog wearing wraparound sunglasses and smoking a cigar and flexing his muscles. On the pants he was flexing all the way down your leg. On the shirt he was flexing across your chest. On the underwear, he was flexing on your crotch. I thought Powerhouse was the baddest thing in the world, I can't even front. I had no friends, I loved dogs, and muscles were cool—that's where I was working from. I had Powerhouse everything, the full range, five of the same outfit in five different colors. It was easy. The pants came with the top, so I knew how to make it work.

Bongani, the other middleman from my CD business, found out I had a date, and he made it his mission to give me a makeover. "You need to up your game," he said. "You cannot go to the dance looking the way you look—for her sake, not yours. Let's go shopping."

I went to my mom and begged her to give me money to buy something to wear for the dance. She finally relented and gave me 2,000 rand, for one outfit. It was the most money she'd ever given me for anything in my life. I told Bongani how much I had to spend, and he said we'd make it work. The trick to looking rich, he told me, is to have one expensive item, and for the rest of the things you get basic, good-looking quality stuff. The nice item will draw everyone's eye, and it'll look like you've spent more than you have.

In my mind nothing was cooler than the leather coats everybody wore in *The Matrix*. *The Matrix* came out while I was in high school and it was my favorite movie at the time. I loved Neo. In my heart I knew: *I am Neo*. He's a nerd. He's useless at everything, but secretly he's a badass superhero. All I needed was a bald, mysterious black man to come into my life and show me the way. Now I had Bongani, black, head shaved, telling me, "You can do it. You're the one." And I was like, "*Yes*. I knew it."

I told Bongani I wanted a leather coat like Keanu Reeves wore, the ankle-length black one. Bongani shut that down. "No, that's not practical. It's cool, but you'll never be able to wear it again." He took me shopping and we bought a calf-length black leather jacket, which would look ridiculous today but at the time, thanks to Neo, was very cool. That alone cost 1,200 rand. Then we finished the outfit with a pair of simple black pants, suede square-toed shoes, and a cream-white knitted sweater.

Once we had the outfit, Bongani took a long look at my enormous Afro. I was forever trying to get the perfect 1970s Michael Jackson Afro. What I had was more Buckwheat: unruly and impossible to comb, like stabbing a pitchfork into a bed of crabgrass.

"We need to fix that fucking hair," Bongani said.

"What do you mean?" I said. "This is just my hair."

"No, we *have* to do something."

Bongani lived in Alexandra. He dragged me there, and we went to talk to some girls from his street who were hanging out on the corner.

"What would you do with this guy's hair?" he asked them.

The girls looked me over.

"He has so much," one of them said. "Why doesn't he cornrow it?"

"Shit, yeah," they said. "That's great!"

I said, "What? Cornrows? No!"

"No, no," they said. "Do it."

Bongani dragged me to a hair salon down the street. We went in and sat down. The woman touched my hair, shook her head, and turned to Bongani.

"I can't work with this sheep," she said. "You have to do something about this."

"What do we need to do?"

"You have to relax it. I don't do that here."

"Okay."

Bongani dragged me to a second salon. I sat down in the chair, and the woman took my hair and started painting this creamy white stuff in it. She was wearing rubber gloves to keep this chemical relaxer off her own skin, which should have been my first clue that maybe this wasn't such a great idea. Once my hair was full of the relaxer, she told me, "You have to try to keep it in for as long as possible. It's going to start burning. When it starts burning, tell me and we'll rinse it out. But the longer you can handle it, the straighter your hair will become."

I wanted to do it right, so I sat in the chair and waited and waited for as long as I could.

I waited too long.

She'd told me to tell her when it started burning. She should have told me to tell her when it started tingling, because by the time it was actually burning it had already taken off several layers of my scalp. I was well past tingling when I started to freak out. *It's burning! It's burning!"* She rushed me over to the sink and started to rinse the relaxer out. What I didn't know is that the chemical doesn't really start to burn until it's being rinsed out. I felt like someone was pouring liquid fire onto my head. When she was done I had patches of acid burns all over my scalp.

I was the only man in the salon; it was all women. It was a window into what women experience to look good on a regular basis. *Why would they ever do this?*, I thought. *This is horrible.* But it worked. My hair was completely straight. The woman combed it back, and I looked like a pimp, a pimp named Slickback.

Bongani then dragged me back to the first salon, and the woman agreed to cornrow my hair. She worked slowly. It took six hours. Finally she said, "Okay, you can look in the mirror." She turned me around in the chair and I looked in the mirror and . . . I had never seen myself like that before. It was like the makeover scenes in my American movies, where they take the dorky guy or girl, fix the hair and change the clothes, and the ugly duckling becomes the swan. I'd been so convinced I'd never get a date that I never tried to look nice for a girl, so I didn't know that I could. The hair was good. My skin wasn't perfect, but it was getting better; the pustules had receded into regular pimples. I looked . . . not bad.

I went home, and my mom squealed when I walked in the door.

"Ooooooh! They turned my baby boy into a pretty little girl! I've got a little girl! You're so pretty!"

"Mom! C'mon. Stop it."

"Is this the way you're telling me that you're gay?"

"What? No. Why would you say that?"

"You know it's okay if you are."

"No, Mom. I'm not gay."

Everyone in my family loved it. They all thought it looked great. My mom did tease the shit out of me, though.

"It's very well done," she said, "but it is way too pretty. You do look like a girl."

The big night finally came. Tom came over to help me get ready. The hair, the clothes, everything came together perfectly. Once I was set, we went to Abel to get the keys to the BMW, and that was the moment the whole night started to go wrong.

It was a Saturday night, end of the week, which meant Abel was drinking with his workers. I walked out to his garage, and as soon as I saw his eyes I knew: He was wasted. *Fuck*. When Abel was drunk he was a completely different person.

"Ah, you look nice!" he said with a big smile, looking me over. "Where are you going?"

"Where am I—Abie, I'm going to the dance."

"Okay. Have fun."

"Um . . . can I get the keys?"

"The keys to what?"

"To the car."

"What car?"

"The BMW. You promised I could drive the BMW to the dance."

"First go buy me some beers," he said.

He gave me his car keys; Tom and I drove to the liquor store. I bought Abel a few cases of beer, drove back, and unloaded it for him.

"Okay," I said, "can I take the BMW now?"

"No."

"What do you mean 'no'?"

"I mean 'no.' I need my car tonight."

"But you promised. You said I could take it."

"Yeah, but I need the car."

I was crushed. I sat there with Tom and begged him for close to half an hour.

"Please."

"No."

"Please."

"Nope."

Finally we realized it wasn't going to happen. We took the shitty Mazda and drove to Babiki's house. I was an hour late picking her up. She was completely pissed off. Tom had to go in and convince her to come out, and eventually she did.

She was even more gorgeous than before, in an amazing red dress, but she was clearly not in a great mood. Inside I was quietly starting to panic, but I smiled and kept trying my gentlemanly best to be a good date, holding the door for her, telling her how beautiful she was. Tom and the sister gave us a send-off and we headed out.

Then I got lost. The dance was being held at some venue in a part of town I wasn't familiar with, and at some point I got completely turned around and had no idea where I was. I drove around for an hour in the dark, going left, going right, doubling back. I was on my cellphone the whole time, desperately calling people, trying to figure out where I was, trying to get directions. Babiki sat next to me in stony silence the whole time, clearly not feeling me or this night *at all*. I was crashing hard. I was late. I didn't know where I was going. I was the worst date she'd ever had in her life.

I finally figured out where I was and we made it to the dance, nearly two hours late. I parked, jumped out, and ran around to get her door. When I opened it, she just sat there.

"Are you ready?" I said. "Let's go in."

"No."

"No? What . . . what do you mean, 'no'?"

"No."

"Okay . . . but why?"

"No."

"But we need to go inside. The dance is inside."

"No."

I stood there for another twenty minutes, trying to convince her to come inside, but she kept saying "no." She wouldn't get out of the car.

Finally, I said, "Okay, I'll be right back."

I ran inside and found Bongani.

"Where have you been?" he said.

"I'm here! But my date's in the car and she won't come in."

"What do you mean she won't come in?"

"I don't know what's going on. Please help me."

We went back out to the parking lot. I took Bongani over to the car, and the second he saw her he lost it. "Jesus in Heaven! This is the most beautiful woman I've ever seen. You said she was beautiful, Trevor, but this is insane." In an instant he completely forgot about helping me with Babiki. He turned and ran back inside and called to the guys. "Guys! You gotta come see this! Trevor got a date! And she's beautiful! Guys! Come out here!"

Twenty guys came running out into the parking lot. They clustered around the car. "Yo, she's so hot!" "Dude, *this* girl came with *Trevor?*" Guys were gawking at her like she was an animal at the zoo. They were asking to take pictures with her. They were calling back to more people inside. "This is insane! Look at Trevor's date! No, no, no, you gotta come and see!"

I was mortified. I'd spent four years of high school carefully avoiding any kind of romantic humiliation whatsoever, and now, on the night of the matric dance, the night of all nights, my humiliation had turned into a circus bigger than the event itself: Trevor the undatable clown thought he was going to have the most beautiful girl at the dance, but he's crashing and burning so let's all go outside and watch.

Babiki sat in the passenger seat, staring straight ahead, refusing to budge. I was outside the car, pacing, stressed out. A friend of mine had a bottle of brandy that he'd smuggled into the dance. "Here," he said, "have some of this." Nothing mattered at that point, so I started drinking. I'd fucked up. The girl didn't like me. The night was done.

Most of the guys eventually wandered back inside. I was sitting on the pavement, taking swigs from the brandy bottle, getting buzzed. At some point Bongani went back over to the car to try one last time to convince Babiki to come in. After a minute his head popped up over the car with this confused look.

"Yo, Trevor," he said, "your date does not speak English."

"What?"

"Your date. She does not speak any English."

"That's not possible."

I got up and walked over to the car. I asked her a question in English and she gave me a blank stare.

Bongani looked at me.

"How did you not know that your date does not speak English?"

"I . . . I don't know."

"Have you never spoken to her?"

"Of course I have—or, wait . . . *have* I?"

I started flashing back through all the times I'd been with Babiki, meeting at her flat, hanging out with her friends, introducing her to Abel. Did I talk to her then? No. Did I talk to her then? No. It was like the scene in *Fight Club* where Ed Norton's character flashes back and realizes he and Brad Pitt have never been in the same room with Helena Bonham Carter at the same time. He realizes he's been punching himself the whole time. *He's* Tyler Durden. In all the excitement of meeting Babiki, the times we were hanging out and getting to know each other, we were never actually speaking to each other. It was always through Tom.

Fucking Tom.

Tom had promised he'd get me a beautiful date for the dance, but he hadn't made any promises about any of her other qualities. Whenever we were together, she was speaking Pedi to Tom, and Tom was speaking English to me. But she didn't speak English, and I didn't speak Pedi. Abel spoke Pedi. He'd learned several South African languages in order to deal with his customers, so he'd spoken with her fluently when they met. But in that moment I realized I'd never actually heard her say anything in English other than: "Yes." "No." "Hi." "Bye." That's it: "Yes." "No." "Hi." "Bye."

Babiki was so shy that she didn't talk much to begin with, and I was so inept with women that I didn't know how to talk to her. I'd never had a girlfriend; I didn't even know what "girlfriend" meant. Someone put a beautiful woman on my arm and said, "She's your girlfriend." I'd been mesmerized by her beauty and just the idea of her—I didn't know I was supposed to talk to her. The naked women on my computer, I'd never had to talk to them, ask them their opinions, ask them about their feelings. And I was afraid I'd open my mouth and ruin the whole thing, so I just nodded and smiled along and let Tom do the talking.

All three of Babiki's older sisters spoke English, and her younger sister Lerato spoke a little. So whenever we hung out with Babiki and her sisters and their friends, a lot of the conversation was in English. The rest of it was going right by me in Pedi or in Sotho, but that's completely normal in South Africa so it never bothered me; I got enough of the gist of the conversation from everyone's English to know what was going on. And the way my mind works with language, even when I'm hearing other languages, they get filtered into English as I'm hearing them. My mind stores them in English. When my grandmother and great-grandmother were hysterically praying to God to destroy the demon that had shit on their kitchen floor, all of that transpired in Xhosa, but it's stored in English. I remember it as English. So whenever I lay in bed at night dreaming about Babiki and the moments we'd spent together, I *felt* like it had transpired in English because that's how I remembered it. And Tom had never said anything about what language she spoke or didn't speak, because why would he care? He just wanted to get his free CDs and get with the sister. Which is how I'd been dating a girl for over a month—the girl I very much believed was my first girlfriend—without ever having had a single conversation with her.

Now the whole night came rushing back and I saw it from her point of view, and it was perfectly obvious to me why she didn't want to get out of the car. She probably hadn't wanted to go to the dance with me in the first place; she probably owed Tom a favor, and Tom can talk anyone into anything. Then I'd left her sitting and waiting for me for an hour and she was pissed off. Then she got into the car and it was the first time we had ever been alone, and she realized I couldn't even hold a conversation with her. I'd driven her around and gotten lost in the dark—a young girl alone in a car in the middle of nowhere with some strange guy, no idea where I was taking her. She was probably terrified. Then we got to the dance and she didn't speak anyone's language. She didn't know anyone. She didn't even know me.

Bongani and I stood outside the car, staring at each other. I didn't know what to do. I tried talking to her in every language I knew. Nothing worked. She only spoke Pedi. I got so desperate that I started trying to talk to her using hand signals.

"Please. You. Me. Inside. Dance. Yes?"

"No."

"Inside. Dance. Please?"

"No."

I asked Bongani if he spoke Pedi. He didn't. I ran inside to the dance and ran around looking for someone who spoke Pedi to help me to convince her to come in. "Do you speak Pedi? Do you speak Pedi? Do you speak Pedi?" Nobody spoke Pedi.

So I never got to go to my matric dance. Other than the three minutes I spent running through it looking for someone who spoke Pedi, I spent the whole night in the parking lot. When the dance ended, I climbed back into the shitty red Mazda and drove Babiki home. We sat in total awkward silence the whole way.

I pulled up in front of her block of flats in Hillbrow, stopped the car, and sat for a moment as I tried to figure out the polite and gentlemanly way to end the evening. Then, out of nowhere, she leaned over and gave me a kiss. Like, a real kiss, a proper kiss. The kind of kiss that made me forget that the whole disaster had just happened. I was so confused. I didn't know what I was supposed to do. She pulled back and I looked deep into her eyes and thought, *I have no idea how girls work*.

I got out of the car, walked around to her side, and opened her door. She gathered up her dress and stepped out and headed toward her flat, and as she turned to go I gave her one last little wave.

"Bye."

"Bye."

PART III

In Germany, no child finishes high school without learning about the Holocaust. Not just the facts of it but the how and the why and the gravity of it—what it means. As a result, Germans grow up appropriately aware and apologetic. British schools treat colonialism the same way, to an extent. Their children are taught the history of the Empire with a kind of disclaimer hanging over the whole thing. "Well, *that* was shameful, now wasn't it?"

In South Africa, the atrocities of apartheid have never been taught that way. We weren't taught judgment or shame. We were taught history the way it's taught in America. In America, the history of racism is taught like this: "There was slavery and then there was Jim Crow and then there was Martin Luther King Jr. and now it's done." It was the same for us. "Apartheid was bad. Nelson Mandela was freed. Let's move on." Facts, but not many, and never the emotional or moral dimension. It was as if the teachers, many of whom were white, had been given a mandate. "Whatever you do, don't make the kids angry."

15

GO HITLER!

When I was in grade nine, three Chinese kids transferred to Sandringham: Bolo, Bruce Lee, and John. They were the only Chinese kids in the school, out of a thousand pupils. Bolo got his nickname because he looked like Bolo Yeung from the Jean-Claude Van Damme movie *Bloodsport*. Bruce Lee's name really was Bruce Lee, which made our lives. Here was this Chinese guy, quiet, good-looking, in great shape, and his name was Bruce Lee. We were like, *This is magic. Thank you, Jesus, for bringing us Bruce Lee*. John was just John, which was weird because of the other two.

I got to know Bolo because he was one of my tuck-shop clients. Bolo's parents were professional pirates. They pirated videogames and sold them at flea markets. As the son of pirates, Bolo did the same thing—he started selling bootleg PlayStation games around school. Kids would give him their PlayStation, and he'd bring it back a few days later with a chip in it that enabled them to play pirated games, which he would then sell them. Bolo was friends with this white kid and fellow pirate named Andrew, who traded in bootleg CDs. Andrew was two grades above me and a real computer geek; he even had a CD writer at home, back when nobody had CD writers.

One day on my tuck-shop rounds, I overheard Andrew and Bolo complaining about the black kids at school. They'd realized that they could take Andrew's and Bolo's merchandise, say "I'll pay you later," and then not pay, because Andrew and Bolo were too scared of black people to go back to ask for the money. I leaned in to their conversation and said, "Listen, you shouldn't get upset. Black people don't have any money, so trying to get more stuff for less money is just what we do. But let me help. I'll be your middleman. You give me the merchandise and I'll sell it, and then I'll handle getting the money. In return, you give me a cut of the sale." They liked the idea right away, and we became partners.

As the tuck-shop guy, I was perfectly positioned. I had my network set up. All I had to do was tap into it. With the money I made selling CDs and videogames, I was able to save up and add new components and more memory to my own computer. Andrew the computer geek showed me how to do it, where to buy the cheapest parts, how to assemble them, how to repair them. He showed me how his business worked, too, how to download music, where to get rewritable CDs in bulk. The only thing I was missing was my own CD writer, because it was the most expensive component. At the time a CD writer cost as much as the rest of the computer, nearly 2,000 rand.

I worked as a middleman for Bolo and Andrew for a year. Then Bolo left school; the rumor was that his parents got arrested. From that point on I worked for Andrew, and then as he was about to matriculate he decided to quit the game. "Trevor," he told me, "you've been a loyal partner." And, as thanks, he bequeathed unto me his CD writer. At the time, black people barely had access to computers, let's start there. But a CD writer? That was the stuff of lore. It was mythical. The day Andrew gave it to me, he changed my life. Thanks to him, I now controlled production, sales, distribution—I had everything I needed to lock down the bootleg business.

I was a natural capitalist. I loved selling stuff, and I was selling something that everybody wanted and nobody else could provide. I sold my discs for 30 rand, around $3. A regular CD in the store cost 100 to 150 rand. Once people started buying from me, they wouldn't buy real CDs ever again—the deal was too good.

I had an instinct for business, but at the time I knew nothing about music, which was odd for someone running a music-pirating business. The only music I knew, still, was Christian music from church, the only music allowed in my mother's house. The CD writer Andrew gave me was a 1x CD writer, which meant it copied at the speed it played. Every day I'd leave school, go to my room, and sit for five to six hours, copying CDs. I had my own surround-sound system built with old car speakers I'd salvaged from the junkers Abel kept in the yard, and I strung them up around the room. Even though I had to sit there while each CD played, for a long time I didn't really listen to them. I knew it was against the dealer's code: Never get high on your own supply.

Thanks to the Internet, I could get anyone anything. I never judged anyone's taste in music. You wanted the new Nirvana, I got you the new Nirvana. You wanted the new DMX, I got you the new DMX. Local South African music was big, but black American music was what people were desperate for, hip-hop and R&B. Jagged Edge was huge. 112 was huge. I sold a lot of Montell Jordan. So much Montell Jordan.

When I started, I had a dial-up connection and a 24k modem. It would take a day to download an album. But technology kept evolving, and I kept reinvesting in the business. I upgraded to a 56k modem. I got faster CD writers, multiple CD writers. I started downloading more, copying more, selling more. That's when I got two middlemen of my own, my friend Tom, who went to Northview, and my friend Bongani, who lived in Alex.

One day Bongani came to me and said, "You know what would

make a lot of money? Instead of copying whole albums, why don't you put the best tracks of different albums onto one CD, because people only wanna hear the songs they like." That sounded like a great idea, so I started making mix CDs. Those sold well. Then a few weeks later Bongani came back and said, "Can you make the tracks fade into one another so the music moves from track one to track two without a break and the beat carries on? It'll be like a DJ playing a complete set the whole night." That sounded like a great idea, too. I downloaded a program called BPM, "beats per minute." It had a graphical interface that looked like two vinyl records side by side, and I could mix and fade between songs, basically everything a DJ can do live. I started making party CDs, and those started selling like hotcakes, too.

Business was booming. By matric I was balling, making 500 rand a week. To put that in perspective, there are maids in South Africa who still earn less than that today. It's a shit salary if you're trying to support a family, but as a sixteen-year-old living at home with no real expenses, I was living the dream.

For the first time in my life I had money, and it was the most liberating thing in the world. The first thing I learned about having money was that it gives you choices. People don't want to be rich. They want to be able to choose. The richer you are, the more choices you have. That is the freedom of money.

With money, I experienced freedom on a whole new level: I went to McDonald's. People in America don't understand, but when an American chain opens in a third-world country, people go crazy. That's true to this day. A Burger King opened for the first time in South Africa last year, and there was a queue around the block. It was an event. Everyone was going around saying, "I have to eat at Burger King. Have you heard? *It's from America.*" The funny thing was that the queue was actually just white people. White people went bat-shit crazy for Burger King. Black people were like, *whatever.* Black people didn't need Burger King. Our hearts were with KFC and McDonald's. The crazy thing

about McDonald's is that we knew about it long before it came, probably from movies. We never even dreamed we would ever get one in
South Africa; McDonald's seemed to us like one of those American
things that is exclusively American and can't go anywhere else. Even
before we ever tasted McDonald's, we knew we'd love it, and we did.
At one point South Africa was opening more McDonald's than any
other country in the world. With Mandela came freedom—and with
freedom came McDonald's. A McDonald's had opened up just two
blocks from our house not long after we moved to Highlands North,
but my mom would never pay for us to eat there. With my own money
I was like, *Let's do this.* I went all in. They didn't have "supersize" at the
time; "large" was the biggest. So I walked up to the counter, feeling
very impressed with myself, and I put down my money and said, "I'll
have a large number one."

I fell in love with McDonald's. McDonald's, to me, tasted like
America. McDonald's *is* America. You see it advertised and it looks
amazing. You crave it. You buy it. You take your first bite, and it blows
your mind. It's even better than you imagined. Then, halfway through,
you realize it's not all it's cracked up to be. A few bites later you're like,
Hmm, there's a lot wrong with this. Then you're done, you miss it like
crazy, and you go back for more.

Once I'd had a taste of America, I never ate at home. I only ate
McDonald's. McDonald's, McDonald's, McDonald's, McDonald's.
Every night my mother would try to cook me dinner.

"Tonight we're having chicken livers."

"No, I'm gonna have McDonald's."

"Tonight we're having dog bones."

"I think I'm gonna go with McDonald's again."

"Tonight we're having chicken feet."

"Hmmmmm . . . Okay, I'm in. But tomorrow I'm eating McDonald's."

The money kept rolling in and I was balling out of control. This is
how balling I was: I bought a cordless telephone. This was before everyone had a cellphone. The range on this cordless phone was strong

enough that I could put the base outside my window, walk the two blocks to McDonald's, order my large number one, walk back home, go up to my room, and fire up my computer, carrying on a conversation the whole time. I was that dude walking down the street holding a giant phone to my ear with the aerial fully extended, talking to my friend. "Yeah, I'm just goin' down to McDonald's . . ."

Life was good, and none of it would have happened without Andrew. Without him, I would never have mastered the world of music piracy and lived a life of endless McDonald's. What he did, on a small scale, showed me how important it is to empower the dispossessed and the disenfranchised in the wake of oppression. Andrew was white. His family had access to education, resources, computers. For generations, while his people were preparing to go to university, my people were crowded into thatched huts singing, *"Two times two is four. Three times two is six. La la la la la."* My family had been denied the things his family had taken for granted. I had a natural talent for selling to people, but without knowledge and resources, where was that going to get me? People always lecture the poor: "Take responsibility for yourself! Make something of yourself!" But with what raw materials are the poor to make something of themselves?

People love to say, "Give a man a fish, and he'll eat for a day. Teach a man to fish, and he'll eat for a lifetime." What they don't say is, "And it would be nice if you gave him a fishing rod." That's the part of the analogy that's missing. Working with Andrew was the first time in my life I realized you need someone from the privileged world to come to you and say, "Okay, here's what you need, and here's how it works." Talent alone would have gotten me nowhere without Andrew giving me the CD writer. People say, "Oh, that's a handout." No. I still have to work to profit by it. But I don't stand a chance without it.

One afternoon I was in my room making a CD when Bongani came over to pick up his inventory. He saw me mixing songs on my computer.

"This is insane," he said. "Are you doing this live?"

"Yeah."

"Trevor, I don't think you understand; you're sitting on a gold mine. We need to do this for a crowd. You need to come to the township and start DJ'ing gigs. No one has ever seen a DJ playing on a computer before."

Bongani lived in Alexandra. Where Soweto is a sprawling, government-planned ghetto, Alexandra is a tiny, dense pocket of a shantytown, left over from the pre-apartheid days. Rows and rows of cinder-block and corrugated-iron shacks, practically stacked on top of one another. Its nickname is Gomorrah because it has the wildest parties and the worst crimes.

Street parties are the best thing about Alexandra. You get a tent, put it up in the middle of the road, take over the street, and you've got a party. There's no formal invitations or guest list. You just tell a few people, word of mouth travels, and a crowd appears. There are no permits, nothing like that. If you own a tent, you have the right to throw a party in your street. Cars creep up to the intersection and the driver will see the party blocking their way and shrug and make a U-turn. Nobody gets upset. The only rule is that if you throw a party in front of somebody's house, they get to come and share your alcohol. The parties don't end until someone gets shot or a bottle gets broken on someone's face. That's how it has to end; otherwise, it wasn't a party.

Back then, most DJs could spin for only a few hours; they were limited by the number of vinyls they could buy. Since parties went all night, you might need five or six DJs to keep the dancing going. But I had a massive hard drive stuffed with MP3s, which is why Bongani was excited when he saw me mixing—he saw a way to corner the market.

"How much music do you have?" he asked.

"Winamp says I can play for a week."

"We'll make a fortune."

Our first gig was a New Year's Eve party the summer we graduated from Sandringham. Bongani and I took my tower, my giant monitor, and all the cables and the keyboard and the mouse. We loaded everything up in a minibus and brought it over to Alex. We took over the street in front of his house, ran the electricity out of his place, set up the computer, set up speakers, and borrowed a tent, and people came. It was explosive. By midnight the whole street was packed from one end to the other. Ours was the biggest New Year's Eve party in Alexandra that year, and to have the biggest party in Alexandra is no joke. All night, from far and wide, people kept coming. The word spread: "There's a light-skinned guy who plays music on a computer. You've never seen anything like it." I DJ'd by myself until dawn. By then me and my friends were so drunk and exhausted that we passed out on the lawn outside Bongani's house. The party was so big it made our reputation in the hood, instantly. Pretty soon we were getting booked all over.

Which was a good thing.

When Bongani and I graduated from high school, we couldn't get jobs. There were no jobs for us to get. The only ways I had to make money were pirating CDs and DJ'ing parties, and now that I'd left Sandringham, the minibus drivers and corner kids in Alexandra were the single biggest market for my CDs. It was also where I was playing the most gigs, so to keep earning I naturally gravitated that way. Most of the white kids I knew were taking a gap year. "I'm going to take a gap year and go to Europe." That's what the white kids were saying. So I said, "I, too, am going to take a gap year. I am going to take a year and go to the township and hang out on the corner." And that's what I did.

There was a low brick wall running down the middle of the road in front of Bongani's house in Alex, and every day Bongani and I and our crew would go sit on the wall. I'd bring my CDs. We'd play music and practice dance moves. We hustled CDs all day and DJ'd parties at night. We started getting booked for gigs in other townships, other hoods.

Thanks to my computer and modem I was getting exclusive tracks few people had access to, but that created a problem for me. Sometimes I'd play the new music at parties and people would stand around going, "What is this? How do you dance to it?" For example, if a DJ plays a song like "Watch Me (Whip/Nae Nae)"—yes, it's a catchy song, but what is a whip? What is a nae nae? For that song to be popular you have to know how to do the whip and the nae nae; new music works at parties only if people know how to dance to it. Bongani decided we needed a dance crew to show people the steps to the songs we were playing. Because we spent our days doing nothing but listening to CDs and coming up with dance moves, our crew from the corner already knew all the songs, so they became our dancers. And hands down the best, most beautiful, most graceful dancer in the crew was Bongani's neighbor, Hitler.

Hitler was a great friend of mine, and good Lord could that guy dance. He was mesmerizing to watch. He had a looseness and a fluidity that defied physics—imagine a jellyfish if it could walk on land. Incredibly handsome, too, tall and lithe and muscular, with beautiful, smooth skin, big teeth, and a great smile, always laughing. And all he did was dance. He'd be up in the morning, blasting house music or hip-hop, practicing moves the whole day.

In the hood, everybody knows who the best dancer in the crew is. He's like your status symbol. When you're poor you don't have cars or nice clothes, but the best dancer gets girls, so that's the guy you want to roll with. Hitler was our guy. There were parties with dance competitions. Kids from every neighborhood would come and bring their best dancers. We'd always bring Hitler, and he almost always won.

When Bongani and I put together a routine for our dance crew, there was no question who was going to be the star attraction. We built the whole set around Hitler. I'd warm the crowd up with a few songs, then the dancers would come out and do a couple of numbers. Once they'd gotten the party started, they'd fan out to form a semicircle around the stage with a gap in the back for Hitler to enter. I'd crank up Redman's "Let's Get Dirty" and start whipping the crowd up even more. *Are you ready?! I can't hear you! Let me hear you make some noise!* People would start screaming, and Hitler would jump into the middle of the semicircle and the crowd would lose it. Hitler would do his thing while the guys circled around him, shouting him on. *"Go Hitler! Go Hit-ler! Go Hit-ler! Go Hit-ler!"* And because this was hip-hop, the crew would do that thing where you shoot your arm out in front of you with your palm flat, bopping it up and down to the beat. *"Go Hit-ler! Go Hit-ler! Go Hit-ler! Go Hit-ler!"* We'd have the whole crowd in a frenzy, a thousand people in the street chanting along with their hands in the air. *"Go Hit-ler! Go Hit-ler! Go Hit-ler! Go Hit-ler!"*

Hitler, although an unusual name, is not unheard-of in South Africa. Part of it has to do with the way a lot of black people pick names. Black people choose their traditional names with great care; those are the names that have deeply personal meanings. But from colonial times through the days of apartheid, black people in South Africa were re-quired to have an English or European name as well—a name that white people could pronounce, basically. So you had your English name, your traditional name, and your last name: Patricia Nombuy-iselo Noah. Nine times out of ten, your European name was chosen at random, plucked from the Bible or taken from a Hollywood celebrity or a famous politician in the news. I know guys named after Mussolini and Napoleon. And, of course, Hitler.

Westerners are shocked and confused by that, but really it's a case of the West reaping what it has sown. The colonial powers carved up Africa, put the black man to work, and did not properly educate him. White people don't talk to black people. So why would black people know what's going on in the white man's world? Because of that, many black people in South Africa don't really know who Hitler was. My own grandfather thought "a hitler" was a kind of army tank that was helping the Germans win the war. Because that's what he took from what he heard on the news. For many black South Africans, the story of the war was that there was someone called Hitler and he was the reason the Allies were losing the war. This Hitler was so powerful that at some point black people had to go help white people fight against him—and if the white man has to stoop to ask the black man for help fighting someone, that someone must be the toughest guy of all time. So if you want your dog to be tough, you name your dog Hitler. If you want your kid to be tough, you name your kid Hitler. There's a good chance you've got an uncle named Hitler. It's just a thing.

At Sandringham, we were taught more about World War II than the typical black kids in the townships were, but only in a basic way. We weren't taught to think critically about Hitler and anti-Semitism and the Holocaust. We weren't taught, for instance, that the architects of apartheid were big fans of Hitler, that the racist policies they put in place were inspired, in part, by the racist policies of the Third Reich. We weren't taught how to think about how Hitler related to the world we lived in. We weren't being taught to think, period. All we were taught was that in 1939 Hitler invaded Poland and in 1941 he invaded the Soviet Union and in 1943 he did something else. They're just facts. Memorize them, write them down for the test, and forget them.

There is also this to consider: The name Hitler does not offend a black South African because Hitler is not the worst thing a black South African can imagine. Every country thinks their history is the most important, and that's especially true in the West. But if black South Africans could go back in time and kill one person, Cecil Rhodes would come up before Hitler. If people in the Congo could go back in time and kill one person, Belgium's King Leopold would come way before Hitler. If Native Americans could go back in time and kill one person, it would probably be Christopher Columbus or Andrew Jackson.

I often meet people in the West who insist that the Holocaust was the worst atrocity in human history, without question. Yes, it was horrific. But I often wonder, with African atrocities like in the Congo, how horrific were they? The thing Africans don't have that Jewish people do have is documentation. The Nazis kept meticulous records, took pictures, made films. And that's really what it comes down to. Holocaust victims count because Hitler counted them. Six million people killed. We can all look at that number and rightly be horrified. But when you read through the history of atrocities against Africans, there are no numbers, only guesses. It's harder to be horrified by a guess. When Portugal and Belgium were plundering Angola and the Congo, they weren't counting the black people they slaughtered. How many black people died harvesting rubber in the Congo? In the gold and diamond mines of the Transvaal?

So in Europe and America, yes, Hitler is the Greatest Madman in History. In Africa he's just another strongman from the history books. In all my time hanging out with Hitler, I never once asked myself, "*Why* is his name Hitler?" His name was Hitler because his mom named him Hitler.

Once Bongani and I added the dancers to our DJ sets, we blew up. We called our group the Black and White Boys. The dancers were called the Springbok Boys. We started getting booked everywhere. Successful black families were moving to the suburbs, but their kids still wanted to have block parties and stay connected to the culture of the townships, so they'd book us to play their parties. Word of mouth traveled. Pretty soon we were getting booked more and more in the suburbs, meeting white people, playing for white people.

One kid we knew from the township, his mother was involved in creating cultural programs for schools. In America they'd be called "diversity programs." They were springing up all over South Africa because we were supposed to be learning about and embracing one another in this post-apartheid era. This kid's mom asked us if we wanted to play at a cultural day at some school in Linksfield, the wealthy suburb south of Sandringham where my pal Teddy had lived. There was going to be all sorts of different dancing and music, and everyone was going to come together and hang out and be cultural. She offered to pay, so we said sure. She sent us the information with the time and place and the name of the school: the King David School. A Jewish school.

The day of the event, we booked a minibus, loaded it up with our gear, and drove over. Once we arrived we waited in the back of the school's assembly hall and watched the acts that went onstage before us, different groups took their turns performing, flamenco dancers, Greek dancers, traditional Zulu musicians. Then we were up. We were billed as the Hip Hop Pantsula Dancers—the South African B-Boys. We set up our sound system onstage. I looked out, and the whole hall was nothing but Jewish kids in their yarmulkes, ready to party.

I got on the mic. "Are you ready to rock out?!"

"Yeahhhhhh!"

"Make some noise!"

"Yeahhhhhh!"

I started playing. The bass was bumping, my crew was dancing, and everyone was having a great time. The teachers, the chaperones, the parents, hundreds of kids—they were all dancing like crazy. Our set was scheduled for fifteen minutes, and at the ten-minute mark came the moment for me to play "Let's Get Dirty," bring out my star dancer, and shut shit down.

I started the song, the dancers fanned out in their semicircle, and I got on the mic.

"Are you guys ready?!"

"Yeahhhhhh!"

"You guys are not ready! Are you *ready*?!"

"*Yeeeaaahhhhhhhh!*"

"All right! Give it up and make some noise for *HIIIIITTTT-LLLLEERRRRRRRRRR*!!!"

Hitler jumped out to the middle of the circle and started killing it. The guys around him were all chanting, *"Go Hit-ler! Go Hit-ler! Go Hit-ler! Go Hit-ler!"* They had their arms out in front of them, bouncing to the rhythm. *"Go Hit-ler! Go Hit-ler! Go Hit-ler! Go Hit-ler!"* And I was right there on the mic leading them along. *"Go Hit-ler! Go Hit-ler! Go Hit-ler! Go Hit-ler!"*

The whole room stopped. No one was dancing. The teachers, the chaperones, the parents, the hundreds of Jewish kids in their yarmulkes—they froze and stared aghast at us up on the stage. I was oblivious. So was Hitler. We kept going. For a good thirty seconds the only sound in the room was the beat of the music and me on the mic yelling, *"Go Hit-ler! Go Hit-ler! Go Hit-ler! Put your hands in the air for Hitler, yo!"*

A teacher ran up behind me and yanked the plug for my system out of the wall. The hall went dead silent, and she turned on me and she was livid. "How *dare* you?! This is disgusting! You horrible, disgusting vile creature! How *dare* you?!"

My mind was racing, trying to figure out what she was talking about. Then it clicked. Hitler had a special dance move called *o spana va*. It means "where you work" and it was very sexual: His hips would gyrate and thrust, like he was fucking the air. That was the move he was doing at the moment the teacher ran out, so clearly the dance was the thing she found so disgusting. But this was a move that African people do all the time. It's a part of our culture. Here we were sharing our culture for a cultural day, and this woman was calling us disgusting. She was offended, and I was offended by her taking offense.

"Lady," I said, "I think you need to calm down."

"I will *not* calm down! How dare you come here and insult us?!"

"This is not insulting anyone. This is who we are!"

"Get out of here! You people are disgusting."

And there it was. *You people.* Now I saw what the deal was: This lady was racist. She couldn't see black men dancing suggestively and not get pissed off. As I started packing up my gear, we kept arguing.

"Listen, lady. We're free now. We're gonna do what we're gonna do. You can't stop us."

"I'll have you know that my people stopped people like you before, and we can stop you again."

She was talking, of course, about stopping the Nazis in World War II, but that's not what I was hearing. Jews in South Africa are just white people. All I was hearing was some white lady shouting about how white people beat us before and they'll beat us again. I said, "You will *never* stop us again, lady"—and here's where I played the trump card— "You'll never stop us, because now we have *Nelson Mandela* on our side! And he *told* us we can do this!"

"*What?!*"

She was so confused. I'd had it. I started cussing her out. "Fuck you, lady. Fuck your program. Fuck your school. Fuck your whole people. Let's go, guys! We're out!"

We didn't walk out of that school. We danced out. We danced down the street pumping our fists in the air. *"Go Hit-ler! Go Hit-ler! Go Hit-ler! Go Hit-ler!"* Because Hitler had shut shit down. Hitler had the most gangster dance moves ever, and those white people didn't know what hit them.

Alexandra was a farm originally named for the wife of the white man who owned it. Like Sophiatown and other black spots populating white areas before apartheid, Alex started out as a squatter settlement where blacks gathered and lived when coming to Johannesburg to find work. What was unique about Alex is that this farmer sold plots of land to some of the black tenants in the time before it was illegal for blacks to own property. So while Sophiatown and other black ghettos were razed and rebuilt as white suburbs, Alex fought and held on and asserted its right to exist. Wealthy white suburbs like Sandton grew around it, but Alex remained. More squatters came and more squatters came, putting up makeshift shacks and shanties. They look like the slums in Mumbai or the favelas in Brazil. The first time I saw the favelas in Rio I said, "Yeah, that's Alexandra, but on a hill."

Soweto was beautiful because, after democracy, you watched Soweto grow. Soweto has become a proper city unto itself. People went from three-room houses to five-room houses to three-bedroom houses with garages. There was room to grow because the piece of land from the government gave you something to build on. Alexandra can't do that. Alex can't get any bigger, because it's pinned in on all sides, and it can't build up, because it's mostly shacks.

When democracy came, people flooded into Alex from the home-lands, building new shacks in the backyards of other shacks with still more shacks attached to the backside of those shacks, growing more dense and more compressed, leaving close to 200,000 people living in a few square kilometers. Even if you go back today, Alex hasn't changed. It can't change. It's physically impossible for it to change. It can only be what it is.

16

THE CHEESE BOYS

My friend Bongani was a short, bald, super-buff guy. He wasn't always that way. His whole life he'd been skinny, and then a bodybuilding magazine found its way into his hands and changed his life. Bongani was one of those people who brought out the best in everybody. He was that friend who believed in you and saw the potential in you that nobody else did, which was why so many of the township kids gravitated toward him, and why I gravitated toward him as well. Bongani was always popular, but his reputation really took off when he beat up one of the more infamous bullies in the school. That cemented his status as sort of the leader and protector of the township kids.

Bongani lived in Alex, but I never visited him there while we were still in school; he'd always come to my house in Highlands North. I'd been to Alex a few times, for brief visits, but I'd never spent any real time there. I'd never been there at night, let's put it that way. Going to Alex during the day is different from going there at night. The place was nicknamed Gomorrah for a reason.

One day after school, not long before we matriculated, Bongani walked up to me on the quad.

"Hey, let's go to the hood," he said.

"The hood?"

At first I had no idea what he was talking about. I knew the word "hood" from rap songs, and I knew the different townships where black people lived, but I had never used the one to describe the other.

The walls of apartheid were coming down just as American hip-hop was blowing up, and hip-hop made it cool to be from the hood. Before, living in a township was something to be ashamed of; it was the bottom of the bottom. Then we had movies like *Boyz n the Hood* and *Menace II Society,* and they made the hood look cool. The characters in those movies, in the songs, they owned it. Kids in the townships started doing the same, wearing their identity as a badge of honor: You were no longer from the township—you were from the hood. Being from Alex gave you way more street cred than living in Highlands North. So when Bongani said, "Let's go to the hood," I was curious about what he meant. I wanted to find out more.

When Bongani took me to Alex we entered as most people do, from the Sandton side. You ride through one of the richest neighborhoods in Johannesburg, past palatial mansions and huge money. Then you go through the industrial belt of Wynberg that cordons off the rich and white from the poor and black. At the entrance to Alex there's the huge minibus rank and the bus station. It's the same bustling, chaotic third-world marketplace you see in James Bond and Jason Bourne movies. It's Grand Central Station but outdoors. Everything's dynamic. Everything's in motion. Nothing feels like it was there yesterday, and nothing feels like it will be there tomorrow, but every day it looks exactly the same.

Right next to the minibus rank, of course, is a KFC. That's one thing about South Africa: There's always a KFC. KFC found the black people. KFC did not play games. They were in the hood before Mc-Donald's, before Burger King, before anyone. KFC was like, "Yo, we're *here* for you."

Once you go past the minibus rank, you're in Alex proper. I've been in few places where there's an electricity like there is in Alex. It's a hive of constant human activity, all day long, people coming and going, gangsters hustling, guys on the corner doing nothing, kids running around. There's nowhere for all that energy to go, no mechanism for it to dissipate, so it erupts periodically in epic acts of violence and crazy parties. One minute it'll be a placid afternoon, people hanging out, doing their thing, and next thing you know there's a cop car chasing gangsters, flying through the streets, a gun battle going off, helicopters circling overhead. Then, ten minutes later, it's like it never happened—everyone's back to hanging out, back to the hustle, coming and going, running around.

Alex is laid out on a grid, a series of avenues. The streets are paved, but the sidewalks are mostly dirt. The color scheme is cinder block and corrugated iron, gray and dark gray, punctuated by bright splashes of color. Someone's painted a wall lime green, or there's a bright-red sign above a takeaway shop, or maybe somebody's picked up a bright-blue piece of sheet metal just by luck. There's little in the way of basic sanitation. Trash is everywhere, typically a garbage fire going down some side street. There's always something burning in the hood.

As you walk, there's every smell you can imagine. People are cooking, eating takeaways in the streets. Some family has a shack that's jury-rigged onto the back of someone else's shack, and they don't have any running water, so they've bathed in a bucket from the outdoor tap and then dumped the dirty water in the street, where it runs into the river of sewerage that's already there because the water system has backed up again. There's a guy fixing cars who thinks he knows what he's doing, but he doesn't. He's dumping old motor oil into the street, and now the oil is combining with the dirty bathwater to make a river of filth running down the street. There's probably a goat hanging around—there's always a goat. As you're walking, sound washes over you, the steady thrum of human activity, people talking in a dozen different languages, chatting, haggling, arguing. There's music playing constantly. You've got traditional South African music coming from one corner, someone blasting Dolly Parton from the next corner, and somebody driving past pumping the Notorious B.I.G.

The hood was a complete sensory overload for me, but within the chaos there was order, a system, a social hierarchy based on where you lived. First Avenue was not cool at all because it was right next to the commotion of the minibus rank. Second Avenue was nice because it had semi-houses that were built when there was still some sort of formal settlement going on. Third, Fourth, and Fifth Avenues were nicer—for the township. These were the established families, the old money. Then from Sixth Avenue on down it got really shitty, more shacks and shanties. There were some schools, a few soccer fields. There were a couple of hostels, giant projects built by the government for housing migrant workers. You never wanted to go there. That's where the serious gangsters were. You only went there if you needed to buy an AK-47.

After Twentieth Avenue you hit the Jukskei River, and on the far side of that, across the Roosevelt Street Bridge, was East Bank, the newest, nicest part of the hood. East Bank was where the government had gone in, cleared out the squatters and their shacks, and started to build actual homes. It was still low-income housing, but decent two-bedroom houses with tiny yards. The families who lived there had a bit of money and usually sent their kids out of the hood to better schools, like Sandringham. Bongani's parents lived in East Bank, at the corner of Roosevelt and Springbok Crescent, and after walking from the minibus rank through the hood, we wound up there, hanging around outside his house on the low brick wall down the middle of Springbok Crescent, doing nothing, shooting the shit. I didn't know it then, but I was about to spend the next three years of my life hanging out at that very spot.

• • •

I graduated from high school when I was seventeen, and by that point life at home had become toxic because of my stepfather. I didn't want to be there anymore, and my mom agreed that I should move out. She helped me move to a cheap, roach-infested flat in a building down the road. My plan, insofar as I had one, was to go to university to be a computer programmer, but we couldn't afford the tuition. I needed to make money. The only way I knew how to make money was selling pirated CDs, and one of the best places to sell CDs was in the hood, because that's where the minibus rank was. Minibus drivers were always looking for new songs because having good music was something they used to attract customers.

Another nice thing about the hood was that it's super cheap. You can get by on next to nothing. There's a meal you can get in the hood called a *kota*. It's a quarter loaf of bread. You scrape out the bread, then you fill it with fried potatoes, a slice of baloney, and some pickled mango relish called *achar*. That costs a couple of rand. The more money you have, the more upgrades you can buy. If you have a bit more money you can throw in a hot dog. If you have a bit more than that, you can throw in a proper sausage, like a bratwurst, or maybe a fried egg. The biggest one, with all the upgrades, is enough to feed three people.

For us, the ultimate upgrade was to throw on a slice of cheese. Cheese was always the thing because it was so expensive. Forget the gold standard—the hood operated on the cheese standard. Cheese on anything was money. If you got a burger, that was cool, but if you got a cheeseburger, that meant you had more money than a guy who just got a hamburger. Cheese on a sandwich, cheese in your fridge, that meant you were living the good life. In any township in South Africa, if you had a bit of money, people would say, "Oh, you're a cheese boy." In essence: You're not really hood because your family has enough money to buy cheese.

In Alex, because Bongani and his crew lived in East Bank, they were considered cheese boys. Ironically, because they lived on the first street just over the river, they were looked down on as the scruff of East Bank and the kids in the nicer houses higher up in East Bank were the cheesier cheese boys. Bongani and his crew would never admit to being cheese boys. They would insist, "We're not cheese. We're hood." But then the real hood guys would say, "Eh, you're not hood. You're cheese." "We're not cheese," Bongani's guys would say, pointing further up East Bank. "They're cheese." It was all a bunch of ridiculous posturing about who was hood and who was cheese.

Bongani was the leader of his crew, the guy who got everyone together and got things moving. Then there was Mzi, Bongani's henchman. Small guy, just wanted to tag along, be in the mix. Bheki was the drinks man, always finding us booze and always coming up with an excuse to drink. Then there was Kakoatse. We called him G. Mr. Nice Guy. All G was interested in was women. If women were in the mix, he was in the game. Then, finally, there was Hitler, the life of the party. Hitler just wanted to dance.

Cheese boys were in a uniquely fucked situation when apartheid ended. It is one thing to be born in the hood and know that you will never leave the hood. But the cheese boy has been shown the world outside. His family has done okay. They have a house. They've sent him to a decent school; maybe he's even matriculated. He has been given more potential, but he has not been given more opportunity. He has been given an awareness of the world that is out there, but he has not been given the means to reach it.

The unemployment rate, technically speaking, was "lower" in South Africa during apartheid, which makes sense. There was slavery—that's how everyone was employed. When democracy came, everyone had to be paid a minimum wage. The cost of labor went up, and suddenly millions of people were out of work. The unemployment rate for young black men post-apartheid shot up, sometimes as high as 50 percent. What happens to a lot of guys is they finish high school and they can't afford university, and even little retail jobs can be hard to come by when you're from the hood and you look and talk a certain way. So, for many young men in South Africa's townships, freedom looks like this: Every morning they wake up, maybe their parents go to work or maybe not. Then they go outside and chill on the corner the whole day, talking shit. They're free, they've been taught how to fish, but no one will give them a fishing rod.

• • •

One of the first things I learned in the hood is that there is a very fine line between civilian and criminal. We like to believe we live in a world of good guys and bad guys, and in the suburbs it's easy to believe that, because getting to know a career criminal in the suburbs is a difficult thing. But then you go to the hood and you see there are so many shades in between.

In the hood, gangsters were your friends and neighbors. You knew them. You talked to them on the corner, saw them at parties. They were a part of your world. You knew them from before they became gangsters. It wasn't, "Hey, that's a crack dealer." It was, "Oh, little Jimmy's selling crack now." The weird thing about these gangsters was that they were all, at a glance, identical. They drove the same red sports car. They dated the same beautiful eighteen-year-old girls. It was strange. It was like they didn't have personalities; they shared a personality. One could be the other, and the other could be the one. They'd each studied how to be *that* gangster.

In the hood, even if you're not a hardcore criminal, crime is in your life in some way or another. There are degrees of it. It's everyone from the mom buying some food that fell off the back of a truck to feed her family, all the way up to the gangs selling military-grade weapons and hardware. The hood made me realize that crime succeeds because crime does the one thing the government doesn't do: crime cares. Crime is grassroots. Crime looks for the young kids who need support and a lifting hand. Crime offers internship programs and summer jobs and opportunities for advancement. Crime gets involved in the community. Crime doesn't discriminate.

My life of crime started off small, selling pirated CDs on the corner. That in itself was a crime, and today I feel like I owe all these artists money for stealing their music, but by hood standards it didn't even qualify as illegal. At the time it never occurred to any of us that we were doing anything wrong—if copying CDs is wrong, why would they make CD writers?

The garage of Bongani's house opened up onto Springbok Cresent.

Every morning we'd open the doors, run an extension cord out into the street, set up a table, and play music. People would walk by and ask, "What is that? Can I get one, please?" Our corner was also where a lot of minibus drivers ended their routes and turned around to loop back to the minibus rank. They'd swing by, place an order, come back, pick it up. Swing by, place an order, come back, pick it up. We spent our whole day running out to them, going back to the garage to make more mixes, and going back out to sell. There was a converted shipping container around the corner where we'd hang out when we got tired of the wall. It had a pay phone installed inside that we'd use to call people. When things were slow we'd wander back and forth between the container and the wall, talking and hanging out with the other people with nothing to do in the middle of the day. We'd talk to drug dealers, talk to gangsters. Every now and then the cops would come crashing through. A day in the life of the hood. Next day, same thing.

Selling slowly evolved into hustling because Bongani saw all the angles and knew how to exploit them. Like Tom, Bongani was a hustler. But where Tom was only about the short con, Bongani had schemes: If we do this, we get that, then we can flip that for the other thing, which gives us the leverage we need to get something bigger. Some minibus drivers couldn't pay up front, for example. "I don't have the money, because I've just started my shift," they'd say. "But I need new music. Can I owe you guys some form of credit? I'll owe you a ride. I'll pay you at the end of my shift, at the end of the week?" So we started letting drivers buy on credit, charging them a bit of interest.

We started making more money. Never more than a few hundred, maybe a thousand rand at a time, but it was all cash on hand. Bongani was quick to realize the position we were in. Cash is the one thing everyone in the hood needs. Everyone's looking for a short-term loan for something, to pay a bill or pay a fine or just hold things together. People started coming to us and asking for money. Bongani would cut a deal, and then he'd come to me. "Yo, we're going to make a deal with this guy. We're going to loan him a hundred, and he's going to give us back one-twenty at the end of the week." I'd say okay. Then the guy would come back and give us 120 rand. Then we did it again. Then we did it some more. We started to double our money, then triple our money.

Cash gave us leverage in the hood's barter economy as well. It's common knowledge that if you're standing at a corner of a main street in the hood, somebody's going to try to sell you something. "Yo, yo, yo, man. You want some weed?" "You wanna buy a VCR?" "You wanna buy a DVD player?" "Yo, I'm selling a TV." That's just how it works.

Let's say we see two guys haggling on the corner, a crackhead trying to sell a DVD player and some working dude who wants it but doesn't have the money because he hasn't got his wages yet. They're going back and forth, but the crackhead wants the money now. Crackheads don't wait. There's no layaway plan with a crackhead. So Bongani steps in and takes the working guy aside.

"Look, I understand you can't pay for the DVD player now," Bongani says. "But how much are you willing to pay for it?"

"I'll pay one-twenty," he says.

"Okay, cool."

Then Bongani takes the crackhead aside.

"How much do you want for the DVD player?"

"I want one-forty."

"Okay, listen. You're a crackhead. This is a stolen DVD player. I'm going to give you fifty."

The crackhead protests a bit, but then he takes the money because he's a crackhead and it's cash and crack is all about the now. Then Bongani goes back to the working guy.

"All right. We'll do one-twenty. Here's your DVD player. It's yours."

"But I don't have the one-twenty."

"It's cool. You can take it now, only instead of one-twenty you give us one-forty when you get your wages."

"Okay."

So now we've invested 50 rand with the crackhead and that gets us 140 from the working guy. But Bongani would see a way to flip it and grow it again. Let's say this guy who bought the DVD player worked at a shoe store.

"How much do you pay for a pair of Nikes with your staff discount?" Bongani would ask.

"I can get a pair of Nikes for one-fifty."

"Okay, instead of you giving us one-forty, we'll give you ten and you get us a pair of Nikes with your discount."

So now this guy's walking away with a DVD player *and* 10 rand in his pocket. He's feeling like he got a good deal. He brings us the Nikes and then we go to one of the cheesier cheese boys up in East Bank and we say, "Yo, dude, we know you want the new Jordans. They're three hundred in the shops. We'll sell them to you for two hundred." We sell him the shoes, and now we've gone and turned 60 rand into 200.

That's the hood. Someone's always buying, someone's always selling, and the hustle is about trying to be in the middle of that whole thing. None of it was legal. Nobody knew where anything came from. The guy who got us Nikes, did he really have a "staff discount"? You don't know. You don't ask. It's just, "Hey, look what I found" and "Cool, how much do you want?" That's the international code.

At first I didn't know not to ask. I remember one time we bought a car stereo or something like that.

"But who did this belong to?" I said.

"Eh, don't worry about it," one of the guys told me. "White people have insurance."

"Insurance?"

"Yeah, when white people lose stuff they have insurance policies that pay them cash for what they've lost, so it's like they've lost nothing."

"Oh, okay," I said. "Sounds nice."

And that was as far as we ever thought about it: When white people lose stuff they get money, just another nice perk of being white.

It's easy to be judgmental about crime when you live in a world wealthy enough to be removed from it. But the hood taught me that everyone has different notions of right and wrong, different definitions of what constitutes crime, and what level of crime they're willing to participate in. If a crackhead comes through and he's got a crate of Corn Flakes boxes he's stolen out of the back of a supermarket, the poor mom isn't thinking, *I'm aiding and abetting a criminal by buying these Corn Flakes*. No. She's thinking, *My family needs food and this guy has Corn Flakes,* and she buys the Corn Flakes.

My own mother, my super-religious, law-abiding mother who used to shit on me about breaking the rules and learning to behave, I'll never forget one day I came home and in the kitchen was a giant box of frozen burger patties, like two hundred of them, from a takeaway place called Black Steer. A burger at Black Steer cost at least 20 rand.

"What the hell is this?" I said.

"Oh, some guy at work had these and was selling them," she said. "I got a great discount."

"But where did he get it from?"

"I don't know. He said he knew somebody who—"

"Mom, he stole it."

"We don't know that."

"We *do* know that. Where the hell is some guy going to get all of these burger patties from, randomly?"

Of course, we ate the burgers. Then we thanked God for the meal.

When Bongani first said to me, "Let's go to the hood," I thought we were going to sell CDs and DJ parties in the hood. It turned out that we were selling CDs and DJing parties in order to capitalize a payday-lending and pawnshop operation in the hood. Very quickly that became our core business.

Every day in the hood was the same. I'd wake up early. Bongani would meet me at my flat and we'd catch a minibus to Alex with my computer, carrying the giant tower and the giant, heavy monitor the whole way. We'd set it up in Bongani's garage, and start the first batch of CDs. Then we'd walk. We'd go down to the corner of Nineteenth and Roosevelt for breakfast. When you're trying to stretch your money, food is where you have to be careful. You have to plan or you'll eat your profits. So every morning for breakfast we eat *vetkoek,* which is fried dough, basically. Those were cheap, like 50 cents a pop. We could buy a bunch of those and have enough energy to sustain us until later on in the day.

Then we'd sit on the corner and eat. While we ate, we'd be picking up orders from the minibus drivers as they went past. After that we'd go back to Bongani's garage, listen to music, lift weights, make the CDs. Around ten or eleven, the drivers would start coming back from their morning routes. We'd take the CDs and head out to the corner for them to pick up their stuff. Then we'd just be on the corner, hanging out, meeting characters, seeing who came by, seeing where the day was going to take us. A guy needs this. A guy's selling that. You never knew what it was going to be.

There was always a big rush of business at lunch. We'd be all over Alexandra, hitting different shops and corners, making deals with everyone. We'd get free rides from the minibus drivers because we'd hop in with them and use it as an opportunity to talk about what music they needed, but secretly we were riding with the guy for free. "Hey, we want to collect orders. We'll talk to you while you drive. What do you need? What music are you looking for? Do you need the new Maxwell? Okay, we got the new Maxwell. Okay, we'll talk to you later. We'll jump out here." Then we'd hop on another ride going wherever we were going next.

After lunch, business would die down, and that's when we'd get our lunch, usually the cheapest thing we could afford, like a smiley with some maize meal. A smiley is a goat's head. They're boiled and covered with chili pepper. We call them smileys because when you're done eating all the meat off it, the goat looks like it's smiling at you from the plate. The cheeks and the tongue are quite delicious, but the eyes are disgusting. They pop in your mouth. You put the eyeball into your mouth and you bite it, and it's just a ball of pus that pops. It has no crunch. It has no chew. It has no flavor that is appetizing in any way.

After lunch we'd head back to the garage, relax, sleep off the meal, and make more CDs. In the afternoons we'd see a lot of moms. Moms loved us. They were some of our best customers. Since moms run the household, they're the ones looking to buy that box of soap that fell off the back of the truck, and they were more likely to buy it from us than from some crackhead. Dealing with crackheads is unpleasant. We were upstanding, well-spoken East Bank boys. We could even charge a premium because we added that layer of respectability to the transaction. Moms are also often the most in need of short-term loans, to pay for this or that for the family. Again, they'd rather deal with us than with some gangster loan shark. Moms knew we weren't going to break anyone's legs if they couldn't pay. We didn't believe in that. Also we weren't capable of it—let's not forget that part. But that's where Bongani's brilliance came in. He always knew what a person could provide pending their failure to pay.

We made some of the craziest trades. Moms in the hood are protective of their daughters, especially if their daughters are pretty. In Alex there were girls who got locked up. They went to school, came straight home, and went straight into the house. They weren't allowed to leave. Boys weren't allowed to talk to them, weren't even allowed to hang around the house—none of that. Some guy was always going on about some locked-away girl: "She's so beautiful. I'll do anything to get with her." But he couldn't. Nobody could.

Then that mom would need a loan. Once we lent her the money, until she paid us back she couldn't chase us away from her house. We'd go by and hang out, chat, make small talk. The daughter would be right there, but the mom couldn't say, "Don't talk to those boys!" The loan gave us access to establish a relationship with the mom. We'd get invited to stay for dinner. Once the mom knew we were nice, upstanding guys, she'd agree to let us take her daughter to a party as long as we promised to get her home safely. So then we'd go to the guy who'd been so desperate to meet the daughter.

"Hey, let's make a deal. We'll bring the girl to your party and you get to hang out with her. How much can you give us?"

"I don't have money," he'd say, "but I have some cases of beer."

"Okay, so tonight we're going to this party. You give us two cases of beer for the party."

"Cool."

Then we'd go to the party. We'd invite the girl, who was usually thrilled to escape her mother's prison. The guy would bring the beer, he'd get to hang out with the girl, we'd write off the mom's debt to show her our gratitude, and we'd make our money back selling the beer. There was always a way to make it work. And often that was the most fun part: working the angles, solving the puzzle, seeing what goes where, who needs what, whom we can connect with who can then get us the money.

At the peak of our operation we probably had around 10,000 rand in capital. We had loans going out and interest coming in. We had our stockpile of Jordans and DVD players we'd bought to resell. We also had to buy blank CDs, hire minibuses to go to our DJ gigs, feed five guys three times a day. We kept track of everything on the computer. Having lived in my mom's world, I knew how to do spreadsheets. We had a Microsoft Excel document laid out: everybody's name, how much they owed, when they paid, when they didn't pay.

After work was when business started to pick up. Minibus drivers picking up one last order, men coming home from work. The men weren't looking for soap and Corn Flakes. They wanted the gear— DVD players, CD players, PlayStation games. More guys would come through selling stuff, too, because they'd been out hustling and stealing all day. There'd be a guy selling a cellphone, a guy selling some leather jackets, a guy selling shoes. There was this one dude who looked like a black version of Mr. Burns from *The Simpsons*. He'd always come by at the end of his shift with the most random useless crap, like an electric toothbrush without the charger. One time he brought us an electric razor.

"What the hell is this?"

"It's an electric razor?"

"An electric razor? We're black. Do you know what these things do to our skin? Do you see anyone around here who can use an electric razor?"

We never knew where he was getting this stuff from. Because you don't ask. Eventually we pieced it together, though: He worked at the airport. It was all crap he was boosting from people's luggage.

Slowly the rush would start to taper off and we'd wind down. We'd make our last collections, go over our CD stock, balance our accounts. If there was a party to DJ that night we'd start getting ready for that. Otherwise, we'd buy a few beers and sit around and drink, talk about the day, listen to the gunshots in the distance. Gunshots went off every night, and we'd always try to guess what kind of gun it was. "That's a nine-millimeter." Usually there'd be a police chase, cop cars flying through after some guy with a stolen car. Then everyone would go home for dinner with their families. I'd take my computer, get back in a minibus, ride home, sleep, and then come back and do it all again the next day.

A year passed. Then two. I had stopped planning for school, and was no closer to having the money to enroll.

The tricky thing about the hood is that you're always working, working, working, and you feel like something's happening, but really nothing's happening at all. I was out there every day from seven a.m. to seven p.m., and every day it was: How do we turn ten rand into twenty? How do we turn twenty into fifty? How do I turn fifty into a hundred? At the end of the day we'd spend it on food and maybe some beers, and then we'd go home and come back and it was: How do we turn ten into twenty? How do we turn twenty into fifty? It was a whole day's work to flip that money. You had to be walking, be moving, be thinking. You had to get to a guy, find a guy, meet a guy. There were many days we'd end up back at zero, but I always felt like I'd been very productive.

Hustling is to work what surfing the Internet is to reading. If you add up how much you read in a year on the Internet—tweets, Facebook posts, lists—you've read the equivalent of a shit ton of books, but in fact you've read no books in a year. When I look back on it, that's what hustling was. It's maximal effort put into minimal gain. It's a hamster wheel. If I'd put all that energy into studying I'd have earned an MBA.

Instead I was majoring in hustling, something no university would give me a degree for.

When I first went into Alex, I was drawn by the electricity and the excitement of it, but more important, I was accepted there, more so than I'd been in high school or anywhere else. When I first showed up, a couple of people raised an eyebrow. "Who's this colored kid?" But the hood doesn't judge. If you want to be there, you can be there. Because I didn't live in the hood I was technically an outsider in the hood, but for the first time in my life I didn't feel like one.

The hood is also a low-stress, comfortable life. All your mental energy goes into getting by, so you don't have to ask yourself any of the big questions. Who am I? Who am I supposed to be? Am I doing enough? In the hood you can be a forty-year-old man living in your mom's house asking people for money and it's not looked down on. You never feel like a failure in the hood, because someone's always worse off than you, and you don't feel like you need to do more, because the biggest success isn't that much higher than you, either. It allows you to exist in a state of suspended animation.

The hood has a wonderful sense of community to it as well. Everyone knows everyone, from the crackhead all the way through to the policeman. People take care of one another. The way it works in the hood is that if any mom asks you to do something, you have to say yes. "Can I send you?" is the phrase. It's like everyone's your mom, and you're everyone's kid.

"Can I send you?"

"Yeah, whaddya need?"

"I need you to go buy milk and bread."

"Yeah, cool."

Then she gives you some money and you go buy milk and bread. As long as you aren't busy and it doesn't cost you anything, you don't say no.

The biggest thing in the hood is that you have to share. You can't get rich on your own. You have money? Why aren't you helping people? The old lady on the block needs help, everyone pitches in. You're buying beer, you buy beer for everyone. You spread it around. Everyone must know that your success benefits the community in one way or another, or you become a target.

The township polices itself as well. If someone's caught stealing, the township deals with them. If someone's caught breaking into a house, the township deals with them. If you're caught raping a woman, pray to God the police find you before the township does. If a woman is being hit, people don't get involved. There are too many questions with a beating. What's the fight about? Who's responsible? Who started it? But rape is rape. Theft is theft. You've desecrated the community.

The hood was strangely comforting, but comfort can be dangerous. Comfort provides a floor but also a ceiling. In our crew, our friend G was like the rest of us, unemployed, hanging out. Then he got a job at a nice clothing store. Every morning he went to work, and the guys would tease him about going to work. We'd see him headed out all dressed up, and everyone would be laughing at him. "Oh, G, look at you in your fancy clothes!" "Oh, G, going to go see the white man today, huh?" "Oh, G, don't forget to bring some books back from the library!"

One morning, after a month of G working at the place, we were hanging out on the wall, and G came out in his slippers and his socks. He wasn't dressed for work.

"Yo, G, what's going on? What's up with the job?"

"Oh, I don't work there anymore."

"Why?"

"They accused me of stealing something and I got fired."

And I'll never forget thinking to myself that it felt like he did it on purpose. He sabotaged himself so that he'd get accepted back into the group again.

The hood has a gravitational pull. It never leaves you behind, but it also never lets you leave. Because by making the choice to leave, you're insulting the place that raised you and made you and never turned you away. And that place fights you back.

As soon as things start going well for you in the hood, it's time to go. Because the hood will drag you back in. It will find a way. There will be a guy who steals a thing and puts it in your car and the cops find it—something. You can't stay. You think you can. You'll start doing better and you'll bring your hood friends out to a nice club, and the next thing you know somebody starts a fight and one of your friends pulls a gun and somebody's getting shot and you're left standing around going, "What just happened?"

The hood happened.

One night I was DJ'ing a party, not in Alex but right outside Alex in Lombardy East, a nicer, middle-class black neighborhood. The police were called about the noise. They came busting in wearing riot gear and pointing machine guns. That's how our police roll. We don't have small and then big. What Americans call SWAT is just our regular police. They came looking for the source of the music, and the music was coming from me. This one cop came over to where I was with my computer and pulled this massive assault rifle on me.

"You gotta shut this down right now."

"Okay, okay," I said. "I'm shutting it down."

But I was running Windows 95. Windows 95 took *forever* to shut down. I was closing windows, shutting down programs. I had one of those fat Seagate drives that damaged easily, and I didn't want to cut the power and possibly damage the drive. This cop clearly didn't give a fuck about any of that.

"Shut it down! Shut it down!"

"I am! I'm shutting it down! I have to close the programs!"

The crowd was getting angry, and the cop was getting nervous. He turned his gun away from me and shot the computer. Only he clearly didn't know anything about computers because he shot the monitor. The monitor exploded but the music kept playing. Now there was chaos—music blaring and everyone running and panicking because of the gunshot. I yanked the power cord out of the tower to shut the thing down. Then the cops started firing tear gas into the crowd.

The tear gas had nothing to do with me or the music. Tear gas is just what the police use to shut down parties in black neighborhoods, like the club turning on the lights to tell everyone to go home.

I lost the hard drive. Even though the cop shot the monitor the explosion somehow fried the thing. The computer would still boot up, but it couldn't read the drive. My music library was gone. Even if I'd had the money for a new hard drive, it had taken me years to amass the music collection. There was no way to replace it. The DJ'ing business was over. The CD-selling business was done. All of a sudden our crew lost its main revenue stream. All we had left was the hustle, and we hustled even harder, taking the bit of cash we had on hand and trying to double it, buying this to flip it for that. We started eating into our savings, and in less than a month we were running on dust.

Then, one evening after work, our friend from the airport, the black Mr. Burns, came by.

"Hey, look what I found," he said.

"What've you got?"

"A camera."

I'll never forget that camera. It was a digital camera. We bought it from him, and I took it and turned it on. It was full of pictures of a nice white family on vacation, and I felt like shit. The other things we'd bought had never mattered to me. Nikes, electric toothbrushes, electric razors. Who cares? Yeah, some guy might get fired because of the pallet of Corn Flakes that went missing from the supermarket, but that's degrees removed. You don't think about it. But this camera had a face. I went through those pictures, knowing how much my family pictures meant to me, and I thought, *I haven't stolen a camera. I've stolen someone's memories. I've stolen part of someone's life.*

It's such a strange thing, but in two years of hustling I never once thought of it as a crime. I honestly didn't think it was bad. *It's just stuff people found. White people have insurance.* Whatever rationalization was handy. In society, we do horrible things to one another because we don't see the person it affects. We don't see their face. We don't see them as people. Which was the whole reason the hood was built in the first place, to keep the victims of apartheid out of sight and out of mind. Because if white people ever saw black people as human, they would see that slavery is unconscionable. We live in a world where we don't see the ramifications of what we do to others, because we don't live with them. It would be a whole lot harder for an investment banker to rip off people with subprime mortgages if he actually had to live with the people he was ripping off. If we could see one another's pain and empathize with one another, it would never be worth it to us to commit the crimes in the first place.

As much as we needed the money, I never sold the camera. I felt too guilty, like it would be bad karma, which I know sounds stupid and it didn't get the family their camera back, but I just couldn't do it. That camera made me confront the fact that there were people on the other end of this thing I was doing, and what I was doing was wrong.

One night our crew got invited to dance in Soweto against another crew. Hitler was going to compete with their best dancer, Hector, who was one of the best dancers in South Africa at the time. This invitation was a huge deal. We were going over there repping our hood. Alex and Soweto have always had a huge rivalry. Soweto was seen as the snobbish township and Alexandra was seen as the gritty and dirty township. Hector was from Diepkloof, which was the nice, well-off part of Soweto. Diepkloof was where the first million-rand houses were built after democracy. "Hey, we're not a township anymore. We're building nice things now." That was the attitude. That's who we were up against. Hitler practiced a whole week.

We took a minibus over to Diepkloof the night of the dance, me and Bongani, Mzi and Bheki and G, and Hitler. Hector won the competition. Then G was caught kissing one of their girls, and it turned into a fight and everything broke down. On our way back to Alex, around one in the morning, as we were pulling out of Diepkloof to get on the freeway, some cops pulled our minibus over. They made everyone get out and they searched it. We were standing outside, lined up alongside the car, when one of the cops came back.

"We've found a gun," he said. "Whose gun is it?"

We all shrugged.

"We don't know," we said.

"Nope, somebody knows. It's somebody's gun."

"Officer, we really don't know," Bongani said.

He slapped Bongani hard across the face.

"You're bullshitting me!"

Then he went down the line, slapping each of us across the face, berating us about the gun. We couldn't do anything but stand there and take it.

"You guys are trash," the cop said. "Where are you from?"

"Alex."

"Ohhhhh, okay, I see. Dogs from Alex. You come here and you rob people and you rape women and you hijack cars. Bunch of fucking hoodlums."

"No, we're dancers. We don't know—"

"I don't care. You're all going to jail until we figure out whose gun this is."

At a certain point we realized what was going on. This cop was shaking us down for a bribe. "Spot fine" is the euphemism everyone uses. You go through this elaborate dance with the cop where you say the thing without saying the thing.

"Can't we do something?" you ask the officer.

"What do you want me to do?"

"We're really sorry, Officer. What can we do?"

"You tell me."

Then you're supposed to make up a story whereby you indicate to the cop how much money you have on you. Which we couldn't do because we didn't have any money. So he took us to jail. It was a public bus. It could have been anyone's gun, but the guys from Alex were the only ones who got arrested. Everyone else in the car was free to go. The cops took us to the police station and threw us in a cell and pulled us out one by one for questioning. When they pulled me aside I had to give my home address: Highlands North. The cop gave me the most confused look.

"You're not from Alex," he said. "What are you doing with these crooks?" I didn't know what to say. He glared at me hard. "Listen here, rich boy. You think it's fun running around with these guys? This isn't play-play anymore. Just tell me the truth about your friends and the gun, and I'll let you go."

I told him no, and he threw me back in the cell. We spent the night, and the next day I called a friend, who said he could borrow the money from his dad to get us out. Later that day the dad came down and paid the money. The cops kept calling it "bail," but it was a bribe. We were never formally arrested or processed. There was no paperwork.

We got out and everything was fine, but it rattled us. Every day we were out in the streets, hustling, trying to act as if we were in some way down with the gangs, but the truth was we were always more cheese than hood. We had created this idea of ourselves as a defense mechanism to survive in the world we were living in. Bongani and the other East Bank guys, because of where they were from, what they looked like—they just had very little hope. You've got two options in that situation. You take the retail job, flip burgers at McDonald's, if you're one of the lucky few who even gets that much. The other option is to toughen up, put up this facade. You can't leave the hood, so you survive by the rules of the hood.

I chose to live in that world, but I wasn't from that world. If anything, I was an imposter. Day to day I was in it as much as everyone else, but the difference was that in the back of my mind I knew I had other options. I could leave. They couldn't.

––––––––––

Once, when I was ten years old, visiting my dad in Yeoville, I needed batteries for one of my toys. My mom had refused to buy me new batteries because, of course, she thought it was a waste of money, so I snuck out to the shops and shoplifted a pack. A security guard busted me on the way out, pulled me into his office, and called my mom.

"We've caught your son shoplifting batteries," he said. "You need to come and fetch him."

"No," she said. "Take him to jail. If he's going to disobey he needs to learn the consequences."

Then she hung up. The guard looked at me, confused. Eventually he let me go on the assumption that I was some wayward orphan, because what mother would send her ten-year-old child to jail?

––––––––––

17

THE WORLD DOESN'T LOVE YOU

My mom never gave me an inch. Anytime I got in trouble it was tough love, lectures, punishment, and hidings. Every time. For every infraction. You get that with a lot of black parents. They're trying to discipline you before the system does. "I need to do this to you before the police do it to you." Because that's all black parents are thinking from the day you're old enough to walk out into the street, where the law is waiting.

In Alex, getting arrested was a fact of life. It was so common that out on the corner we had a sign for it, a shorthand, clapping your wrists together like you were being put in handcuffs. Everyone knew what that meant.

"Where's Bongani?"

Wrist clap.

"Oh, shit. When?"

"Friday night."

"Damn."

My mom hated the hood. She didn't like my friends there. If I brought them back to the house, she didn't even want them coming inside. "I don't like those boys," she'd say. She didn't hate them personally; she hated what they represented. "You and those boys get into so much shit," she'd say. "You must be careful who you surround yourself with because where you are can determine who you are."

She said the thing she hated most about the hood was that it didn't pressure me to become better. She wanted me to hang out with my cousin at his university.

"What's the difference if I'm at university or I'm in the hood?" I'd say. "It's not like I'm going to university."

"Yes, but the pressure of the university is going to get you. I know you. You won't sit by and watch these guys become better than you. If you're in an environment that is positive and progressive, you too will become that. I keep telling you to change your life, and you don't. One day you're going to get arrested, and when you do, don't call me. I'll tell the police to lock you up just to teach you a lesson."

Because there were some black parents who'd actually do that, not pay their kid's bail, not hire their kid a lawyer—the ultimate tough love. But it doesn't always work, because you're giving the kid tough love when maybe he just needs love. You're trying to teach him a lesson, and now that lesson is the rest of his life.

One morning I saw an ad in the paper. Some shop was having a clearance sale on mobile phones, and they were selling them at such a ridiculous price I knew Bongani and I could flip them in the hood for a profit. This shop was out in the suburbs, too far to walk and too out-of-the-way to take a minibus. Fortunately my stepfather's workshop and a bunch of old cars were in our backyard.

I'd been stealing Abel's junkers to get around since I was fourteen. I would say I was test driving them to make sure they'd been repaired correctly. Abel didn't think that was funny. I'd been caught many times, caught and subjected to my mother's wrath. But that had never stopped me from doing anything.

Most of these junkers weren't street legal. They didn't have proper registrations or proper number plates. Luckily, Abel also had a stack of old number plates in the back of the garage. I quickly learned I could just put one on an old car and hit the road. I was nineteen, maybe twenty, not thinking about any of the ramifications of this. I stopped by Abel's garage when no one was around, picked up one of the cars, the red Mazda I'd taken to the matric dance, slapped some old plates on it, and set off in search of discounted cell phones.

I got pulled over in Hillbrow. Cops in South Africa don't give you a reason when they pull you over. Cops pull you over because they're cops and they have the power to pull you over; it's as simple as that. I used to watch American movies where cops would pull people over and say, "You didn't signal" or "Your taillight's out." I'd always wonder, *Why do American cops bother lying?* One thing I appreciate about South Africa is that we have not yet refined the system to the point where we feel the need to lie.

"Do you know why I pulled you over?"

"Because you're a policeman and I'm a black person?"

"That's correct. License and registration, please."

When the cop pulled me over, it was one of those situations where I wanted to say, "Hey, I know you guys are racially profiling me!" But I couldn't argue the case because I was, at that moment, actually breaking the law. The cop walked up to my window, asked me the standard cop questions. Where are you going? Is this your car? Whose car is this? I couldn't answer. I completely froze.

Being young, funnily enough, I was more worried about getting in trouble with my parents than with the law. I'd had run-ins with the cops in Alexandra, in Soweto, but it was always more about the circumstance: a party getting shut down, a raid on a minibus. The law was all around me, but it had never come down on me, Trevor, specifically. And when you haven't had much experience with the law, the law appears rational—cops are dicks for the most part, but you also recognize that they're doing a job.

Your parents, on the other hand, are not rational at all. They have served as judge, jury, and executioner for your entire childhood, and it feels like they give you a life sentence for every misdemeanor. In that moment, when I should have been scared of the cop, all I was thinking was *Shit shit shit; I'm in so much trouble when I get home.*

The cop called in the number-plate registration and discovered that it didn't match the car. Now he was really on my case. "This car is not in your name! What's going on with these plates?! Step out of the vehicle!" It was only then that I realized: *Ohhhhh, shit. Now I'm in* real *trouble.* I stepped out of the car, and he put the cuffs on me and told me I was being arrested on suspicion of driving a stolen vehicle. He took me in, and the car was impounded.

The Hillbrow police station looks exactly like every other police station in South Africa. They were all built by the same contractor at the height of apartheid—separate nodes in the central nervous system of a police state. If you were blindfolded and taken from one to the other, you probably wouldn't even know that you'd changed locations. They're sterile, institutional, with fluorescent lights and cheap floor tile, like a hospital. My cop walked me in and sat me down at the front booking desk. I was charged and fingerprinted.

In the meantime, they'd been checking out the car, which wasn't going well for me, either. Whenever I borrowed cars from Abel's workshop, I tried to take the junkers rather than a real client's car; I thought I'd get in less trouble that way. That was a mistake. The Mazda, being one of Abel's junkers, didn't have a clear title of ownership. If it had had an owner, the cops would have called the owner, the owner would have explained that the car had been dropped off for repairs, and the whole thing would have been sorted out. Since the car didn't have an owner, I couldn't prove I hadn't stolen it.

Carjackings were common in South Africa at the time, too. So common you weren't even surprised when they happened. You'd have a friend coming over for a dinner party and you'd get a call.

"Sorry. Got carjacked. Gonna be late."

"Ah, that sucks. Hey, guys! Dave got carjacked."

"Sorry, Dave!"

And the party would continue. And that's if the person survived the carjacking. Often they didn't. People were getting shot for their cars all the time. Not only could I not prove I hadn't stolen the car, I couldn't prove I hadn't murdered someone for it, either. The cops were grilling me. "You kill anyone to get that car, boy? Eh? You a killer?"

I was in deep, deep trouble. I had only one lifeline: my parents. One call would have fixed everything. "This is my stepfather. He's a mechanic. I borrowed his car when I shouldn't have." Done. At worst I'd get a slap on the wrist for driving a car that wasn't registered. But what would I be getting at home?

I sat there in the police station—arrested for suspicion of grand theft auto, a plausible suspect for carjacking or murder—and debated whether I should call my parents or go to jail. With my stepfather I was thinking, *He might actually kill me*. In my mind that was an entirely realistic scenario. With my mother I was thinking, *She's going to make this worse. She's not the character witness I want right now. She won't help me.* Because she'd told me she wouldn't. "If you ever get arrested, don't call me." I needed someone sympathetic to my plight, and I didn't believe she was that person. So I didn't call my parents. I decided I didn't need them. I was a man. I could go it alone. I used my call to phone my cousin and told him not to tell anyone what had happened while I figured out what to do—now I just had to figure out what to do.

I'd been picked up late in the afternoon, so by the time I was processed it was close to lights-out. I was spending the night in jail, like it or not. It was at that point that a cop pulled me aside and told me what I was in for.

The way the system works in South Africa is that you're arrested and held in a cell at the police station until your bail hearing. At the hearing, the judge looks at your case, hears arguments from the opposing sides, and then he either dismisses the charges or sets bail and a trial date. If you can make bail, you pay and go home. But there are all sorts of ways your bail hearing can go wrong: You get some court-appointed lawyer who hasn't read your case and doesn't know what's going on. Your family can't pay your bail. It could even be that the court's backed up. "Sorry, we're too busy. No more hearings today." It doesn't matter the reason. Once you leave jail, you can't go back to jail. If your situation isn't resolved that day, you go to prison to await trial. In prison you're housed with the people awaiting trial, not with the general population, but even the awaiting-trial section is incredibly dangerous because you have people picked up for traffic violations all the way up to proper hardened criminals. You're stuck there together, and you can be there for days, weeks, maybe months. It's the same way in America. If you're poor, if you don't know how the system works, you can slip through the cracks, and the next thing you know you're in this weird purgatory where you're not in prison but you're not not in prison. You haven't been convicted of any crime, but you're still locked up and can't get out.

This cop pulled me aside and said, "Listen, you don't want to go to your bail hearing. They'll give you a state attorney who won't know what's going on. He'll have no time for you. He'll ask the judge for a postponement, and then maybe you'll go free or maybe you won't. Trust me, you don't want to do that. You have the right to stay here for as long as you like. You want to meet with a lawyer and set yourself up before you go anywhere near a court or a judge." He wasn't giving me this advice out of the goodness of his heart. He had a deal with a defense attorney, sending him clients in exchange for a kickback. He handed me the attorney's business card, I called him, and he agreed to take my case. He told me to stay put while he handled everything.

Now I needed money, because lawyers, as nice as they are, don't do anything for free. I called a friend and asked him if he could ask his dad to borrow some money. He said he'd handle it. He talked to his dad, and the lawyer got his retainer the next day.

With the lawyer taken care of, I felt like I had things under control.

I was feeling pretty slick. I'd handled the situation, and, most important, Mom and Abel were none the wiser.

When the time came for lights-out a cop came and took my stuff. My belt, my wallet, my shoelaces.

"Why do you need my shoelaces?"

"So you don't hang yourself."

"Right."

Even when he said that, the gravity of my situation still wasn't sinking in. Walking to the station's holding cell, looking around at the other six guys in there, I was thinking, *This is no big deal. Everything's gonna be cool. I'm gonna get out of this.* I thought that right up until the moment the cell door clanged shut behind me and the guard yelled, "Lights out!" That's when I thought, *Oh, shit. This is real.*

The guards had given me a mat and a scratchy blanket. I rolled them out on the concrete floor and tried to get comfortable. Every bad prison movie I'd ever seen was racing through my head. I was thinking, *I'm gonna get raped. I'm gonna get raped. I'm gonna get raped.* But of course I didn't get raped, because this wasn't prison. It was jail, and there's a big difference, as I would soon come to understand.

I woke up the next morning with that fleeting sensation where you think something has all been a dream. Then I looked around and remembered that it wasn't. Breakfast came, and I settled in to wait.

A day in jail is mostly silence punctuated by passing guards shouting profanities at you, doing roll call. Inside the holding cell nobody says anything. Nobody walks into a jail cell and says, "Hi, guys! I'm Brian!" Because everyone is afraid, and no one wants to appear vulnerable. Nobody wants to be the bitch. Nobody wants to be the guy getting killed. I didn't want anyone to know that I was just a kid in for a traffic charge, so I reached back in my mind for all the stereotypes of what I imagined people act like in prison, and then I tried to act like that.

In South Africa, everyone knows that colored gangsters are the most ruthless, the most savage. It's a stereotype that's fed to you your whole life. The most notorious colored gangs are the Numbers Gangs: the 26s, the 27s, the 28s. They control the prisons. They're known for being brutally violent—maiming, torturing, raping, cutting off people's heads—not for the sake of making money but just to prove how ruthless and savage they are, like Mexican drug cartels. In fact a lot of these gangs base their thing on those Mexican gangs. They have the same look: the Converse All Stars with the Dickies pants and the open shirt buttoned only at the top.

By the time I was a teenager, anytime I was profiled by cops or security guards, it usually wasn't because I was black but because I looked colored. I went to a club once with my cousin and his friend. The bouncer searched Mlungisi, waved him in. He searched our friend, waved him in. Then he searched me and got up in my face.

"Where's your knife?"

"I don't have a knife."

"I know you have a knife somewhere. Where is it?"

He searched and searched and finally gave up and let me in, looking me over like I was trouble.

"No *shit* from you! Okay?"

I figured that if I was in jail people were going to assume I was the kind of colored person who ends up in jail, a violent criminal. So I played it up. I put on this character; I played the stereotype. Anytime the cops asked me questions I started speaking in broken Afrikaans with a thick colored accent. Imagine a white guy in America, just dark enough to pass for Latino, walking around jail doing bad Mexican-gangster dialogue from the movies. *"Shit's about to get loco,* ese." That's basically what I was doing—the South African version of that. This was my brilliant plan to survive incarceration. But it worked. The guys in the cell with me, they were there for drunk driving, for domestic abuse, for petty theft. They had no idea what real colored gangsters were like. Everyone left me alone.

We were all playing a game, only nobody knew we were playing it. When I walked in that first night, everyone was giving me this look: "I'm dangerous. Don't fuck with me." So I went, "Shit, these people are hardened criminals. I shouldn't be here, because I am not a criminal." Then the next day everything turned over quickly. One by one, guys left to go to their hearings, I stayed to wait for my lawyer, and new people started to pitch up. Now I was the veteran, doing my colored-gangster routine, giving the new guys the same look: "I'm dangerous. Don't fuck with me." And they looked at me and went, "Shit, he's a hardened criminal. I shouldn't be here, because I am not like him." And round and round we went.

At a certain point it occurred to me that every single person in that cell might be faking it. We were all decent guys from nice neighborhoods and good families, picked up for unpaid parking tickets and other infractions. We could have been having a great time sharing meals, playing cards, and talking about women and soccer. But that didn't happen, because everyone had adopted this dangerous pose and nobody talked because everyone was afraid of who the other guys were pretending to be. Now those guys were going to get out and go home to their families and say, "Oh, honey, that was rough. Those were some real criminals in there. There was this one colored guy. Man, he was a killer."

Once I had the game sorted out, I was good again. I relaxed. I was back to thinking, *I got this. This is no big deal.* The food was actually decent. For breakfast they brought you these peanut butter sandwiches on thick slices of bread. Lunch was chicken and rice. The tea was too hot, and it was more water than tea, but it was drinkable. There were older, hard-time prisoners close to parole, and their detail was to come and clean the cells and circulate books and magazines for you to read. It was quite relaxing.

There was one point when I remember eating a meal and saying to myself, *This isn't so bad. I hang around with a bunch of dudes. There's no chores. No bills to pay. No one constantly nagging me and telling me what to do. Peanut butter sandwiches? Shit, I eat peanut butter sandwiches all the time. This is pretty sweet. I could do this.* I was so afraid of the ass-whooping waiting for me at home that I genuinely considered going to prison. For a brief moment I thought I had a plan. "I'll go away for a couple of years, come back, and say I was kidnapped, and mom will never know and she'll just be happy to see me."

On the third day, the cops brought in the largest man I'd ever seen. This guy was *huge*. Giant muscles. Dark skin. Hardened face. He looked like he could kill all of us. Me and the other prisoners who'd been acting tough with one another—the second he walked in our tough-guy routines were over. Everyone was terrified. We all stared at him. "Oh, fuck . . ."

For whatever reason this guy was half naked when the cops picked him up. He was wearing clothes the police had scrounged up for him at the station, this torn-up wifebeater that was way too small, pants so short on him they looked like capris. He looked like a black version of the Incredible Hulk.

This guy went and sat alone in the corner. Nobody said a word. Everyone watched and waited, nervously, to see what he would do. Then one of the cops came back and called the Hulk over; they needed information from him. The cop started asking him a bunch of questions, but the guy kept shaking his head and saying he didn't understand. The cop was speaking Zulu. The Hulk was speaking Tsonga. Black person to black person, and neither could understand the other— the Tower of Babel. Few people in South Africa speak Tsonga, but since my stepfather was Tsonga I had picked it up along the way. I overheard the cop and the other guy going back and forth with nothing getting across, so I stepped in and translated for them and sorted everything out.

Nelson Mandela once said, "If you talk to a man in a language he understands, that goes to his head. If you talk to him in his language, that goes to his heart." He was so right. When you make the effort to speak someone else's language, even if it's just basic phrases here and there, you are saying to them, "I understand that you have a culture and identity that exists beyond me. I see you as a human being."

That is exactly what happened with the Hulk. The second I spoke to him, this face that had seemed so threatening and mean lit up with gratitude. *"Ah, na khensa, na khensa, na khensa. Hi wena mani? Mufana wa mukhaladi u xitiela kwini xiTsonga? U huma kwini?"* "Oh, thank you, thank you, thank you. Who are you? How does a colored guy know Tsonga? Where are you from?"

Once we started talking I realized he wasn't the Hulk at all. He was the sweetest man, a gentle giant, the biggest teddy bear in the world. He was simple, not educated. I'd assumed he was in for murder, for squashing a family to death with his bare hands, but it wasn't anything like that. He'd been arrested for shoplifting PlayStation games. He was out of work and needed money to send to his family back home, and when he saw how much these games sold for he thought he could steal a few and sell them to white kids and make a lot of money. As soon as he told me that, I knew he wasn't some hardened criminal. I know the world of pirated things—stolen videogames have no value because it's cheaper and less risky to copy them, like Bolo's parents did.

I tried to help him out a bit. I told him my trick of putting off your bail hearing to get your defense together, so he stayed in the cell, too, biding his time, and we hit it off and hung out for a few days, having a good time, getting to know each other. No one else in the cell knew what to make of us, the ruthless colored gangster and his menacing, Hulk-like friend. He told me his story, a South African story that was all too familiar to me: The man grows up under apartheid, working on a farm, part of what's essentially a slave labor force. It's a living hell but it's at least something. He's paid a pittance but at least he's paid. He's told where to be and what to do every waking minute of his day. Then apartheid ends and he doesn't even have that anymore. He finds his way to Johannesburg, looking for work, trying to feed his children back home. But he's lost. He has no education. He has no skills. He doesn't know what to do, doesn't know where to be. The world has been taught to be scared of him, but the reality is that he is scared of the world because he has none of the tools necessary to cope with it. So what does he do? He takes shit. He becomes a petty thief. He's in and out of jail. He gets lucky and finds some construction work, but then he gets laid off from that, and a few days later he's in a shop and he sees some Play-Station games and he grabs them, but he doesn't even know enough to know that he's stolen something of no value.

I felt terrible for him. The more time I spent in jail, the more I realized that the law isn't rational at all. It's a lottery. What color is your skin? How much money do you have? Who's your lawyer? Who's the judge? Shoplifting PlayStation games was less of an offense than driving with bad number plates. He had committed a crime, but he was no more a criminal than I was. The difference was that he didn't have any friends or family to help him out. He couldn't afford anything but a state attorney. He was going to go stand in the dock, unable to speak or understand English, and everyone in the courtroom was going to assume the worst of him. He was going to go to prison for a while and then be set free with the same nothing he had going in. If I had to guess, he was around thirty-five, forty years old, staring down another thirty-five, forty years of the same.

The day of my hearing came. I said goodbye to my new friend and wished him the best. Then I was handcuffed and put in the back of a police van and driven to the courthouse to meet my fate. In South African courts, to minimize your exposure and your opportunities for escape, the holding cell where you await your hearing is a massive pen below the courtroom; you walk up a set of stairs into the dock rather than being escorted through the corridors. What happens in the holding cell is you're mixed in with the people who've been in prison awaiting trial for weeks and months. It's a weird mix, everything from white-collar criminals to guys picked up on traffic stops to real, hardcore criminals covered with prison tattoos. It's like the cantina scene from *Star Wars*, where the band's playing music and Han Solo's in the corner and all of the bad guys and bounty hunters from all over the universe are hanging out—a wretched hive of scum and villainy, only there's no music and there's no Han Solo.

I was with these people for only a brief window of time, but in that moment I saw the difference between prison and jail. I saw the difference between criminals and people who've committed crimes. I saw the hardness in people's faces. I thought back on how naive I'd been just hours before, thinking jail wasn't so bad and I could handle it. I was now truly afraid of what might happen to me.

When I walked into that holding pen, I was a smooth-skinned, fresh-faced young man. At the time, I had a giant Afro, and the only way to control it was to have it tied back in this ponytail thing that looked really girly. I looked like Maxwell. The guards closed the door behind me, and this creepy old dude yelled out in Zulu from the back, *"Ha, ha, ha! Hhe madoda! Angikaze ngibone indoda enhle kangaka! Sizoba nobusuku obuhle!"* "Yo, yo, yo! Damn, guys. I've never seen a man this beautiful before. It's gonna be a good night tonight!"

Fuuuuuuuuuuck.

Right next to me as I walked in was a young man having a complete meltdown, talking to himself, bawling his eyes out. He looked up and locked eyes with me, and I guess he thought I looked like a kindred soul he could talk to. He came straight at me and started crying about how he'd been arrested and thrown in jail and the gangs had stolen his clothes and his shoes and raped him and beat him every day. He wasn't some ruffian. He was well-spoken, educated. He'd been waiting for a year for his case to be heard; he wanted to kill himself. That guy put the fear of God in me.

I looked around the holding cell. There were easily a hundred guys in there, all of them spread out and huddled into their clearly and unmistakably defined racial groups: a whole bunch of black people in one corner, the colored people in a different corner, a couple of Indians off to themselves, and a handful of white guys off to one side. The guys who'd been with me in the police van, the second we walked in, they instinctively, automatically, walked off to join the groups they belonged to. I froze.

I didn't know where to go.

I looked over at the colored corner. I was staring at the most notorious, most violent prison gang in South Africa. I looked like them, but

I wasn't them. I couldn't go over there doing my fake gangster shit and have them discover I was a fraud. No, no, no. That game was over, my friend. The last thing I needed was colored gangsters up against me.

But then what if I went to the black corner? I know that I'm black and I identify as black, but I'm not a black person on the face of it, so would the black guys understand why I was walking over? And what kind of shit would I start by going there? Because going to the black corner as a perceived colored person might piss off the colored gangs even more than going to the colored corner as a fake colored person. Because that's what had happened to me my entire life. Colored people would see me hanging out with blacks, and they'd confront me, want to fight me. I saw myself starting a race war in the holding cell.

"Hey! Why are you hanging out with the blacks?"

"Because I am black."

"No, you're not. You're colored."

"Ah, yes. I know it looks that way, friend, but let me explain. It's a funny story, actually. My father is white and my mother is black and race is a social construct, so . . ."

That wasn't going to work. Not here.

All of this was happening in my head in an instant, on the fly. I was doing crazy calculations, looking at people, scanning the room, assessing the variables. *If I go here, then this. If I go there, then that.* My whole life was flashing before me—the playground at school, the *spaza* shops in Soweto, the streets of Eden Park—every time and every place I ever had to be a chameleon, navigate between groups, explain who I was. It was like the high school cafeteria, only it was the high school cafeteria from hell because if I picked the wrong table I might get beaten or stabbed or raped. I'd never been more scared in my life. But I still had to pick. Because racism exists, and you have to pick a side. You can say that you don't pick sides, but eventually life will force you to pick a side.

That day I picked white. They just didn't look like they could hurt me. It was a handful of average, middle-aged white dudes. I walked over to them. We hung out for a while, chatted a bit. They were mostly in for white-collar crimes, money schemes, fraud and racketeering. They'd be useless if anyone came over looking to start trouble; they'd get their asses kicked as well. But they weren't going to do anything to me. I was safe.

Luckily the time went by fairly quickly. I was in there for only an hour before I was called up to court, where a judge would either let me go or send me to prison to await trial. As I was leaving, one of the white guys reached over to me. "Make sure you don't come back down here," he said. "Cry in front of the judge; do whatever you have to do. If you go up and get sent back down here, your life will never be the same."

Up in the courtroom, I found my lawyer waiting. My cousin Mlungisi was there, too, in the gallery, ready to post my bail if things went my way.

The bailiff read out my case number, and the judge looked up at me. "How are you?" he said.

I broke down. I'd been putting on this tough-guy facade for nearly a week, and I just couldn't do it anymore.

"I–I'm not fine, Your Honor. I'm not fine."

He looked confused. "What?!"

I said, "I'm not fine, sir. I'm really suffering."

"Why are you telling me this?"

"Because you asked how I was."

"Who asked you?"

"You did. You just asked me."

"I didn't say, 'How are you?' I said, 'Who are you?' Why would I waste time asking 'How are you?'! This is jail. I know everyone is suffering down there. If I asked everyone 'How are you?' we'd be here all day. I said, 'Who are you?' State your name for the record."

"Trevor Noah."

"Okay. Now we can carry on."

The whole courtroom started laughing, so then I started laughing, too. But now I was even more petrified because I didn't want the judge to think I wasn't taking him seriously because I was laughing.

It turned out that I needn't have been worried. Everything that happened next took only a few minutes. My lawyer had talked to the prosecutor and everything had been arranged beforehand. He presented my case. I had no priors. I wasn't dangerous. There were no objections from the opposing side. The judge assigned my trial date and set my bail, and I was free to go.

I walked out of court and the light of day hit my face and I said, "Sweet *Jesus*, I am never going back there again." It had been only a week, in a cell that wasn't terribly uncomfortable with food that wasn't half bad, but a week in jail is a long, long time. A week without shoelaces is a long, long time. A week with no clocks, with no sun, can feel like an eternity. The thought of anything worse, the thought of doing real time in a real prison, I couldn't even imagine.

I drove with Mlungisi to his place, took a shower, and slept there. The next day he dropped me back at my mom's house. I strolled up the driveway acting real casual. My plan was to say I'd been crashing with Mlungisi for a few days. I walked into the house like nothing had happened. "Hey, Mom! What's up?" Mom didn't say anything, didn't ask me any questions. I was like, *Okay. Cool. We're good.*

I stayed for most of the day. Later in the afternoon we were sitting at the kitchen table, talking. I was telling all these stories, going on about everything Mlungisi and I had been up to that week, and I caught my mom giving me this look, slowly shaking her head. It was a different look than I had ever seen her give before. It wasn't "One day, I'm going to catch you." It wasn't anger or disapproval. It was disappointment. She was hurt.

"What?" I said. "What is it?"

She said, "Boy, who do you think paid your bail? Hmm? Who do you think paid your lawyer? Do you think I'm an idiot? Did you think no one would tell me?"

The truth came spilling out. Of course she'd known: the car. It had been missing the whole time. I'd been so wrapped up in dealing with jail and covering my tracks I'd forgotten that the proof of my crime was right there in the yard, the red Mazda missing from the driveway. And of course when I called my friend and he'd asked his dad for the money for the lawyer, the dad had pressed him on what the money was for and, being a parent himself, had called my mother immediately. She'd given my friend the money to pay the lawyer. She'd given my cousin the money to pay my bail. I'd spent the whole week in jail thinking I was so slick. But she'd known everything the whole time.

"I know you see me as some crazy old bitch nagging at you," she said, "but you forget the reason I ride you so hard and give you so much shit is because I love you. Everything I have ever done I've done from a place of love. If I don't punish you, the world will punish you even worse. The world doesn't love you. If the police get you, the police don't love you. When I beat you, I'm trying to save you. When they beat you, they're trying to kill you."

———————

My favorite thing to eat as a kid, and still my favorite dessert of all time, was custard and jelly, what Americans would call Jell-O. One Saturday my mom was planning for a big family celebration and she made a huge bowl of custard and jelly and put it in the fridge. It had every flavor: red, green, and yellow. I couldn't resist it. That whole day, every time I walked past the fridge I'd pop my head in with a spoon and sneak a bite. This was a giant bowl, meant to last for a week for the whole family. I finished it in one day by myself.

That night I went to bed and I got absolutely butchered by mosquitoes. Mosquitoes love to feast on me, and when I was a kid it was bad. They would destroy me at night. I would wake up covered with bites and feel ill to my stomach and itchy all over. Which was exactly what happened this particular Sunday morning. Covered with mosquito bites, my stomach bloated with custard and jelly, I could barely get out of bed. I felt like I was going to vomit. Then my mom walked in.

"Get dressed," she said. "We're going to church."

"I don't feel well."

"That's why we're going to church. That's where Jesus is going to heal you."

"Eh, I'm not sure that's how it works."

My mom and I had different ideas about how Jesus worked. She believed that you pray to Jesus and then Jesus pitches up and does the thing that you need. My views on Jesus were more reality-based.

"Why don't I take medicine," I said, "and then pray to Jesus to thank him for giving us the doctors who invented medicine, because medicine is what makes you feel better, not Jesus."

"You don't need medicine if you have Jesus. Jesus will heal you. Pray to Jesus."

"But is medicine not a blessing from Jesus? And if Jesus gives us medicine and we do not take the medicine, are we not denying the grace that he has given us?"

Like all of our debates about Jesus, this conversation went nowhere.

"Trevor," she said, "if you don't go to church you're going to get worse. You're lucky you got sick on Sunday, because now we're going to church and you can pray to Jesus and Jesus is going to heal you."

"That sounds nice, but why don't I just stay home?"

"No. Get dressed. We're going to church."

———

18

MY MOTHER'S LIFE

Once I had my hair cornrowed for the matric dance, I started getting attention from girls for the first time. I actually went on dates. At times I thought that it was because I looked better. At other times I thought it was because girls liked the fact that I was going through as much pain as they did to look good. Either way, once I found success, I wasn't going to mess with the formula. I kept going back to the salon every week, spending hours at a time getting my hair straightened and cornrowed. My mom would just roll her eyes. "I could never date a man who spends more time on his hair than I do," she'd say.

Monday through Saturday my mom worked in her office and puttered around her garden dressed like a homeless person. Then Sunday morning for church she'd do her hair and put on a nice dress and some high heels and she looked like a million bucks. Once she was all done up, she couldn't resist teasing me, throwing little verbal jabs the way we'd always do with each other.

"Now who's the best-looking person in the family, eh? I hope you enjoyed your week of being the pretty one, 'cause the queen is back, baby. You spent four hours at the salon to look like that. I just took a shower."

She was just having fun with me; no son wants to talk about how hot his mom is. Because, truth be told, she was beautiful. Beautiful on the outside, beautiful on the inside. She had a self-confidence about her that I never possessed. Even when she was working in the garden, dressed in overalls and covered in mud, you could see how attractive she was.

I can only assume that my mother broke more than a few hearts in her day, but from the time I was born, there were only two men in her life, my father and my stepfather. Right around the corner from my father's house in Yeoville, there was a garage called Mighty Mechanics. Our Volkswagen was always breaking down, and my mom would take it there to get it repaired. We met this really cool guy there, Abel, one of the auto mechanics. I'd see him when we went to fetch the car. The car broke down a lot, so we were there a lot. Eventually it felt like we were there even when there was nothing wrong with the vehicle. I was six, maybe seven. I didn't understand everything that was happening. I just knew that suddenly this guy was around. He was tall, lanky and lean but strong. He had these long arms and big hands. He could lift car engines and gearboxes. He was handsome, but he wasn't good-looking. My mom liked that about him; she used to say there's a type of ugly that women find attractive. She called him Abie. He called her Mbuyi, short for Nombuyiselo.

I liked him, too. Abie was charming and hilarious and had an easy, gracious smile. He loved helping people, too, especially anyone in distress. If someone's car broke down on the freeway, he pulled over to see what he could do. If someone yelled "Stop, thief!" he was the guy who gave chase. The old lady next door needed help moving boxes? He's that guy. He liked to be liked by the world, which made his abuse even harder to deal with. Because if you think someone is a monster and the whole world says he's a saint, you begin to think that you're the bad person. *It must be my fault this is happening* is the only conclusion you can draw, because why are you the only one receiving his wrath?

Abel was always cool with me. He wasn't trying to be my dad, and my dad was still in my life, so I wasn't looking for anyone to replace him. *That's mom's cool friend* is how I thought of him. He started coming out to stay with us in Eden Park. Some nights he'd want us to crash with him at his converted garage flat in Orange Grove, which we did. Then I burned down the white people's house, and that was the end of that. From then on we lived together in Eden Park.

One night my mom and I were at a prayer meeting and she took me aside.

"Hey," she said. "I want to tell you something. Abel and I are going to get married."

Instinctively, without even thinking, I said, "I don't think that's a good idea."

I wasn't upset or anything. I just had a sense about the guy, an intuition. I'd felt it even before the mulberry tree. That night hadn't changed my feelings toward Abel; it had only shown me, in flesh and blood, what he was capable of.

"I understand that it's hard," she said. "I understand that you don't want a new dad."

"No," I said. "It's not that. I like Abel. I like him a lot. But you shouldn't marry him." I didn't know the word "sinister" then, but if I had I probably would have used it. "There's just something not right about him. I don't trust him. I don't think he's a good person."

I'd always been fine with my mom dating this guy, but I'd never considered the possibility of him becoming a permanent addition to our family. I enjoyed being with Abel the same way I enjoyed playing with a tiger cub the first time I went to a tiger sanctuary: I liked it, I had fun with it, but I never thought about bringing it home.

If there was any doubt about Abel, the truth was right there in front of us all along, in his name. He was Abel, the good brother, the good son, a name straight out of the Bible. And he lived up to it as well. He was the firstborn, dutiful, took care of his mother, took care of his siblings. He was the pride of his family.

But Abel was his English name. His Tsonga name was Ngisaveni. It means "Be afraid."

Mom and Abel got married. There was no ceremony, no exchange of rings. They went and signed the papers and that was it. A year or so later, my baby brother, Andrew, was born. I only vaguely remember my mom being gone for a few days, and when she got back there was now this thing in the house that cried and shat and got fed, but when you're nine years older than your sibling, their arrival doesn't change much for you. I wasn't changing diapers; I was out playing arcade games at the shop, running around the neighborhood.

The main thing that marked Andrew's birth for me was our first trip to meet Abel's family during the Christmas holidays. They lived in Tzaneen, a town in Gazankulu, what had been the Tsonga homeland under apartheid. Tzaneen has a tropical climate, hot and humid. The white farms nearby grow some of the most amazing fruit—mangoes, lychees, the most beautiful bananas you've ever seen in your life. That's where all the fruit we export to Europe comes from. But on the black land twenty minutes down the road, the soil has been decimated by years of overfarming and overgrazing. Abel's mother and his sisters were all traditional, stay-at-home moms, and Abel and his younger brother, who was a policeman, supported the family. They were all very kind and generous and accepted us as part of the family right away.

Tsonga culture, I learned, is extremely patriarchal. We're talking about a world where women must bow when they greet a man. Men and women have limited social interactions. The men kill the animals, and the women cook the food. Men are not even allowed in the kitchen. As a nine-year-old boy, I thought this was fantastic. I wasn't allowed to do anything. At home my mom was forever making me do chores—wash the dishes, sweep the house—but when she tried to do that in Tzaneen, the women wouldn't allow it.

"Trevor, make your bed," my mom would say.

"No, no, no, no," Abel's mother would protest. "Trevor must go outside and play."

I was made to run off and have fun while my girl step-cousins had to clean the house and help the women cook. I was in heaven.

My mother loathed every moment of being there. For Abel, a first-born son who was bringing home his own firstborn son, this trip was a huge deal. In the homelands, the firstborn son almost becomes the father/husband by default because the dad is off working in the city. The firstborn son is the man of the house. He raises his siblings. His mom treats him with a certain level of respect as the dad's surrogate. Since this was Abel's big homecoming with Andrew, he expected my mother to play her traditional role, too. But she refused.

The women in Tzaneen had a multitude of jobs during the day. They prepared breakfast, prepared tea, prepared lunch, did the washing and the cleaning. The men had been working all year in the city to support the family, so this was their vacation, more or less. They were at leisure, waited on by the women. They might slaughter a goat or something, do whatever manly tasks needed to be done, but then they would go to an area that was only for men and hang out and drink while the women cooked and cleaned. But my mom had been working in the city all year, too, and Patricia Noah didn't stay in anyone's kitchen. She was a free-roaming spirit. She insisted on walking to the village, going where the men hung out, talking to the men as equals.

The whole tradition of women bowing to the men, my mom found that absurd. But she didn't refuse to do it. She overdid it. She made a mockery of it. The other women would bow before men with this po-lite little curtsy. My mom would go down and cower, groveling in the dirt like she was worshipping a deity, and she'd stay down there for a long time, like a *really* long time, long enough to make everyone very uncomfortable. That was my mom. Don't fight the system. Mock the system. To Abel, it looked like his wife didn't respect him. Every other man had some docile girl from the village, and here he'd come with this modern woman, a Xhosa woman no less, a culture whose women were thought of as particularly loudmouthed and promiscuous. The two of them fought and bickered the whole time, and after that first trip my mother refused to go back.

Up to that point I'd lived my whole life in a world run by women, but after my mom and Abel were married, and especially after Andrew was born, I watched him try to assert himself and impose his ideas of what he thought his family should be. One thing that became clear early on was that those ideas did not include me. I was a reminder that my mom had lived a life before him. I didn't even share his color. His family was him, my mom, and the new baby. My family was my mom and me. I actually appreciated that about him. Sometimes he was my buddy, sometimes not, but he never pretended our relationship was anything other than what it was. We'd joke around and laugh together. We'd watch TV together. He'd slip me pocket money now and again after my mother said I'd had enough. But he never gave me a birthday present or a Christmas present. He never gave me the affection of a father. I was never his son.

Abel's presence in the house brought with it new rules. One of the first things he did was kick Fufi and Panther out of the house.

"No dogs in the house."

"But we've always had the dogs in the house."

"Not anymore. In an African home, dogs sleep outside. People sleep inside."

Putting the dogs in the yard was Abel's way of saying, "We're going to do things around here the way they're supposed to be done." When they were just dating, my mother was still the free spirit, doing what she wanted, going where she wanted. Slowly, those things got reined in. I could feel that he was trying to rein in our independence. He even got upset about church. "You cannot be at church the whole day," he'd say. "My wife is gone all day, and what will people say? 'Why is his wife not around? Where is she? Who goes to church for the whole day?' No, no, no. This brings disrespect to me."

He tried to stop her from spending so much time at church, and one of the most effective tools he used was to stop fixing my mother's car. It would break down, and he'd purposefully let it sit. My mom couldn't afford another car, and she couldn't get the car fixed somewhere else. You're married to a mechanic and you're going to get your car fixed by another mechanic? That's worse than cheating. So Abel became our only transport, and he would refuse to take us places. Ever defiant, my mother would take minibuses to get to church.

Losing the car also meant losing access to my dad. We had to ask Abel for rides into town, and he didn't like what they were for. It was an insult to his manhood.

"We need to go to Yeoville."

"Why are you going to Yeoville?"

"To see Trevor's dad."

"What? No, no. How can I take my wife and her child and drop you off there? You're insulting me. What do I tell my friends? What do I tell my family? My wife is at another man's house? The man who made that child with her? No, no, no."

I saw my father less and less. Not long after, he moved down to Cape Town.

Abel wanted a traditional marriage with a traditional wife. For a long time I wondered why he ever married a woman like my mom in the first place, as she was the opposite of that in every way. If he wanted a woman to bow to him, there were plenty of girls back in Tzaneen being raised solely for that purpose. The way my mother always explained it, the traditional man wants a woman to be subservient, but he never falls in love with subservient women. He's attracted to independent women. "He's like an exotic bird collector," she said. "He only wants a woman who is free because his dream is to put her in a cage."

When we first met Abel, he smoked a lot of weed. He drank, too, but it was mostly weed. Looking back, I almost miss his pothead days because the weed mellowed him out. He'd smoke, chill, watch TV, and fall asleep. I think subconsciously it was something he knew he needed to do to take the edge off his anger. He stopped smoking after he and my mom got married. She made him stop for religious reasons—the body is a temple and so on. But what none of us saw coming was that when he stopped smoking weed he just replaced it with alcohol. He started drinking more and more. He never came home from work sober. An average day was a six-pack of beer after work. Weeknights he'd have a buzz on. Some Fridays and Saturdays he just didn't come home.

When Abel drank, his eyes would go red, bloodshot. That was the clue I learned to read. I always thought of Abel as a cobra: calm, perfectly still, then explosive. There was no ranting and raving, no clenched fists. He'd be very quiet, and then out of nowhere the violence would come. The eyes were my only clue to stay away. His eyes were everything. They were the eyes of the Devil.

Late one night we woke up to a house filled with smoke. Abel hadn't come home by the time we'd gone to bed, and I'd fallen asleep in my mother's room with her and Andrew, who was still a baby. I jerked awake to her shaking me and screaming. *"Trevor! Trevor!"* There was smoke everywhere. We thought the house was burning down.

My mom ran down the hallway to the kitchen, where she discovered the kitchen on fire. Abel had driven home drunk, blind drunk, drunker than we'd ever seen him before. He'd been hungry, tried to heat up some food on the stove, and passed out on the couch while it was cooking. The pot had burned itself out and burned up the kitchen wall behind the stove, and smoke was billowing everywhere. She turned off the stove and opened the doors and the windows to try to air the place out. Then she went over to the couch and woke him up and started berating him for nearly burning the house down. He was too drunk to care.

She came back into the bedroom, picked up the phone, and called my grandmother. She started going on and on about Abel and his drinking. "This man, he's going to kill us one day. He almost burnt the house down . . ."

Abel walked into the bedroom, very calm, very quiet. His eyes were blood red, his eyelids heavy. He put his finger on the cradle and hung up the call. My mom lost it.

"How dare you! Don't you hang up my phone call! What do you think you're doing?!"

"You don't tell people what's happening in this house," he said.

"Oh, please! You're worried about what the world is thinking? Worry about this world! Worry about what your family is thinking!"

Abel towered over my mother. He didn't raise his voice, didn't get angry.

"Mbuyi," he said softly, "you don't respect me."

"Respect?! You almost burned down our house. Respect? Oh, please! Earn your respect! You want me to respect you as a man, then act like a man! Drinking your money in the streets, and where are your child's diapers?! Respect?! Earn your respect—"

"Mbuyi—"

"You're not a man; you're a child—"

"Mbuyi—"

"I can't have a child for a husband—"

"Mbuyi—"

"I've got my own children to raise—"

"Mbuyi, shut up—"

"A man who comes home drunk—"

"Mbuyi, shut up—"

"And burns down the house with his children—"

"Mbuyi, shut up—"

"And you call yourself a father—"

Then out of nowhere, like a clap of thunder when there were no clouds, *crack!*, he smacked her across the face. She ricocheted off the wall and collapsed like a ton of bricks. I'd never seen anything like it. She went down and stayed down for a good thirty seconds. Andrew started screaming. I don't remember going to pick him up, but I clearly remember holding him at some point. My mom pulled herself up and struggled back to her feet and launched right back into him. She'd clearly been knocked for a loop, but she was trying to act more with-it than she was. I could see the disbelief in her face. This had never happened to her before in her life. She got right back in his face and started shouting at him.

"Did you just hit me?"

The whole time, in my head, I kept thinking the same thing Abel was saying. *Shut up, Mom. Shut up. You're going to make it worse.* Because I knew, as the receiver of many beatings, the one thing that doesn't help is talking back. But she wouldn't stay quiet.

"Did you just hit me?"

"Mbuyi, I told you—"

"No man has ever! Don't think you can control me when you can't even control—"

Crack! He hit her again. She stumbled back but this time didn't fall. She scrambled, grabbed me, and grabbed Andrew.

"Let's go. We're leaving."

We ran out of the house and up the road. It was the dead of night, cold outside. I was wearing nothing but a T-shirt and sweatpants. We walked to the Eden Park police station, over a kilometer away. My mom marched us in, and there were two cops on duty at the front desk.

"I'm here to lay a charge," she said.

"What are you here to lay a charge about?"

"I'm here to lay a charge against the man who hit me."

To this day I'll never forget the patronizing, condescending way they spoke to her.

"Calm down, lady. Calm down. Who hit you?"

"My husband."

"Your husband? What did you do? Did you make him angry?"

"Did I . . . what? No. He hit me. I'm here to lay a charge against—"

"No, no. Ma'am. Why do you wanna make a case, eh? You sure you want to do this? Go home and talk to your husband. You do know once you lay charges you can't take them back? He'll have a criminal record. His life will never be the same. Do you really want your husband going to jail?"

My mom kept insisting that they take a statement and open a case, and they actually refused—they refused to write up a charge sheet.

"This is a family thing," they said. "You don't want to involve the police. Maybe you want to think it over and come back in the morning."

Mom started yelling at them, demanding to see the station commander, and right then Abel walked into the station. He'd driven down. He'd sobered up a bit, but he was still drunk, driving into a police station. That didn't matter. He walked over to the cops, and the station turned into a boys' club. Like they were a bunch of old pals.

"Hey, guys," he said. "You know how it is. You know how women can be. I just got a little angry, that's all."

"It's okay, man. We know. It happens. Don't worry."

I had never seen anything like it. I was nine years old, and I still thought of the police as the good guys. You get in trouble, you call the police, and those flashing red-and-blue lights are going to come and save you. But I remember standing there watching my mom, flabbergasted, horrified that these cops wouldn't help her. That's when I realized the police were not who I thought they were. They were men first, and police second.

We left the station. My mother took me and Andrew, and we went out to stay with my grandmother in Soweto for a while. A few weeks later, Abel drove over and apologized. Abel was always sincere and heartfelt with his apologies: He didn't mean it. He knows he was wrong. He'll never do it again. My grandmother convinced my mom that she should give Abel a second chance. Her argument was basically, "All men do it." My grandfather, Temperance, had hit her. Leaving Abel was no guarantee it wouldn't happen again, and at least Abel was willing to apologize. So my mom decided to give him another chance. We drove back to Eden Park together, and for years, nothing—for *years* Abel didn't lay a finger on her. Or me. Everything went back to the way it was.

Abel was an amazing mechanic, probably one of the best around at the time. He'd been to technical college, graduated first in his class. He'd had job offers from BMW and Mercedes. His business thrived on referrals. People would bring their cars from all over the city for him to fix because he could work miracles on them. My mom truly believed in him. She thought she could raise him up, help him make good on his potential, not merely as a mechanic but as the owner of his own workshop.

As headstrong and independent as my mom is, she remains the woman who gives back. She gives and gives and gives; that is her nature. She refused to be subservient to Abel at home, but she did want him to succeed as a man. If she could make their marriage a true marriage of equals, she was willing to pour herself into it completely, the same way she poured herself into her children. At some point, Abel's boss decided to sell Mighty Mechanics and retire. My mom had some money saved, and she helped Abel buy it. They moved the workshop from Yeoville to the industrial area of Wynberg, just west of Alex, and Mighty Mechanics became the new family business.

When you first go into business there are so many things nobody tells you. That's especially true when you're two young black people, a secretary and a mechanic, coming out of a time when blacks had never been allowed to own businesses at all. One of the things nobody tells you is that when you buy a business you buy its debt. After my mom and Abel opened up the books on Mighty Mechanics and came to a full realization of what they'd bought, they saw how much trouble the company was already in.

The garage gradually took over our lives. I'd get out of school and walk the five kilometers from Maryvale to the workshop. I'd sit for hours and try to do my homework with the machines and repairs going on around me. Inevitably Abel would get behind schedule on a car, and since he was our ride, we'd have to wait for him to finish before we could go home. It started out as "We're running late. Go nap in a car, and we'll tell you when we're leaving." I'd crawl in the backseat of some sedan, they'd wake me up at midnight, and we'd drive all the way back out to Eden Park and crash. Then pretty soon it was "We're running late. Go sleep in a car, and we'll wake you for school in the morning." We started sleeping at the garage. At first it was one or two nights a week, then three or four. Then my mom sold the house and put that money into the business as well. She went all in. She gave up everything for him.

From that point on we lived in the garage. It was a warehouse, basically, and not the fancy, romantic sort of warehouse hipsters might one day turn into lofts. No, no. It was a cold, empty space. Gray concrete floors stained with oil and grease, old junk cars and car parts everywhere. Near the front, next to the roller door that opened onto the street, there was a tiny office built out of drywall for doing paperwork and such. In the back was a kitchenette, just a sink, a portable hot plate, and some cabinets. To bathe, there was only an open wash basin, like a janitor's sink, with a showerhead rigged up above.

Abel and my mom slept with Andrew in the office on a thin mattress they'd roll out on the floor. I slept in the cars. I got really good at sleeping in cars. I know all the best cars to sleep in. The worst were the cheap ones, Volkswagens, low-end Japanese sedans. The seats barely reclined, no headrests, cheap fake-leather upholstery. I'd spend half the night trying not to slide off the seat. I'd wake up with sore knees because I couldn't stretch out and extend my legs. German cars were wonderful, especially Mercedes. Big, plush leather seats, like couches. They were cold when you first climbed in, but they were well insulated and warmed up nicely. All I needed was my school blazer to curl up under, and I could get really cozy inside a Mercedes. But the best, hands-down, were American cars. I used to pray for a customer to come in with a big Buick with bench seats. If I saw one of those, I'd be like, *Yes!* It was rare for American cars to come in, but when they did, boy, was I in heaven.

Since Mighty Mechanics was now a family business, and I was family, I also had to work. There was no more time for play. There wasn't even time for homework. I'd walk home, the school uniform would come off, the overalls would go on, and I'd get under the hood of some sedan. I got to a point where I could do a basic service on a car by myself, and often I did. Abel would say, "That Honda. Minor service." And I'd get under the hood. Day in and day out. Points, plugs, condensers, oil filters, air filters. Install new seats, change tires, swap headlights, fix taillights. Go to the parts shop, buy the parts, back to the workshop. Eleven years old, and that was my life. I was falling behind in school. I wasn't getting anything done. My teachers used to come down on me.

"Why aren't you doing your homework?"

"I can't do my homework. I have work, at home."

We worked and worked and worked, but no matter how many hours we put in, the business kept losing money. We lost everything. We couldn't even afford real food. There was one month I'll never forget, the worst month of my life. We were so broke that for weeks we ate nothing but bowls of *marogo*, a kind of wild spinach, cooked with caterpillars. Mopane worms, they're called. Mopane worms are literally the cheapest thing that only the poorest of poor people eat. I grew up poor, but there's poor and then there's "Wait, I'm eating worms." Mopane worms are the sort of thing where even people in Soweto would be like, "Eh . . . no." They're these spiny, brightly colored caterpillars the size of your finger. They're nothing like escargot, where someone took a snail and gave it a fancy name. They're fucking worms. They have black spines that prick the roof of your mouth as you're eating them. When you bite into a mopane worm, it's not uncommon for its yellow-green excrement to squirt into your mouth.

For a while I sort of enjoyed the caterpillars. It was like a food adventure, but then over the course of weeks, eating them every day, day after day, I couldn't take it anymore. I'll never forget the day I bit a mopane worm in half and that yellow-green ooze came out and I thought, "I'm eating caterpillar shit." Instantly I wanted to throw up. I snapped and ran to my mom crying. "I don't want to eat caterpillars anymore!" That night she scraped some money together and bought us chicken. As poor as we'd been in the past, we'd never been without food.

That was the period of my life I hated the most—work all night, sleep in some car, wake up, wash up in a janitor's sink, brush my teeth in a little metal basin, brush my hair in the rearview mirror of a Toyota, then try to get dressed without getting oil and grease all over my school clothes so the kids at school won't know I live in a garage. Oh, I hated it so much. I hated cars. I hated sleeping in cars. I hated working on cars. I hated getting my hands dirty. I hated eating worms. I hated it all.

I didn't hate my mom, or even Abel, funnily enough. Because I saw how hard everyone was working. At first I didn't know about the mistakes being made on the business level that were making it hard, so it just felt like a hard situation. But eventually I started to see why the business was hemorrhaging money. I used to go around and buy auto parts for Abel, and I learned that he was buying his parts on credit. The vendors were charging him a crazy markup. The debt was crippling the company, and instead of paying off the debt he was drinking what little cash he made. Brilliant mechanic, horrible businessman.

At a certain point, in order to try to save the garage, my mother quit her job at ICI and stepped in to help him run the workshop. She brought her office skills to the garage full-time and started keeping the books, making the schedule, balancing the accounts. And it was going well, until Abel started to feel like she was running his business. People started commenting on it as well. Clients were getting their cars on time, vendors were getting paid on time, and they would say, "Hey, Abie, this workshop is going so much better now that your wife has taken over." That didn't help.

We lived in the workshop for close to a year, and then my mom had had enough. She was willing to help him, but not if he was going to drink all the profits. She had always been independent, self-sufficient, but she'd lost that part of herself at the mercy of someone else's failed dream. At a certain point she said, "I can't do this anymore. I'm out of this. I'm done." She went out and got a job as a secretary with a real-estate developer, and somehow, between that and borrowing against whatever equity was left in Abel's workshop, she was able to get us the house in Highlands North. We moved, the workshop was seized by Abel's creditors, and that was the end of that.

Growing up I suffered no shortage of my mother's old school, Old Testament discipline. She spared no rod and spoiled no child. With Andrew, she was different. He got spankings at first, but they tapered off and eventually went away. When I asked her why I got beatings and Andrew didn't, she made a joke about it like she does with everything. "I beat you like that because you could take it," she said. "I can't hit your little brother the same way because he's a skinny little stick. He'll break. But you, God gave you that ass for whipping." Even though she was kidding, I could tell that the reason she didn't beat Andrew was because she'd had a genuine change of heart on the matter. It was a lesson she'd learned, oddly enough, from me.

I grew up in a world of violence, but I myself was never violent at all. Yes, I played pranks and set fires and broke windows, but I never attacked people. I never hit anyone. I was never angry. I just didn't see myself that way. My mother had exposed me to a different world than the one she grew up in. She bought me the books she never got to read. She took me to the schools that she never got to go to. I immersed myself in those worlds and I came back looking at the world a different way. I saw that not all families are violent. I saw the futility of violence, the cycle that just repeats itself, the damage that's inflicted on people that they in turn inflict on others.

I saw, more than anything, that relationships are not sustained by violence but by love. Love is a creative act. When you love someone you create a new world for them. My mother did that for me, and with the progress I made and the things I learned, I came back and created a new world and a new understanding for her. After that, she never raised her hand to her children again. Unfortunately, by the time she stopped, Abel had started.

In all the times I received beatings from my mom, I was never scared of her. I didn't like it, certainly. When she said, "I hit you out of love," I didn't necessarily agree with her thinking. But I understood that it was discipline and it was being done for a purpose. The first time Abel hit me I felt something I had never felt before. I felt terror.

I was in grade six, my last year at Maryvale. We'd moved to Highlands North, and I'd gotten in trouble at school for forging my mom's signature on some document; there was some activity I didn't want to participate in, so I'd signed the release in her name to get out of it. The school called my mom, and she asked me about it when I got home that afternoon. I was certain she was going to punish me, but this turned out to be one of those times when she didn't care. She said I should have just asked her; she would have signed the form anyway. Then Abel, who'd been sitting in the kitchen with us, watching the whole thing, said, "Hey, can I talk to you for a second?" Then he took me into this tiny room, a walk-in pantry off the kitchen, and he closed the door behind us.

He was standing between me and the door, but I didn't think anything of it. It didn't occur to me to be scared. Abel had never tried to discipline me before. He'd never even given me a lecture. It was always "Mbuyi, your son did this," and then my mother would handle it. And this was the middle of the afternoon. He was completely sober, which made what happened next all the more terrifying.

"Why did you forge your mother's signature?" he said.

I started making up some excuse. "Oh, I, uh, forgot to bring the form home—"

"Don't lie to me. Why did you forge your mom's signature?"

I started stammering out more bullshit, oblivious to what was coming, and then out of nowhere it came.

The first blow hit me in the ribs. My mind flashed: *It's a trap!* I'd never been in a fight before, had never learned how to fight, but I had this instinct that told me to get in close. I had seen what those long arms could do. I'd seen him take down my mom, but more important, I'd seen him take down grown men. Abel never hit people with a punch; I never saw him punch another person with a closed fist. But he had this ability to hit a grown man across his face with an open hand and they'd crumple. He was that strong. I looked at his arms and I knew, *Don't be on the other end of those things*. I ducked in close and he kept hitting and hitting, but I was in too tight for him to land any solid blows. Then he caught on and he stopped hitting and started trying to grapple and wrestle me. He did this thing where he grabbed the skin on my arms and pinched it between his thumb and forefinger and twisted hard. Jesus, that hurt.

It was the most terrifying moment of my life. I had never been that scared before, ever. Because there was no purpose to it—that's what made it so terrifying. It wasn't discipline. Nothing about it was coming from a place of love. It didn't feel like something that would end with me learning a lesson about forging my mom's signature. It felt like something that would end when he wanted it to end, when his rage was spent. It felt like there was something inside him that wanted to destroy me.

Abel was much bigger and stronger than me, but being in a confined space was to my advantage because he didn't have the room to maneuver. As he grappled and punched I somehow managed to twist and wriggle my way around him and slip out the door. I was quick, but Abel was quick as well. He chased me. I ran out of the house and jumped over the gate, and I ran and I ran and I ran. The last time I turned around he was rounding the gate, coming out of the yard after me. Until I turned twenty-five years old, I had a recurring nightmare of the look on his face as he came around that corner.

The moment I saw him I put my head down and ran. I ran like the Devil was chasing me. Abel was bigger and faster, but this was my neighborhood. You couldn't catch me in my neighborhood. I knew every alley and every street, every wall to climb over, every fence to slip through. I was ducking through traffic, cutting through yards. I have no idea when he gave up because I never looked back. I ran and ran and ran, as far as my legs would carry me. I was in Bramley, three neighborhoods away, before I stopped. I found a hiding place in some bushes and crawled inside and huddled there for what felt like hours.

You don't have to teach me a lesson twice. From that day until the day I left home, I lived like a mouse in that house. If Abel was in a room, I was out of the room. If he was in one corner, I was in the other corner. If he walked into a room, I would get up and act like I was going to the kitchen, then when I reentered the room, I would make sure I was close to the exit. He could be in the happiest, friendliest mood. Didn't matter. Never again did I let him come between me and a door. Maybe a couple of times after that I was sloppy and he'd land a punch or a kick before I could get away, but I never trusted him again, not for a moment.

It was different for Andrew. Andrew was Abel's son, flesh of his flesh, blood of his blood. Despite being nine years younger than me,

Andrew was really the eldest son in that house, Abel's firstborn, and that accorded him a respect that I and even my mother never enjoyed. And Andrew had nothing but love for that man, despite his shortcomings. Because of that love, I think, out of all of us, Andrew was the only one who wasn't afraid. He was the lion tamer, only he'd been raised by the lion—he couldn't love the beast any less despite knowing what it was capable of. For me, the first glint of anger or madness from Abel and I was gone. Andrew would stay and try to talk Abel down. He'd even get between Abel and Mom. I remember one night when Abel threw a bottle of Jack Daniel's at Andrew's head. It just missed him and exploded on the wall. Which is to say that Andrew stayed long enough to get the bottle thrown at him. I wouldn't have stuck around long enough for Abel to get a bead on me.

When Mighty Mechanics went under, Abel had to get his cars out. Someone was taking over the property; there were liens against his assets. It was a mess. That's when he started running his workshop out of our yard. It's also when my mother divorced him.

In African culture there's legal marriage and traditional marriage. Just because you divorce someone legally doesn't mean they are no longer your spouse. Once Abel's debts and his terrible business decisions started impacting my mother's credit and her ability to support her sons, she wanted out. "I don't have debts," she said. "I don't have bad credit. I'm not doing these things with you." We were still a family and they were still traditionally married, but she divorced him in order to separate their financial affairs. She also took her name back.

Because Abel had started running an unlicensed business in a residential area, one of the neighbors filed a petition to get rid of us. My mom applied for a license to be able to operate a business on the property. The workshop stayed, but Abel kept running it into the ground, drinking his money. At the same time, my mother started moving up at the real-estate company she worked for, taking on more responsibilities and earning a better salary. His workshop became like a side hobby almost. He was supposed to pay for Andrew's school fees and groceries, but he started falling behind even on that, and soon my mom was paying for everything. She paid the electricity. She paid the mortgage. He literally contributed nothing.

That was the turning point. When my mother started making more money and getting her independence back—that's when we saw the dragon emerge. The drinking got worse. He grew more and more violent. It wasn't long after coming for me in the pantry that Abel hit my mom for the second time. I can't recall the details of it, because now it's muddled with all the other times that came after it. I do remember that the police were called. They came out to the house this time, but again it was like a boys' club. "Hey, guys. These women, you know how they are." No report was made. No charges were filed.

Whenever he'd hit her or come after me, my mom would find me crying afterward and take me aside. She'd give me the same talk every time.

"Pray for Abel," she'd say. "Because he doesn't hate us. He hates himself."

To a kid this makes no sense. "Well, if he hates himself," I'd say, "why doesn't he kick himself?"

Abel was one of those drinkers where once he was gone you'd look into his eyes and you didn't even see the same person. I remember one night he came home fuckdrunk, stumbling through the house. He stumbled into my room, muttering to himself, and I woke up to see him whip out his dick and start pissing on the floor. He thought he was in the bathroom. That's how drunk he would get—he wouldn't know which room in the house he was in. There were so many nights he would stumble into my room thinking it was his and kick me out of bed and pass out. I'd yell at him, but it was like talking to a zombie. I'd go sleep on the couch.

He'd get wasted with his crew in the backyard every evening after work, and many nights he'd end up fighting with one of them. Someone would say something Abel didn't like, and he'd beat the shit out of him. The guy wouldn't show up for work Tuesday or Wednesday, but then by Thursday he'd be back because he needed the job. Every few weeks it was the same story, like clockwork.

Abel kicked the dogs, too. Fufi, mostly. Panther was smart enough to stay away, but dumb, lovable Fufi was forever trying to be Abel's friend. She'd cross his path or be in his way when he'd had a few, and he'd give her the boot. After that she'd go and hide somewhere for a while. Fufi getting kicked was always the warning sign that shit was about to go down. The dogs and the workers in the yard often got the first taste of his anger, and that would let the rest of us know to lie low. I'd usually go find Fufi wherever she was hiding and be with her.

The strange thing was that when Fufi got kicked she never yelped or cried. When the vet diagnosed her as deaf, he also found out she had some condition where she didn't have a fully developed sense of touch. She didn't feel pain. Which was why she would always start over with Abel like it was a new day. He'd kick her, she'd hide, then she'd be right back the next morning, wagging her tail. "Hey. I'm here. I'll give you another chance."

And he always got the second chance. The Abel who was likable and charming never went away. He had a drinking problem, but he was a nice guy. We had a family. Growing up in a home of abuse, you struggle with the notion that you can love a person you hate, or hate a person you love. It's a strange feeling. You want to live in a world where someone is good or bad, where you either hate them or love them, but that's not how people are.

There was an undercurrent of terror that ran through the house, but the actual beatings themselves were not that frequent. I think if they had been, the situation would have ended sooner. Ironically, the good times in between were what allowed it to drag out and escalate as far as it did. He hit my mom once, then the next time was three years later, and it was just a little bit worse. Then it was two years later, and it was just a little bit worse. Then it was a year later, and it was just a little bit worse. It was sporadic enough to where you'd think it wouldn't happen again, but it was frequent enough that you never forgot it was possible. There was a rhythm to it. I remember one time, after one terrible incident, nobody spoke to him for over a month. No words, no eye contact, no conversations, nothing. We moved through the house as strangers, at different times. Complete silent treatment. Then one morning you're in the kitchen and there's a nod. "Hey." "Hey." Then a week later it's "Did you see the thing on the news?" "Yeah." Then the next week there's a joke and a laugh. Slowly, slowly, life goes back to how it was. Six months, a year later, you do it all again.

One afternoon I came home from Sandringham and my mom was very upset and worked up.

"This man is unbelievable," she said.

"What happened?"

"He bought a gun."

"What? A *gun*? What do you mean, 'He bought a gun'?"

A gun was such a ridiculous thing in my world. In my mind, only cops and criminals had guns. Abel had gone out and bought a 9mm Parabellum Smith & Wesson. Sleek and black, menacing. It didn't look cool like guns in movies. It looked like it killed things.

"Why did he buy a gun?" I asked.

"I don't know."

She said she'd confronted him about it, and he'd gone off on some nonsense about the world needing to learn to respect him.

"He thinks he's the policeman of the world," she said. "And that's the problem with the world. We have people who cannot police themselves, so they want to police everyone else around them."

Not long after that, I moved out. The atmosphere had become toxic for me. I'd reached the point where I was as big as Abel. Big enough to punch back. A father does not fear retribution from his son, but I was not his son. He knew that. The analogy my mom used was that there were now two male lions in the house. "Every time he looks at you he sees your father," she'd say. "You're a constant reminder of another man. He hates you, and you need to leave. You need to leave before you become like him."

It was also just time for me to go. Regardless of Abel, our plan had always been for me to move out after school. My mother never wanted me to be like my uncle, one of those men, unemployed and still living at home with his mother. She helped me get my flat, and I moved out. The flat was only ten minutes away from the house, so I was always around to drop in to help with errands or have dinner once in a while. But, most important, whatever was going on with Abel, I didn't have to be involved.

At some point my mom moved to a separate bedroom in the house, and from then on they were married in name only, not even cohabitating but coexisting. That state of affairs lasted a year, maybe two. Andrew had turned nine, and in my world I was counting down until he turned eighteen, thinking that would finally free my mom from this abusive man. Then one afternoon my mom called and asked me to come by the house. A few hours later, I popped by.

"Trevor," she said. "I'm pregnant."

"Sorry, what?"

"I'm pregnant."

"What?!"

Good Lord, I was furious. I was so angry. She herself seemed resolute, as determined as ever, but with an undertone of sadness I had never seen before, like the news had devastated her at first but she'd since reconciled herself to the reality of it.

"How could you let this happen?"

"Abel and I, we made up. I moved back into the bedroom. It was just one night, and then . . . I became pregnant. I don't know how."

She didn't know. She was forty-four years old. She'd had her tubes tied after Andrew. Even her doctor had said, "This shouldn't be possible. We don't know how this happened."

I was boiling with rage. All we had to do was wait for Andrew to grow up, and it was going to be over, and now it was like she'd re-upped on the contract.

"So you're going to have this child with this man? You're going to stay with this man another eighteen years? Are you crazy?"

"God spoke to me, Trevor. He told me, 'Patricia, I don't do anything by mistake. There is nothing I give you that you cannot handle.' I'm pregnant for a reason. I know what kind of kids I can make. I know what kind of sons I can raise. I can raise this child. I will raise this child."

Nine months later Isaac was born. She called him Isaac because in the Bible Sarah gets pregnant when she's like a hundred years old and she's not supposed to be having children and that's what she names her son.

Isaac's birth pushed me even further away. I visited less and less. Then I popped by one afternoon and the house was in chaos, police cars out front, the aftermath of another fight.

He'd hit her with a bicycle. Abel had been berating one of his workers in the yard, and my mom had tried to get between them. Abel was furious that she'd contradicted him in front of an employee, so he picked up Andrew's bike and he beat her with it. Again she called the police, and the cops who showed up this time actually knew Abel. He'd fixed their cars. They were pals. No charges were filed. Nothing happened.

That time I confronted him. I was big enough now.

"You can't keep doing this," I said. "This is not right."

He was apologetic. He always was. He didn't puff out his chest and get defensive or anything like that.

"I know," he said. "I'm sorry. I don't like doing these things, but you know how your mom is. She can talk a lot and she doesn't listen. I feel like your mom doesn't respect me sometimes. She came and disrespected me in front of my workers. I can't have these other men looking at me like I don't know how to control my wife."

After the bicycle, my mom hired contractors she knew through the real-estate business to build her a separate house in the backyard, like a little servants' quarters, and she moved in there with Isaac.

"This is the most insane thing I've ever seen," I told her.

"This is all I can do," she said. "The police won't help me. The government won't protect me. Only my God can protect me. But what

I can do is use against him the one thing that he cherishes, and that is his pride. By me living outside in a shack, everyone is going to ask him, 'Why does your wife live in a shack outside your house?' He's going to have to answer that question, and no matter what he says, everyone will know that something is wrong with him. He loves to live for the world. Let the world see him for who he is. He's a saint in the streets. He's a devil in this house. Let him be seen for who he is."

When my mom had decided to keep Isaac, I was so close to writing her off. I couldn't stand the pain anymore. But seeing her hit with a bicycle, living like a prisoner in her own backyard, that was the final straw for me. I was a broken person. I was done.

"This thing?" I told her. "This dysfunctional thing? I won't be a part of it. I can't live this life with you. I refuse. You've made your decision. Good luck with your life. I'm going to live mine."

She understood. She didn't feel betrayed or abandoned at all.

"Honey, I know what you're going through," she said. "At one point, I had to disown my family to go off and live my own life, too. I understand why you need to do the same."

So I did. I walked out. I didn't call. I didn't visit. Isaac came and I went, and for the life of me I could not understand why she wouldn't do the same: leave. Just leave. Just fucking leave.

I didn't understand what she was going through. I didn't understand domestic violence. I didn't understand how adult relationships worked; I'd never even had a girlfriend. I didn't understand how she could have sex with a man she hated and feared. I didn't know how easily sex and hatred and fear can intertwine.

I was angry with my mom. I hated him, but I blamed her. I saw Abel as a choice she'd made, a choice she was continuing to make. My whole life, telling me stories about growing up in the homelands, being abandoned by her parents, she had always said, "You cannot blame anyone else for what you do. You cannot blame your past for who you are. You are responsible for you. You make your own choices."

She never let me see us as victims. We *were* victims, me and my mom, Andrew and Isaac. Victims of apartheid. Victims of abuse. But I was never allowed to think that way, and I didn't see her life that way. Cutting my father out of our lives to pacify Abel, that was her choice. Supporting Abel's workshop was her choice. Isaac was her choice. She had the money, not him. She wasn't dependent. So in my mind, she was the one making the decision.

It is so easy, from the outside, to put the blame on the woman and say, "You just need to leave." It's not like my home was the only home where there was domestic abuse. It's what I grew up around. I saw it in the streets of Soweto, on TV, in movies. Where does a woman go in a society where that is the norm? When the police won't help her? When her own family won't help her? Where does a woman go when she leaves one man who hits her and is just as likely to wind up with another man who hits her, maybe even worse than the first? Where does a woman go when she's single with three kids and she lives in a society that makes her a pariah for being a manless woman? Where she's seen as a whore for doing that? Where does she go? What does she do?

But I didn't comprehend any of that at the time. I was a boy with a boy's understanding of things. I distinctly remember the last time we argued about it, too. It was sometime after the bicycle, or when she was moving into her shack in the backyard. I was going off, begging her for the thousandth time.

"Why? Why don't you just leave?"

She shook her head. "Oh, baby. No, no, no. I can't leave."

"Why not?"

"Because if I leave he'll kill us."

She wasn't being dramatic. She didn't raise her voice. She said it totally calm and matter-of-fact, and I never asked her that question again.

Eventually she did leave. What prompted her to leave, what the final breaking point was, I have no idea. I was gone. I was off becoming a comedian, touring the country, playing shows in England, hosting radio shows, hosting television shows. I'd moved in with my cousin

Mlungisi and made my own life separate from hers. I couldn't invest myself anymore, because it would have broken me into too many pieces. But one day she bought another house in Highlands North, met someone new, and moved on with her life. Andrew and Isaac still saw their dad, who, by that point, was just existing in the world, still going through the same cycle of drinking and fighting, still living in a house paid for by his ex-wife.

Years passed. Life carried on.

Then one morning I was in bed around ten a.m. and my phone rang. It was on a Sunday. I know it was on a Sunday because everyone else in the family had gone to church and I, quite happily, had not. The days of endlessly schlepping back and forth to church were no longer my problem, and I was lazily sleeping in. The irony of my life is that whenever church is involved is when shit goes wrong, like getting kidnapped by violent minibus drivers. I'd always teased my mom about that, too. "This church thing of yours, all this Jesus, what good has come of it?"

I looked over at my phone. It was flashing my mom's number, but when I answered, it was Andrew on the other end. He sounded perfectly calm.

"Hey, Trevor, it's Andrew."

"Hey."

"How are you?"

"Good. What's up?"

"Are you busy?"

"I'm sort of sleeping. Why?"

"Mom's been shot."

Okay, so there were two strange things about the call. First, why would he ask me if I was busy? Let's start there. When your mom's been shot, the first line out of your mouth should be "Mom's been shot." Not "How are you?" Not "Are you busy?" That confused me. The second weird thing was when he said, "Mom's been shot," I didn't ask, "Who shot her?" I didn't have to. He said, "Mom's been shot," and my mind automatically filled in the rest: "Abel shot mom."

"Where are you now?" I said.

"We're at Linksfield Hospital."

"Okay, I'm on my way."

I jumped out of bed, ran down the corridor, and banged on Mlungisi's door. "Dude, my mom's been shot! She's in the hospital." He jumped out of bed, too, and we got in the car and raced to the hospital, which luckily was only fifteen minutes away.

At that point, I was upset but not terrified. Andrew had been so calm on the phone, no crying, no panic in his voice, so I was thinking, *She must be okay. It must not be that bad.* I called him back from the car to find out more.

"Andrew, what happened?"

"We were on our way home from church," he said, again totally calm. "And Dad was waiting for us at the house, and he got out of his car and started shooting."

"But where? Where did he shoot her?"

"He shot her in her leg."

"Oh, okay," I said, relieved.

"And then he shot her in the head."

When he said that, my body just let go. I remember the exact traffic light I was at. For a moment there was a complete vacuum of sound, and then I cried tears like I had never cried before. I collapsed in heaving sobs and moans. I cried as if every other thing I'd cried for in my life had been a waste of crying. I cried so hard that if my present crying self could go back in time and see my other crying selves, it would slap them and say, "That shit's not worth crying for." My cry was not a cry of sadness. It was not catharsis. It wasn't me feeling sorry for myself. It was an expression of raw pain that came from an inability of my body to express that pain in any other way, shape, or form. She was my mom. She was my teammate. It had always been me and her together, me and her against the world. When Andrew said, "shot her in the head," I broke in two.

The light changed. I couldn't even see the road, but I drove through the tears, thinking, *Just get there, just get there, just get there.* We pulled up to the hospital, and I jumped out of the car. There was an outdoor sitting area by the entrance to the emergency room. Andrew was standing there waiting for me, alone, his clothes smeared with blood. He still looked perfectly calm, completely stoic. Then the moment he looked up and saw me he broke down and started bawling. It was like he'd been holding it together the whole morning and then everything broke loose at once and he lost it. I ran to him and hugged him and he cried and cried. His cry was different from mine, though. My cry was one of pain and anger. His cry was one of helplessness.

I turned and ran into the emergency room. My mom was there in triage on a gurney. The doctors were stabilizing her. Her whole body was soaked in blood. There was a hole in her face, a gaping wound above her lip, part of her nose gone.

She was as calm and serene as I'd ever seen her. She could still open one eye, and she turned and looked up at me and saw the look of horror on my face.

"It's okay, baby," she whispered, barely able to speak with the blood in her throat.

"It's not okay."

"No, no, I'm okay, I'm okay. Where's Andrew? Where's your brother?"

"He's outside."

"Go to Andrew."

"But Mom—"

"*Shh*. It's okay, baby. I'm fine."

"You're not fine, you're—"

"*Shhhhhh*. I'm fine, I'm fine, I'm fine. Go to your brother. Your brother needs you."

The doctors kept working, and there was nothing I could do to help her. I went back outside to be with Andrew. We sat down together, and he told me the story.

They were coming home from church, a big group, my mom and Andrew and Isaac, her new husband and his children and a whole bunch of his extended family, aunts and uncles, nieces and nephews. They had just pulled into the driveway when Abel pulled up and got out of his car. He had his gun. He looked right at my mother.

"You've stolen my life," he said. "You've taken everything away from me. Now I'm going to kill all of you."

Andrew stepped in front of his father. He stepped right in front of the gun.

"Don't do this, Dad, please. You're drunk. Just put the gun away."

Abel looked down at his son.

"No," he said. "I'm killing everybody, and if you don't walk away I will shoot you first."

Andrew stepped aside.

"His eyes were not lying," he told me. "He had the eyes of the Devil. In that moment I could tell my father was gone."

For all the pain I felt that day, in hindsight, I have to imagine that Andrew's pain was far greater than mine. My mom had been shot by a man I despised. If anything, I felt vindicated; I'd been right about Abel all along. I could direct my anger and hatred toward him with no shame or guilt whatsoever. But Andrew's mother had been shot by Andrew's father, a father he loved. How does he reconcile his love with that situation? How does he carry on loving both sides? Both sides of himself?

Isaac was only four years old. He didn't fully comprehend what was happening, and as Andrew stepped aside, Isaac started crying.

"Daddy, what are you doing? Daddy, what are you doing?"

"Isaac, go to your brother," Abel said.

Isaac ran over to Andrew, and Andrew held him. Then Abel raised his gun and he started shooting. My mother jumped in front of the gun to protect everyone, and that's when she took the first bullet, not in her leg but in her butt cheek. She collapsed, and as she fell to the ground she screamed.

"Run!"

Abel kept shooting and everyone ran. They scattered. My mom was struggling to get back to her feet when Abel walked up and stood over her. He pointed the gun at her head point-blank, execution-style. Then he pulled the trigger. Nothing. The gun misfired. *Click!* He pulled the trigger again, same thing. Then again and again. *Click! Click! Click! Click!* Four times he pulled the trigger, and four times the gun misfired. Bullets were popping out of the ejection port, falling out of the gun, falling down on my mom and clattering to the ground.

Abel stopped to see what was wrong with the gun. My mother jumped up in a panic. She shoved him aside, ran for the car, jumped into the driver's seat.

Andrew ran behind and jumped into the passenger seat next to her. Just as she turned the ignition, Andrew heard one last gunshot, and the windshield went red. Abel had fired from behind the car. The bullet went into the back of her head and exited through the front of her face, and blood sprayed everywhere. Her body slumped over the steering wheel. Andrew, reacting without thinking, pulled my mom to the passenger side, flipped over her, jumped into the driver's seat, slammed the car into gear, and raced to the hospital in Linksfield.

I asked Andrew what happened to Abel. He didn't know. I was filled with rage, but there was nothing I could do. I felt completely impotent, but I still felt I had to do something. So I took out my phone and I called him—I called the man who'd just shot my mom, and he actually picked up.

"Trevor."

"You killed my mom."

"Yes, I did."

"You *killed* my *mom*!"

"Yes. And if I could find you, I would kill you as well."

Then he hung up. It was the most chilling moment. It was terrifying. Whatever nerve I'd worked up to call him I immediately lost. To this day I don't know what I was thinking. I don't know what I expected to happen. I was just enraged.

I kept asking Andrew questions, trying to get more details. Then, as we were talking, a nurse came outside looking for me.

"Are you the family?" she asked.

"Yes."

"Sir, there's a problem. Your mother was speaking a bit at first.

She's stopped now, but from what we've gathered she doesn't have health insurance."

"What? No, no. That can't be true. I know my mom has health insurance."

She didn't. As it turned out, a few months prior, she'd decided, "This health insurance is a scam. I never get sick. I'm going to cancel it." So now she had no health insurance.

"We can't treat your mother here," the nurse said. "If she doesn't have insurance we have to send her to a state hospital."

"*State hospital?!* What—no! You can't. My mom's been shot in the head. You're going to put her back on a gurney? Send her out in an ambulance? She'll die. You need to treat her right now."

"Sir, we can't. We need a form of payment."

"I'm your form of payment. I'll pay."

"Yes, people say that, but without a guarantee—"

I pulled out my credit card.

"Here," I said. "Take this. I'll pay. I'll pay for everything."

"Sir, hospital can be very expensive."

"I don't care."

"Sir, I don't think you understand. Hospital can be *really* expensive."

"Lady, I have money. I'll pay anything. Just help us."

"Sir, you don't understand. We have to do so many tests. One test alone could cost two, three thousand rand."

"Three thousan—what? Lady, this is my mother's life we're talking about. I'll pay."

"Sir, you don't understand. Your mother has been shot. In her brain. She'll be in ICU. One night in ICU could cost you fifteen, twenty thousand rand."

"Lady, are you not listening to me? This is my mother's *life*. This is her *life*. Take the money. Take all of it. I don't care."

"*Sir!* You don't understand. I've seen this happen. Your mother could be in the ICU for weeks. This could cost you five hundred thousand, six hundred thousand. Maybe even millions. You'll be in debt for the rest of *your* life."

I'm not going to lie to you: I paused. I paused *hard*. In that moment, what I heard the nurse saying was, "All of your money will be gone," and then I started to think, *Well . . . what is she, fifty? That's pretty good, right? She's lived a good life.*

I genuinely did not know what to do. I stared at the nurse as the shock of what she'd said sunk in. My mind raced through a dozen different scenarios. *What if I spend that money and then she dies anyway? Do I get a refund?* I actually imagined my mother, as frugal as she was, waking up from a coma and saying, "You spent *how much?* You idiot. You should have saved that money to look after your brothers." And what about my brothers? They would be my responsibility now. I would have to raise the family, which I couldn't do if I was millions in debt, and it was always my mother's solemn vow that raising my brothers was the one thing I would never have to do. Even as my career took off, she'd refused any help I offered. "I don't want you paying for your mother the same way I had to pay for mine," she'd say. "I don't want you raising your brothers the same way Abel had to raise his."

My mother's greatest fear was that I would end up paying the black tax, that I would get trapped by the cycle of poverty and violence that came before me. She had always promised me that I would be the one to break that cycle. I would be the one to move forward and not back. And as I looked at that nurse outside the emergency room, I was petrified that the moment I handed her my credit card, the cycle would just continue and I'd get sucked right back in.

People say all the time that they'd do anything for the people they love. But would you really? Would you do anything? Would you give everything? I don't know that a child knows that kind of selfless love. A mother, yes. A mother will clutch her children and jump from a moving car to keep them from harm. She will do it without thinking. But I don't think the child knows how to do that, not instinctively. It's something the child has to learn.

I pressed my credit card into the nurse's hand.

"Do whatever you have to do. Just please help my mom."

We spent the rest of the day in limbo, waiting, not knowing, pacing around the hospital, family members stopping by. Several hours later, the doctor finally came out of the emergency room to give us an update.

"What's happening?" I asked.

"Your mother is stable," he said. "She's out of surgery."

"Is she going to be okay?"

He thought for a moment about what he was going to say.

"I don't like to use this word," he said, "because I'm a man of science and I don't believe in it. But what happened to your mother today was a miracle. I never say that, because I hate it when people say it, but I don't have any other way to explain this."

The bullet that hit my mother in the butt, he said, was a through-and-through. It went in, came out, and didn't do any real damage. The other bullet went through the back of her head, entering below the skull at the top of her neck. It missed the spinal cord by a hair, missed the medulla oblongata, and traveled through her head just underneath the brain, missing every major vein, artery, and nerve. With the trajectory the bullet was on, it was headed straight for her left eye socket and would have blown out her eye, but at the last second it slowed down, hit her cheekbone instead, shattered her cheekbone, ricocheted off, and came out through her left nostril. On the gurney in the emergency room, the blood had made the wound look much worse than it was. The bullet took off only a tiny flap of skin on the side of her nostril, and it came out clean, with no bullet fragments left inside. She didn't even need surgery. They stopped the bleeding, stitched her up in back, stitched her up in front, and let her heal.

"There was nothing we can do, because there's nothing we need to do," the doctor said.

My mother was out of the hospital in four days. She was back at work in seven.

The doctors kept her sedated the rest of that day and night to rest. They told all of us to go home. "She's stable," they said. "There's nothing you can do here. Go home and sleep." So we did.

I went back first thing the next morning to be with my mother in her room and wait for her to wake up. When I walked in she was still asleep. The back of her head was bandaged. She had stitches in her face and gauze covering her nose and her left eye. She looked frail and weak, tired, one of the few times in my life I'd ever seen her look that way.

I sat close by her bed, holding her hand, waiting and watching her breathe, a flood of thoughts going through my mind. I was still afraid I was going to lose her. I was angry at myself for not being there, angry at the police for all the times they didn't arrest Abel. I told myself I should have killed him years ago, which was ridiculous to think because I'm not capable of killing anyone, but I thought it anyway. I was angry at the world, angry at God. Because all my mom does is pray. If there's a fan club for Jesus, my mom is definitely in the top 100, and this is what she gets?

After an hour or so of waiting, she opened her unbandaged eye. The second she did, I lost it. I started bawling. She asked for some water and I gave her a cup, and she leaned forward a bit to sip through the straw. I kept bawling and bawling and bawling. I couldn't control myself.

"*Shh,*" she said. "Don't cry, baby. *Shhhhh.* Don't cry."

"How can I not cry, Mom? You almost died."

"No, I wasn't going to die. I wasn't going to die. It's okay. I wasn't going to die."

"But I thought you were dead." I kept bawling and bawling. "I thought I'd lost you."

"No, baby. Baby, don't cry. Trevor. Trevor, listen. Listen to me. Listen."

"What?" I said, tears streaming down my face.

"My child, you must look on the bright side."

"*What?* What are you talking about, 'the bright side'? Mom, you were shot in the face. There is no bright side."

"Of course there is. Now you're officially the best-looking person in the family."

She broke out in a huge smile and started laughing. Through my tears, I started laughing, too. I was bawling my eyes out and laughing hysterically at the same time. We sat there and she squeezed my hand and we cracked each other up the way we always did, mother and son, laughing together through the pain in an intensive-care recovery room on a bright and sunny and beautiful day.

When my mother was shot, so much happened so quickly. We were only able to piece the whole story together after the fact, as we collected all the different accounts from everyone who was there. Waiting around at the hospital that day, we had so many unanswered questions, like, What happened to Isaac? Where was Isaac? We only found out after we found him and he told us.

When Andrew sped off with my mom, leaving the four-year-old alone on the front lawn, Abel walked over to his youngest, picked him up, put the boy in his car, and drove away. As they drove, Isaac turned to his dad.

"Dad, why did you kill Mom?" he asked, at that point assuming, as we all did, that my mom was dead.

"Because I'm very unhappy," Abel replied. "Because I'm very sad."

"Yeah, but you shouldn't kill Mom. Where are we going now?"

"I'm going to drop you off at your uncle's house."

"And where are you going?"

"I'm going to kill myself."

"But don't kill yourself, Dad."

"No, I'm going to kill myself."

The uncle Abel was talking about was not a real uncle but a friend. He dropped Isaac off with this friend and then he drove off. He spent that day and went to everyone, relatives and friends, and said his goodbyes. He even told people what he had done. "This is what I've done. I've killed her, and I'm now on the way to kill myself. Goodbye." He spent the whole day on this strange farewell tour, until finally one of his cousins called him out.

"You need to man up," the cousin said. "This is the coward's way. You need to turn yourself in. If you were man enough to do this, you have to be man enough to face the consequences."

Abel broke down and handed his gun over to the cousin, the cousin drove him to the police station, and Abel turned himself in.

He spent a couple of weeks in jail, waiting for a bail hearing. We filed a motion opposing bail because he'd shown that he was a threat. Since Andrew and Isaac were still minors, social workers started getting involved. We felt like the case was open-and-shut, but then one day, after a month or so, we got a call that he'd made bail. The great irony was that he got bail because he told the judge that if he was in jail, he couldn't earn money to support his kids. But he wasn't supporting his kids—my mom was supporting the kids.

So Abel was out. The case slowly ground its way through the legal system, and everything went against us. Because of my mother's miraculous recovery, the charge was only attempted murder. And because no domestic violence charges had ever been filed in all the times my mother had called the police to report him, Abel had no criminal record. He got a good lawyer, who continued to lean on the court about the fact that he had children at home who needed him. The case never went to trial. Abel pled guilty to attempted murder. He was given three years' probation. He didn't serve a single day in prison. He kept joint custody of his sons. He's walking around Johannesburg today, completely free. The last I heard he still lives somewhere around Highlands North, not too far from my mom.

The final piece of the story came from my mom, who could only tell us her side after she woke up. She remembered Abel pulling up and pointing the gun at Andrew. She remembered falling to the ground after getting shot in the ass. Then Abel came and stood over her and pointed his gun at her head. She looked up and looked at him straight down the barrel of the gun. Then she started to pray, and that's when the gun misfired. Then it misfired again. Then it misfired again, and again. She jumped up, shoved him away, and ran for the car. Andrew leapt in beside her and she turned the ignition and then her memory went blank.

To this day, nobody can explain what happened. Even the police didn't understand. Because it wasn't like the gun didn't work. It fired, and then it didn't fire, and then it fired again for the final shot. Anyone who knows anything about firearms will tell you that a 9mm handgun cannot misfire in the way that gun did. But at the crime scene the police had drawn little chalk circles all over the driveway, all with spent shell casings from the shots Abel fired, and then these four bullets, intact, from when he was standing over my mom—nobody knows why.

My mom's total hospital bill came to 50,000 rand. I paid it the day we left. For four days we'd been in the hospital, family members visiting, talking and hanging out, laughing and crying. As we packed up her things to leave, I was going on about how insane the whole week had been.

"You're lucky to be alive," I told her. "I still can't believe you didn't have any health insurance."

"Oh but I do have insurance," she said.

"You do?"

"Yes. Jesus."

"Jesus?"

"Jesus."

"Jesus is your health insurance?"

"If God is with me, who can be against me?"

"Okay, Mom."

"Trevor, I prayed. I told you I prayed. I don't pray for nothing."

"You know," I said, "for once I cannot argue with you. The gun, the bullets—I can't explain any of it. So I'll give you that much." Then I couldn't resist teasing her with one last little jab. "But where was your Jesus to pay your hospital bill, hmm? I know for a fact that He didn't pay that."

She smiled and said, "You're right. He didn't. But He blessed me with the son who did."

———

ACKNOWLEDGMENTS

For nurturing my career these past years and steering me down the road that led to this book, I owe many thanks to Norm Aladjem, Derek Van Pelt, Sanaz Yamin, Rachel Rusch, Matt Blake, Jeff Endlich, and Jill Fritzo.

For making this book deal happen and keeping it on track during a very tight and hectic time, I would like to thank Peter McGuigan and his team at Foundry Literary + Media, including Kirsten Neuhaus, Sara DeNobrega, and Claire Harris. Also, many thanks to Tanner Colby for helping me put my story on the page.

For seeing the potential in this book and making it a reality, I would like to thank everyone at Random House and Spiegel & Grau, including my editor Chris Jackson, publishers Julie Grau and Cindy Spiegel,

Tom Perry, Greg Mollica, Susan Turner, Andrea DeWerd, Leigh Marchant, Barbara Fillon, Dhara Parikh, Rebecca Berlant, Kelly Chian, Nicole Counts, and Gina Centrello.

For bringing this book home to South Africa and making sure it is published with the utmost care, I would like to thank everyone at Pan Macmillan South Africa, including Sean Fraser, Sandile Khumalo, Andrea Nattrass, Rhulani Netshivhera, Sandile Nkosi, Nkateko Traore, Katlego Tapala, Wesley Thompson, and Mia van Heerden.

For reading this manuscript in its early stages and sharing thoughts and ideas to make it the finished product you hold in your hands, I owe my deepest gratitude to Khaya Dlanga, David Kibuuka, Anele Mdoda, Ryan Harduth, Sizwe Dhlomo, and Xolisa Dyeshana.

And, finally, for bringing me into this world and making me the man I am today, I owe the greatest debt, a debt I can never repay, to my mother.

ABOUT THE AUTHOR

TREVOR NOAH is a comedian from South Africa.

trevornoah.com
Facebook.com/OfficialTrevorNoah
Twitter: @Trevornoah
Instagram: @trevornoah

ABOUT THE TYPE

This book was set in Fournier, a typeface named for Pierre-Simon Fournier (1712–68), the youngest son of a French printing family. He started out engraving woodblocks and large capitals, then moved on to fonts of type. In 1736 he began his own foundry and made several important contributions in the field of type design; he is said to have cut 147 alphabets of his own creation. Fournier is probably best remembered as the designer of St. Augustine Ordinaire, a face that served as the model for the Monotype Corporation's Fournier, which was released in 1925.